OUTRAGEOUS
MISFITS

BRIAN BRADLEY

OUTRAGEOUS MISFITS

Female Impersonator Craig Russell
and His Wife, Lori Russell Eadie

DUNDURN
TORONTO

Publisher: Scott Fraser | Acquiring editor: Rachel Spence | Editor: Dominic Farrell
Designer: Laura Boyle
Cover image: Ron Bull/Toronto Star (1982)
The Music Of The Night from THE PHANTOM OF THE OPERA. Music by Andrew Lloyd Webber. Lyrics by Charles Hart. Additional Lyrics by Richard Stilgoe. © Copyright 1986 Andrew Lloyd Webber licensed to The Really Useful Group Ltd. International Copyright Secured All Rights Reserved. *Reprinted by Permission of Hal Leonard LLC*

Printer: Marquis Book Printing Inc.

Library and Archives Canada Cataloguing in Publication

Title: Outrageous misfits : female impersonator Craig Russell and his wife, Lori Russell Eadie / Brian Bradley.
Names: Bradley, Brian, 1982- author.
Description: Includes bibliographical references and index.
Identifiers: Canadiana (print) 20200164155 | Canadiana (ebook) 20200164171 | ISBN 9781459746978 (softcover) | ISBN 9781459746985 (PDF) | ISBN 9781459746992 (EPUB)
Subjects: LCSH: Russell, Craig (Vocalist) | LCSH: Eadie, Lori Russell. | LCSH: Female impersonators—Canada—Biography. | LCSH: Actors—Canada—Biography. | LCSH: Entertainers—Canada—Biography. | LCGFT: Biographies.
Classification: LCC PN2638.R87 B73 2020 | DDC 792.02/8092—dc23

We acknowledge the support of the Canada Council for the Arts and the Ontario Arts Council for our publishing program. We also acknowledge the financial support of the Government of Ontario, through the Ontario Book Publishing Tax Credit and Ontario Creates, and the Government of Canada.

VISIT US AT

 dundurn.com | @dundurnpress | dundurnpress | dundurnpress

Dundurn
3 Church Street, Suite 500
Toronto, Ontario, Canada
M5E 1M2

For my outrageous sister Jocelyn.

And for anyone who has ever struggled.
You are seen, you are understood, you are loved.

You're mad as a hatter, darling. But that's alright because so am I. So am I. I've never known anyone worth knowing who wasn't a positive fruitcake.

— Craig Russell as character Robin Turner in *Outrageous!* (1977)

CONTENTS

AUTHOR'S NOTE

This biography, about Russell Craig Eadie (Craig Russell) and Lori (Jenkins) Russell Eadie, touches on sixty years of gay history in Toronto with a particular emphasis on the Toronto gay community from the 1960s through to the 1980s.

Much has changed in that time, including our understanding and acknowledgement of gender and sexual identities. Everyone has a place in the history highlighted in this book but to be true to the gay community as it was understood in Craig and Lori's time, this text mostly identifies gay and lesbian people in respect to historical events and venues I have cited.

You will also note that I have used the broad term *gay community*. Do not confuse this to mean a community of gay males. In the context of this history, the term *gay community* includes people of all gender and sexual identities and their allies. To me and my book subjects, we all have a place within it.

PREFACE

This is a biography about a man who grew up wanting to be a star and his No. 1 fan, a woman who later became his wife.

It sounds like a familiar set-up — a relationship between a man and a woman that is relatable, even predictable. But a lot is different about the stories of this particular man and woman, and you might come to the conclusion that these two people are unlike anyone you have ever known.

Craig Eadie, better known as Craig Russell, and Lori (Jenkins) Russell Eadie had similar backgrounds and interests. They grew up and built their careers in Toronto. They loved the arts, the rush of performance, the thrill of curtain call, and the adulation of an audience. Craig made his living performing on the stage and dabbling in film and television. Lori worked in theatre, too, but she preferred life backstage in the land of wardrobe, where she was a dresser for some of the most highly touted theatrical productions in Canadian theatre history.

Craig's career was built from a teenage love of great dame female entertainers like Judy Garland, Marlene Dietrich, Tallulah Bankhead, and Bette Davis. Sexpot actress Mae West was his idol and, as president of his (initially fake) Mae West Fan Club, he went to work as her personal secretary in California. Who gets to do something like that? Craig did. He was charmed, in a way, and larger than life. He was destined to be onstage and with the stars.

His art fits into the world of drag, but Craig insisted he was not a drag queen. He was a female impressionist. He was really good at what he did. He was an excellent singer, and his comedy had perfect timing. His impressions were so finely tuned, he imitated gestures down to the wiggle of a pinky finger, the wink of an eye, or the flick of a cigarette. One reviewer said he was able to "stir an audience the way the ladies themselves did or do." Another said that no one "could handle the big ladies of stage and screen so well. All you have to do is sit there, sip your suds and pick your lower jaw off the floor every now and then."

Eventually joined by some of the best musicians from Canada, the United States, and Germany, Craig toured the world impersonating the ladies he loved and played in some of the grandest venues for audiences who never would have given such a queer man the time of day outside of a theatre. His talent gave him a key to the mainstream entertainment world from which his beloved entertainers came. He went on to star in a movie credited as a groundbreaking film for gay culture and a force that pushed the Canadian film scene forward.

I was thirteen years old, incredibly naive, and living in a small francophone community outside Sudbury, Ontario, when I first heard the name Craig Russell. I was watching something rather bland on television, and all of a sudden, this colourful, flamboyant man was mentioned in a commercial promoting a documentary. I remember it so clearly — his coiffed hair and eye makeup, talk of a friendship with actress Mae West, brazen footage of him singing in a wig and gown, and mention that self-confidence eluded him despite his incredible success.

I had immediate questions. Who was this effeminate man in makeup? Was he a cross-dresser? He lived with an old-lady movie star? And he got to make a movie? Why did he get to do things like this?

Craig was like no one I'd ever known. I figured he was likely gay. I didn't know any gay people, nor did I see any in the television shows or movies I watched. Was this what gay men were like? I was skeptical, wondering why there'd be a documentary about someone like that and why it was worth talking about. I had so much to learn about the world.

A decade later I was a journalism graduate with an interest in social history and biography when Craig's name crossed my path again. I was researching Margaret Gibson, a celebrated writer who suffered from schizophrenia, and an article about her mentioned Craig. They had been friends and roommates. I wondered what that could have been like.

I looked up one of their shared friends in the phone book and called her up, telling her I had an interest in both Margaret, the writer who struggled with what she called madness, and Craig, the flamboyant female impressionist who seemed so unrecognized and misunderstood. I got more than I bargained for.

That conversation spawned so much intrigue that I spent the next decade of my life researching and learning about Craig. Initially it was a hobby, but by 2017 my efforts were full-time, and I knew there was a book to be written about his life. His story had talents to be celebrated, intrigues to be understood, and curious situations to be explained.

In learning about Craig, I came to learn about Lori, a shy and demure theatre-loving file clerk who joined his world of make-believe and became his wife. What a turn of events that must have been for her. Who gets to marry their favourite movie star? How did that happen? What was their marriage like? I had to know. I became just as enamoured with Lori as I was with Craig, and a biography about one became a biography about two.

And what lives they lived. As if they weren't both outrageous and interesting enough, Craig and Lori's life and their careers coincided with gay liberation. In the years after the Stonewall Riots in the United States, Toronto had its first annual gay pride week, gay bars quietly opened along Yonge Street, the local drag scene began to take shape, and there was a push to include sexual orientation in the Ontario Human Rights Code. The atmosphere was as motivating as it was frightening. Police raided bathhouses, and homophobic thugs lurked around parks and protests. Numerous men turned up murdered after frequenting popular gay establishments.

Craig and Lori were not necessarily politically engaged in the changing times, but they shared the notion they could do as they pleased with no apologies or regrets. They defied gender conventions and eschewed the heteronormative. Their lives and careers blossomed at the beginning of the throbbing sexual revolution and new-wave counterculture brought to the stage, radio, television, and film by icons like David Bowie, Freddie Mercury, Carole Pope, and Boy George.

Craig and Lori were strange people, square pegs in a world of round holes. Unusual. Misfits. That is a challenging existence, but their challenges did not stop there.

Few people knew about it, but Craig's life was gripped by mental illness. Mental health was not only poorly understood when he was alive, it simply was not a conversation that was had. Craig self-medicated, and his choice of cocaine led to years of drug dependency. There wasn't a conversation about addiction then, either. It was a vicious cycle from which he could not recover.

Lori faced her own traumas. She had a physically and emotionally abusive parent, was a survivor of rape, and suffered multiple accidents that broke her body and took from her spirit. Suffering from his own mental illness, Craig was at times abusive, too. Lori never realized she was a victim of abuse, nor did she see that, in her dependency, she was an enabler and her behaviour demonstrated an unhealthy obsession with Craig.

Few knew about their challenges, and in time, friends, fans, and even some family came to look at both of them with raised eyebrows. Opinions and reactions to their outlandish behaviour shifted from delightful curiosity to confusion and embarrassment. That judgment compounded Craig's and Lori's challenges, putting another ceiling over them that they could not break through, even after having seemingly broken through every possible barrier.

What people missed is this: as outrageous and nonconformist as they were, Craig and Lori were just like you and me. They were two vulnerable, sensitive people who yearned for love and belonging. For a while I thought that must be why I was driven to learn about them; I could relate to those sentiments. But then I realized that love and a sense of belonging are things we all need and crave, no matter who we are or where we come from.

Research for this book included nearly one hundred interviews; the reviewing of books, movies, audiotapes, letters, and promotional materials; and countless news and feature articles from Canada, the United States, Germany, and the Netherlands. I shared coffee and meals with Craig's and Lori's families and friends, reviewed family photo albums and scrapbooks, listened to their favourite music, toured one of Toronto's greatest theatres with two backstage crew members, danced and sang along at drag shows in the

Gay Village, and went to performances by some of their favourite musicians. I even got a lesson in cosmetics from Craig's young cousin, a professional makeup artist who shares Craig's passion for theatre and transformation.

I was blessed to receive journals, day planners, and an unpublished manuscript belonging to Lori, which were of great insight and allowed me to speak clearly about her feelings, impressions, and experiences. Craig was a little harder: half the time he spoke in character as one of his ladies, and he hid his emotions behind his impressions. But through meaningful interviews with people who knew him and corroboration with other sources, I feel comfortable speaking for him. I feel I knew Craig and Lori. I have written of their lives and experiences as I understand them.

This book is meant to acknowledge the wonderful aspects of Craig's and Lori's lives, identify their strengths, and celebrate their successes. It can't be denied that they made mistakes around every success they enjoyed, dealing with crushing challenges that haunted and hindered them more than anyone realized. But there is a humanity to be recognized where we fall. I have done that here.

Craig's and Lori's difficulties are an equal part of the story of the lives of two people who can only be described as outrageous misfits, who at face value seem so unusual and different, but in reality, could not have been more relatable.

CHAPTER ONE
ALL OF ME

Lori Jenkins had planned a way to meet Craig Russell for weeks.

It was February 1978, and Craig was set to be a guest at a concert at the hip and happening El Mocambo club on Spadina Avenue in Toronto. Lori dropped everything to go. At last she could meet the man she adored. It was a great opportunity to show him the tapestry she had made of his likeness. Maybe she could give it to him. At the very least she could tell him how much she loved him.

Lori was a high school student with a love for the drama club when she first heard about Craig Russell, an impressionist of Hollywood's greatest female entertainers. Craig was making a name for himself in the world then, taking his one-of-a-kind act on the road with a packed touring schedule across North America, Europe, and the United Kingdom. He also had a starring role in the just released, critically acclaimed film *Outrageous!* He'd come a long way from his Mae West Fan Club and Toronto drag-show days. Lori was hooked before she even saw him perform.

When a project came up in Lori's art class, she chose Craig as her subject. She spent weeks carefully sewing a tapestry of Craig as Mae West, Barbra Streisand, and Carol Channing, using colourful thread, feathers, sequins, and rhinestones. She called it *All About Craig*, a play on the title of the film *All About Eve*. Lori was so proud of the final product that she had her brother take photos on slide film before she submitted the tapestry to be included in a student installation downtown.

Lori loved the whole entertainment scene — art, drama, and music — but preferred live theatre. It didn't matter to her whether it was gay or straight, and she did not discriminate in her choice of venues. She saw *A Chorus Line* at the Royal Alexandra Theatre, David Bowie at Maple Leaf Gardens, Shirley MacLaine at the O'Keefe Centre, and B.B. King at the Ontario Place Forum. Café des Copains was her favourite cabaret theatre and Club David's was her favourite disco.

When she wasn't out at a venue somewhere downtown, Lori loved to watch popular talk shows hosted by Alan Hamel and Brian Linehan to see the biggest stars. She liked the interviews so much that she'd make notes about them in her journal. She wrote most of her entries backwards. It was an act of defiance to her mother, who always told her she was backwards.

When Lori liked an entertainer, she would be consumed. Case in point: When she first saw entertainer Peter Allen on Linehan's interview show, *City Lights*, she ran out to Sam the Record Man's flagship store on Yonge Street to buy all of his albums. Lori listened to them — all of them — in time to see him at the Colonial Tavern jazz club, where she made a request for a song she already knew from memory.

Peter's flamboyant persona was right up Lori's alley. She preferred versatile performers who could sing, act, and be funny, but who were also seductive and had vibrant sexualities that teased at gender norms and sexual identity. She loved Freddie Mercury and David Bowie. Lori was elusive when it came to her own sexuality. A part of her was shy; a part of her liked to keep people guessing.

More than any other art form, Lori loved female impersonators, now better known as drag queens. Drag was thriving in Toronto in the 1960s and 1970s. The St. Charles Tavern, the Manatee, Club 511, and the August Club were popular gay clubs that featured drag on their stages. In clubs that accepted female patrons, Lori saw shows by Canadian drag queens Michelle DuBarry, Georgie Girl, Jackie Loren, Michelle Ross, Murray Cooper, Ronnie Holliday, Danny Love, and Rusty Ryan as they were building their careers. She did not see drag as a novelty or something only gay men did.

She respected it as an art form and put drag performers on the same pedestal as other, more mainstream entertainers.

The El Mocambo was drag friendly, too. It was a hot spot in Toronto in those days. The El Mo was popular among the younger generation who wanted rock 'n' roll when other clubs played disco. Blondie, the Ramones, and Joan Jett played there. The Rolling Stones recorded part of their *Love You Live* album there in 1977 and made headlines when they partied there with Margaret Trudeau, wife of then Canadian prime minister Pierre Trudeau.

Lori was no stranger to the El Mo either, and on February 15, 1978, Peter Allen was on the bill. With Craig rumoured to be a special guest, Lori arrived at the venue early, took a table near the stage, and kept her eyes peeled for him. She was so excited she was almost giddy. This was it. This was her chance.

Craig was excited to go, too, but for different reasons. An appearance at the El Mo was a great opportunity for the self-professed "promosexual" to get another mention in newspapers ahead of his planned engagement at the Royal York Hotel later that month. He headed to the club ahead of showtime, entourage in tow, hoping to see reporters he knew.

But the first person who spotted him was Lori. Not missing a beat, she zipped over to his table, squeezed by his bodyguard, and in one breath introduced herself and gave him a photo slide of her *All About Craig* tapestry. She told him she was his biggest fan, explained her artwork with pride, and said she wanted him to have it.

Craig took the sudden demand for his attention in stride. He met fans often and was used to having them around at events and parties. He took some time with most, and he often invited them to hang around and go on to the next venue with him. He was no different with Lori, but since their time was short, he suggested they exchange phone numbers.

Craig did not have any added interest in this particular fan. He was not attracted to her, and was not looking to take her to bed. Lori did not stand out in that way. She was soap-and-water beautiful. She was plainly dressed, a little masculine, and she didn't look femme at all. She fit right in with the popular androgynous look of the time. Her beauty came out in her adoration and enthusiasm; when she was excited, she beamed.

A poster from Craig's days touring the U.S. in the mid-1970s.

To Lori, all that mattered was this moment. She was obsessed with Craig, just as Craig had been with his own idol, Mae West. Lori's entire sense of self-worth at that time was tied to the fact that this movie star seemed to want to get to know her.

Craig wants the tapestry, she thought. *He wants to get to know me.*

She was so thrilled that she documented the exchange in her journal with little mention of Peter Allen's concert at the El Mo that night. Meeting her star was the highlight of her day, her week, and her year. Her world had changed.

Lori never did reach Craig by phone to arrange the handing over of her gift. Undeterred, Lori got in touch with his mother, Norma Hurst, and asked to come over for tea. Norma agreed, and a week later Lori excitedly handed over her tapestry and talked Norma's ear off. Norma was touched by the gesture but found the whole exchange odd. She gave the tapestry to her sister Cathryn who, like Lori, documented everything she could about Craig's career.

Lori met Craig again five months later, in July 1978, when *Outrageous!* screened at the New Yorker Theatre (now the CAA Theatre) on Yonge Street. Craig was away performing in the United States when the film premiered at the 1977 Festival of Festivals in Toronto, so the red carpet was rolled out again for a flashy screening. True to form, Lori knew Craig would be there. She sat through three screenings of the film before he arrived for the fourth.

The energy at the New Yorker couldn't have been higher. Craig arrived with Canadian actress Barbara Hamilton on his arm and an entourage of people around him, including bandmates and a scattering of his family, friends, and fans. Photographer David Street trailed him, too, snapping away with his camera. This star knew how to *arrive*.

Just as she had at the El Mo, Lori took notice of Craig's arrival right away, squeezed to the front of the crowd, handed him a new photo of the tapestry, and asked for his autograph. As Craig signed for her, David called for his attention and the two of them looked up as he snapped yet another shot. David published a photo collection on Craig the next year. The photo with Lori is included, forever capturing the moment.

Craig and Lori entered the theatre separately but by happenstance were seated close together. As a VIP, Craig was treated to chocolate, strawberries,

Craig as Carol Channing in 1978 on the publicity circuit to support Outrageous!

and champagne, and taking notice of the close proximity of his self-professed No. 1 fan, he slipped the treats to her throughout the film. She was delighted, easy to please. He liked this enthusiasm. He also couldn't help but notice she had memorized his lines from beginning to end.

Smitten, Lori followed Craig after the screening to the flashy club Wonder Bar down the block where he and his entourage were celebrating. Lori and Craig picked up their conversation and talked about the tapestry, his performances, and *Outrageous!* Craig was in a casual, celebratory mood. The movie was rocketing him to superstar status.

Lori was increasingly intense. She couldn't help it. She told him flat out that she loved him.

"Wait until we get away from all the bullshit and we get to know each other better," he told her, apprehensive, but intrigued.

Craig loved to be loved. Not only had he worked hard in his career and felt he'd earned that adoration, but also the fact that this stranger professed to love him temporarily filled a longing that he worked to hide. He didn't often feel loved, even in the presence of family, friends, and crowds of people. It was part of a mental illness he didn't have words to explain.

Lori kept on with her theatre-loving life through the next three years. She worked an administrative job by day and spent her evenings and weekends in cinemas, theatres, and clubs. She went to see everyone from Peter Donato to Cher to Diana Ross.

She also kept up her adoration of Craig and his work. She would eventually see *Outrageous!* more than thirty times. She watched and recorded all his TV appearances and kept a book of newspaper clippings. She sent him fan letters. They were written backwards, just like her journal entries.

They didn't meet when Craig returned to Toronto in December 1978 to perform at Massey Hall, but Lori made sure to be there. She shouted, "Bravo! Bravo!" so loudly from her seat that he could hear her from the stage. Lori borrowed a 35 mm camera with telephoto lens for the show and took seventy-two shots of him performing. She was so excited to see the end result that she tried to develop the film herself even though she didn't really know how.

Craig was all over the world in those years. In addition to a packed touring schedule from Las Vegas to London to Sydney, he had countless TV appearances and charity performances with almost constant coverage in newspapers and magazines. One day he'd be performing in a television special; the next he'd be at a children's hospital charity auction. He was everywhere.

He had two more runs at the Imperial Room in Toronto's Royal York Hotel, and in May 1981 he was set to star in a theatre production called *Hogtown* at the Bayview Playhouse Theatre. It was his first play. Craig was good in his role, but his relationships with the producer, director, musical director, and other cast members were rocky, making Lori a welcome reprieve when she reintroduced herself. It didn't take long. She had tickets for all preview performances and every weekend performance once it opened.

Now in need of a friend, Craig invited Lori for drinks at his aunt's midtown apartment, where he was staying. He was grateful to have an ally and pulled out all the stops to impress her. He made them rum and Cokes, showed her a fan letter she had sent him, and pulled out the now infamous tapestry. He then played her German actress and singer Marlene Dietrich's rendition of the song "I Wish You Love."

As Marlene sang the sweet lyrics, Lori started to cry. Her emotions were as fragile as they were intense. It wasn't just the song that was getting to her. It was time with her star.

I've never heard the song before in my life, and here I am beside my idol, listening to a love song, she thought to herself. *I can't believe my fortune in being invited over by Craig.*

Lori must have been quite the sight. When his aunt arrived and introductions were made, she asked if Lori was on drugs.

Craig and Lori chatted about *Hogtown* and his planned summer engagements. He told her he needed a dresser to manage his wardrobe and assist him before and during his performances. It wasn't exactly a job offer, but Lori jumped at the idea and offered her services. So what if she didn't have any formal training in wardrobe? She wanted nothing more than to be around Craig all the time.

Craig agreed they could give it a try, but cautioned her on one point. If their working relationship was going to succeed, she would have to be more assertive. Assertive? Really? It was an odd piece of feedback considering the lengths she had gone to in order to meet and get to know him, but Lori nonetheless took it to heart.

The following Sunday Lori arrived at the Bayview Playhouse Theatre ahead of the afternoon performance even though she wasn't expected until the evening show. She was ready to work and walked in with the attitude that she belonged there and had been part of it all along. When Craig inquired about her unexpected arrival, she held her ground.

"I'm trying to be more assertive," she said proudly and matter-of-factly.

Craig was amused. He had his dresser. Through the rest of the play's run, he taught Lori about all his characters and impressions, how to maintain and set his wigs, how to care for his gowns, and how to prepare his accessories. She worked before and after the show with all of his materials, and stayed side stage through each performance for quick costumes changes.

Lori was a willing and compliant assistant. She lapped up as much responsibility as she could find. She took on all the shopping for supplies, including makeup, wig products, pantyhose, hairbrushes, bobby pins, earrings, razors, and spirits. She kept careful track of each item's cost, before and after tax, in a book of expenditures with a photo of Craig taped on the inside cover. One container of ivory face powder cost $4.73. Two packs of fake eyelashes cost $5.55. A carton of cigarettes and two lighters cost $9.72.

Lori's responsibilities also extended to getting Craig out of bed. One morning she arrived at his apartment and found him passed out in his bedroom, nude with his penis exposed and erect. She was embarrassed and flustered at the scene, but she had a job to do. Lori got him dressed, nudged him into their waiting limousine, and went to work on his nails as he continued sleeping on the drive to an appearance on the television show *Backstage*.

Craig took notice of her efforts and seriousness in building a career in the theatre. He thought she was someone he could mentor. It made him feel strong. Now that she had her work as a dresser down, he told Lori it was time she adopted a stage name to be more professional. Lori Jenkins was far too plain for the theatre world.

Together, they settled on the name "Lori Westman." Westman was Lori's mother's maiden name. It also reminded Craig of his beloved Mae. The name and their pairing seemed to fit perfectly.

* * *

In late July 1981, Craig and Lori were off to Provincetown, Massachusetts, for a seasonal engagement in the Madeira Room at the Pilgrim House hotel.

Provincetown has a thriving arts scene with multiple theatres, performance groups, and long-standing events. Entertainers from all over the world descend every summer, taking up residence and engagements that pack houses into the fall. The shows are so popular that some theatregoers move in right alongside the actors, singers, and playwrights to watch all the theatre and live entertainment they can get.

Craig called it P-P town. He had spent several summers there over the years, but now with Lori he had a permanent backstage crew member to support him. He couldn't have found anyone more dedicated.

Lori reported to Craig's cottage every day at noon and took care of any messages he needed handled. That included mailing replies to fan letters, and shopping in markets and shops for flowers and new jewellery. She'd then go over his costumes, make alterations and repairs as needed, and give them a fresh steam cleaning. They'd take a break for dinner and then head to the theatre for two shows nightly, with Craig performing onstage and Lori just behind the curtain for costume changes.

Lori wanted everything to be perfect and left no detail untouched. She dressed in a tuxedo to look professional, and she made sure Craig's gowns sparkled, his wigs were perfectly set, and his costume changes were quick and efficient. She added small details for his characters — a feather boa here, a pair of sunglasses there — and hauled her mother's trunk onto the sparse stage as a prop. During the live show, she snuck away from her side-stage post to blend in with the crowd and liven things up during the Q & A segment of the show.

"Do you believe in love at first sight?" Lori asked Craig from the audience during the show one night. He was dressed as Mae.

"Yeah, it saves a lot of time!" Mae replied to audience laughter.

Away from the theatre, Lori picked up Craig's housekeeping work. The two lived separately, but she took it upon herself to keep his cottage tidy and see that his linens and towels were fresh and clean. She wanted movie star treatment for her star. Craig knew what she was up to and thanked her in advance before he returned home one night with two men to find a

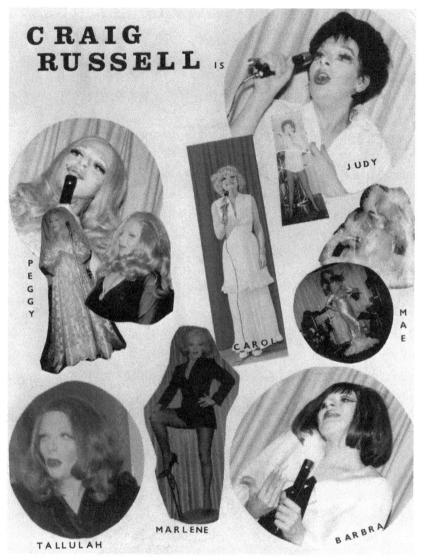

An early poster of Craig's performing days.

freshly made bed for them to share. As much as she wanted to share a bed with him instead, Lori was more pleased to have found his approval.

With their close existence in Provincetown, Lori grew accustomed to Craig's habits, preferences, and idiosyncrasies. She knew he preferred to eat alone, so she left him for most meals. She cleaned up his hair when he would shave his head to make wearing wigs easier. She kept Disaronno Originale liqueur on hand in his dressing room, knowing he liked to sip it with a cigarette between shows. One night she spilled some of the liqueur on a line of cocaine he asked her to leave for him on a compact. They licked it later, at his urging. Their tongues were numb and their eyes twinkled at the rush of the drug.

Craig was a frequent drug user. He believed drugs like cocaine improved his performances and made him livelier. What he hadn't yet told Lori was that he had been diagnosed with manic depression but had shunned prescription drugs to treat it because the downers prescribed by his doctor made it impossible to perform. This was his livelihood. He needed to focus and perform well to make his living.

"With drugs, you become totally insensitive to everything but your mission," he told her years later. "You put blinkers on, without regard to your personal life."

A lack of regard would be the right way to describe some of Craig's behaviour. Anywhere he stayed or lived was often messy and would be nearly destroyed by the end of his stay, with furniture broken, walls damaged, and linens ruined. Lori wrote that Craig wiped soot from the fireplace all over the kitchen walls, cupboards, dishes, and glasses in his cottage that summer. He threw out a bunch of her music cassettes, and one night he melted one on the stove burner.

"Evil, capital E–Evil!" Craig said with a laugh, imitating actress Bette Davis as he melted a tape that included actress Joan Crawford, Davis's real-life rival.

Lori didn't complain, even in her journals. When he was moody, she would remove herself from the situation. When he was angry with her, she would be hurt but take the jab at her feelings. She asked no questions and she made no demands. Lori was a child of abuse and had lived through years of physical trauma. She was almost immune to pain.

But Craig's erratic behaviour was an increasing problem that even he recognized. He didn't feel he could control himself. He didn't know how to keep his moods in check and their volatility confused and embarrassed him at times. He once asked Lori why she put up with it and why she didn't stand up for herself when he was behaving poorly. He admitted he was terrified.

"I'm sorry for being abrupt," he gingerly told her one night after he snapped at her for attempting to clean. He elaborated that he took his anger out on her simply because she always seemed to be there.

"You've got me," he assured her, with two kisses on the forehead.

"You've got me, too!" she eagerly countered, situation forgotten.

Another night, as an apology, he wrote her a poem about how having her there helped him realize how beautiful his world was.

Tuesdays were nights off. Craig would take Lori around to other venues he liked and introduce her to fans he'd met over his previous stays and artists like female impressionist Charles Pierce, singer Maxene Andrews from the Andrews Sisters harmony trio, and comedian Beverly Cardella, who went by the stage name Pudgy. One night Craig did Lori's makeup and told her she had the same hair colour as Mae West. She took the comparison as a big compliment. They celebrated Mae's birthday that August, even though she had died the year before.

It was a charmed time for Lori. The previous three months had been a whirlwind. She went from having a somewhat solitary existence to being the close, trusted assistant to a global star whom she adored and loved. Her love grew more and more each day as she took his small acts of kindness, tenderness, and support as grand gestures. A Post-it Note hello was a love letter. A gift of Joy perfume was a forever memory.

The intensity of Lori's feelings for Craig had not ebbed. He saw that. But the feeling was not mutual and he found her adoration increasingly overwhelming. He cared for Lori, was willing to mentor her, and wanted to support her, but the line was drawn. They were friends, not lovers. Boundaries were needed.

He had to put a pin in it, but he didn't know exactly how. He tried to tell her in his own way. When he couldn't find the words, he tried a humorous act or gesture to get his message across. One day he left Lori a note, asking for space.

"Too close for comfort, don't fence me in," he wrote. "In the past seven months, Lori, I have had to face a whole bunch of realities … Timing is everything. Use your keen sense and instinct and you'll know what to do. I need a road manager, not a shadow. Brighten up. You're my Number One!"

She replied with a note telling him, "You're my star, always shining bright."

Another night when Lori again made her loving feelings known, Craig dove into an impression of the character Jane Hudson from the film *What Ever Happened to Baby Jane?*

"I don't fuck fans, Blanche," he said, pushing Lori around in a wheelchair, acting every bit as crazed as Jane in the film.

Lori laughed but didn't get the point.

Craig's drug-induced manic behaviour continued and worsened into September. Taking notice, a friend from the Pilgrim House reached out to Lori with concern. It was like an intervention, but the addict wasn't there. The friend wanted Lori to take action and stop Craig's drug use.

"Craig is doing too much cocaine," she said, concerned. "He doesn't need to do it at all. Perhaps you, Lori, can get through to him."

The friend continued that she thought Craig and Lori were much more than an idol and a fan. They were "whole together … apart they were only a half." Together they were "one soul."

With those two words, the point of the meeting was lost. Their observed closeness was the only point Lori heard. Her heart swelled. She didn't press the drug issue further.

The summer stay ended abruptly. Craig told Lori he had a heated discussion with the owner of the Pilgrim House and the rest of his shows there were cancelled. It was another tie severed for Craig, another relationship lost. They had been coming undone in his life for almost three years. Lori had no idea.

Craig was enraged by the circumstances. He not only insisted they leave town, he also told Lori she was no longer employed and to go home to Toronto alone. She would have to look out for herself. He did not need her anymore.

Lori was shocked and devastated but left quickly, just as he wanted. She got as far as Boston on the trip home when she realized they hadn't talked about what to do with his wigs and gowns. He couldn't perform without them. He might not want to employ her, but his materials had to be taken care of. The show could not go on without them.

She adjusted her tickets and went right back to Provincetown, as determined to assertively stand up for what she wanted to do as when she had gone to work as his dresser four months earlier. It didn't take long to find her star. He had nowhere to go.

"Why are you dragging this thing out?" Craig asked her. "Your term of employment has ended, and it's time to lead your own life."

Lori held her ground and fibbed. She wasn't there for him, she said. She was planning to stick around to get some sun, so she might as well take care of everything as he figured out where he was going next. She would not be dissuaded in that decision.

Craig was exasperated and spent. He had no fight left; in fact, it was somewhat of a relief to have someone fight for him and not against him. He needed the love. He pulled her on to his lap and they cuddled through the evening. They didn't speak about her supposed firing again.

To make up for his coldness, Craig invited Lori to join him at the Crown & Anchor where he booked a final show. Victorious, she agreed. She was proud of herself for standing up for what she wanted to do. That wasn't something she had done before. It did not matter that she had to lie.

Singer Houston Allred, a dynamic entertainer plucked from the cabaret theatre scene, was performing in the lounge at the Crown & Anchor when Craig and Lori arrived the next day. Houston took notice of them, pointed Craig out to the small crowd, and told the audience Craig was "an extremely brilliant man who is far ahead of his time."

Craig's resolve softened. Lori beamed with pride.

Houston then sang the Charles Aznavour tune "What Makes a Man" and dedicated it to Craig. On a break the trio fell into conversation. Knowing nothing about all that had transpired, including Lori's true feelings for Craig, Houston had nothing but praise for her. He told her she was a "tremendous influence" on Craig's life and a help for his "suicidal tendencies."

Suicide? Lori wondered. *When did he say he wanted to kill himself?*

There was so much Lori had yet to learn. Before she had a chance to question Houston's comment, the singer had more praise. He told Lori she brought a calming influence to Craig's high-energy persona, with his diva-like reputation, mood swings, and demands. If Craig were smart, he'd be wise to keep her around.

At the end of the weekend, when Lori finally headed back to Toronto, it was set. Lori Jenkins would always be there for Craig Russell, no matter what.

Craig would come to depend on that.

CHAPTER TWO

REAL MEN

One of the best Christmas gifts Craig ever received was a pair of earrings. His grandmother Bessie Hall gave them to him when he was just five years old.

Bessie knew there was something different about her grandson. He was not like most little boys. He was loud and flamboyant, and he gestured frequently and effeminately. He had character, and at a very young age he could transform himself and impersonate people.

When he was nine, Craig donned a red velvet coat, pants with a shiny black belt, and a matching hat for the family Christmas party. The Halls had their own little Santa Claus to hand out gifts to delighted aunts, uncles, and cousins that year. Craig loved the attention. It was his first taste of transformation.

As he would write years later, he was "a Hollywood child who happened to be born in Canada."

Russell Craig Eadie was born at Toronto General Hospital on January 10, 1948, and was adopted by Russell Eadie and his wife, Norma Hall. They gave their first and only child his adoptive father's name but called him by his middle name.

Russell was on leave from the Canadian Navy when he met Norma. They got married and worked together in an insurance company in Scarborough just before Craig was born. Russell was a man's man with traditional values who wanted to build a nuclear family and a white-picket-fence life in the suburbs. A son to carry on the family name suited him just fine.

Norma gave no inclination that she yearned for the joys of mother-hood when they married. In her mind it was something married couples just did. She'd prove herself a good mother to Craig, devoted to all of his needs. She shared the joys of babyhood and toddlerhood with her childless sisters, Melba and Cathryn.

Craig was a cute, chunky baby, with rosy cheeks, curly blond hair, and a baby face he kept well into grade school. He didn't stand out for his looks as much as he did for his personality. He was lively and mischievous, always animated and seeking the attention of adults. He liked to make them laugh, and he liked to play off other people's quirks or annoyances.

When he saw that his antics amused his mother, in particular, he kept going. On several occasions little Craig imitated Lucille Ball by wrapping a towel around his head, pouting his lips, and copying Lucy's gestures. That had Norma in stitches. Craig and his mother shared a love of music, and they spent hours listening to her records and singing. Norma thought her boy would make a fine addition to a church choir someday.

"He was very, not precocious, but unique as a child," his aunt Cathryn would later say. "He was always mimicking people. We probably egged him on a bit."

An entertaining child was a good fit in the Hall family. They were party people. They'd host big bashes at their house and cottage, with family and friends coming out in their best clothes for nights of food, music, drinking, and dancing. Craig loved that energy. The party would continue after the guests left, as little Craig kept his mother and aunts laughing imitating the people who'd been there.

It was at his uncle Howard Hall's wedding to Zula Jackson in 1951 where Craig took a liking to fashion. A photo shows him joyous with a big smile as he watched the bride and groom walk down the aisle in their formal wear. The dresses and accessories other women were wearing mesmerized him, too. He liked the glitz and glamour of it all. Back at

The moment little Craig Eadie, age three, fell in love with femininity in 1951.

home, he started to dress up in his mother's clothes and shoes. Norma and her family let him be. They never questioned his interest in girls' things. Whatever makes him happy, everyone said, thinking Craig would probably just outgrow it.

Russell, however, was not amused. He had a very specific idea of what boys should be like and how they should behave. Boys were not to have an interest in girls' things or wear girls' clothes, nor were they to be silly and generate attention. They were to be well-behaved, disciplined, and in control. An early school photo of Craig shows a lad with a tight, military crewcut and a starched white collared shirt. Yet with his rosy cheeks, long eyelashes, and easy smile, he was almost pretty. He did not fit the image of the disciplined son his father wanted.

Russell expressed his displeasure with an iron fist. He had a son, not a daughter. He not only disapproved of his effeminate son, but he also disapproved of his wife's acceptance of him.

Russell and Norma's relationship was rocky as their little boy grew up. Norma's sister Cathryn told the family of an afternoon in Russell and Norma's insurance office where the couple had a fight that culminated in Russell hitting Norma. The Hall family believed Russell was drinking heavily and philandering with other women, out living life on terms he could control. Not surprisingly, the marriage failed.

Craig was shaken by his parents' divorce. Already confused as to why his father did not accept him, he now had to face the breakup of his household. Now he would have two homes and two beds. In one, he was accepted; in the other, he longed to feel wanted.

To make matters worse, Craig was torn from Norma for a while. Divorce was not common in the 1950s, and the division of home and children did not necessarily favour mothers. Norma believed the best way to keep custody of Craig was to leave him with her mother in Port Perry through the proceedings. The little town was a nice, quiet place for kids, and Craig would have two of his cousins to play with.

Bessie took Craig under her wing and the two became close. Knowing her grandson's interest in performing, Bessie signed him up for music lessons. He took piano from his aunt Zula's mother, Gertrude Jackson, and joined the children's choir at Port Perry United Church. He would later sing with the St. James Cathedral choir in Toronto. Craig excelled in music and had a good singing voice with impressive range, but he grew fidgety with the formality of performances. He never did well when he had to adhere to any kind of protocol.

"I wanted to do jokes and patter but it didn't fit into the show," he wrote years later. "I wish I could have sung like Peggy Lee."

After his parents' divorce was settled, Craig moved back in with Norma. She raised him in Toronto with help from Cathryn and Melba. They were like a pack of den mothers around a cub. Norma was the provider with the rules and values. She was practical, logical, and the voice of reason. Melba was the disciplinarian — "whatever Melba said, you did," a family friend remembers. Cathryn provided devotion, sweetness, and love. But still, Craig longed for the father who didn't seem to want him.

Craig found distraction in movies and television. He loved to watch variety shows and late-night movies, long after he should have been in bed. He wasn't much of a fan of wholesome kids' shows like *The Mickey Mouse Club*, *Father Knows Best*, and *Leave It to Beaver*. Instead, he was drawn to adult programs like *I Love Lucy*, *The Loretta Young Show*, and *The Jackie Gleason Show*. He liked characters, music, comedy, and the sound of audience laughter and applause.

It was while watching these shows that Craig was drawn to female entertainers. But it was about more than the fashion now. He had grown fascinated by femininity, and strong women appealed to him. It empowered him.

"Feminine strength is stronger, more enduring, oh, more reliable than masculine strength," he said. "The males I know pretend to be strong through attitude, posture, voice. Women can sit and play at being feminine and underneath there's a core that comes from being strong."

Strong is not a word that would have been used to describe Craig at age twelve. Hitting puberty, he was an emotional eater and his weight ballooned to 160 pounds. He avoided gym class at school because he didn't understand sports. He fumbled with what to do and was relentlessly teased as a result. Embarrassed, he wouldn't interact with other boys and tried to blend in with the girls.

"There's nothing worse than a fat person jiggling around and pretending to be athletic," he said. "When my report card came out, there was no mark for phys. ed. Instead of a grade the teacher just wrote in 'unknown.' That got me into hot water."

He began to act out. He was the class clown and caused disruptions at school, wanting attention. He skipped more classes, wrote obscenities in school books, and regularly prank called one of his teachers. It was all a cry for help. Craig was struggling. He felt unloved and misunderstood, and he didn't know where he belonged.

He found comfort listening to his records. The first record he ever owned was a live recording of Judy Garland, *Judy at Carnegie Hall*. He cherished the troubled star and all of her songs. She had talent and was an impressive vocalist, and the vulnerability in her delivery intrigued him. He connected with her.

But Craig needed more than records. Norma thought her son needed his father, and she had him move in with Russell in the Scarborough neighbourhood of West Hill, reasoning that Russell could provide the security and strength Craig couldn't seem to find. She thought the two could bond, and Russell could see Craig into manhood.

It wasn't a good decision. Russell no more accepted Craig as a preteen with a love for Judy Garland than he did when his son was an effeminate toddler. Craig said Russell burned his women's fashion magazines, was scornful of his records of female entertainers, and scoffed when Craig used makeup to cover his prominent teenage acne.

Cosmetics were particularly important for him. While others were busy making out, he was busy making up. He often said he carried his face in a bag. But the young teenage Craig was ridiculed at school for that practice. Eventually, other kids — and even some adults — harassed Craig at home with prank calls about the queer boy and his girly ways. Russell was furious at his son for that.

"He didn't think I was trying hard enough to become one of the boys," Craig said. "That put my head into a terrible space for quite a while and I used up a lot of Kleenex."

Russell and Craig were also not aligned morally. Craig said that one day Russell sat him down with gin and a cigarette and made him have both, in hopes his son would be sick and never touch either again. It had the opposite effect. Craig said he felt high and fabulous.

Craig Eadie, second from right in the second row from the back, publicly overweight and privately unhappy.

It was a temporary reprieve. Craig didn't feel fabulous at home. He never found acceptance. Russell loved his child, but he did not have the son he knew how to have. Craig wanted badly to please his father, but he couldn't change or hide who he was. Defeated, he concluded that his father "didn't want a fag for a son."

That may have been true, but there may have been another reason for Russell's rejection of Craig, one not spoken of openly. It had to do with Craig's biological parentage.

Norma quietly told the Hall family that one of Craig's biological parents was one of Russell's siblings. That was how they adopted him. The sibling was young, thought to be promiscuous, and suspected of having mental health problems. It was impossible to keep and raise the baby, so compounded with the personal struggles at hand, Craig's birth became a point of deeply rooted shame for the Eadie family.

"Mental illness was strong within the family, I believe," an Eadie family member says, speaking on a condition of anonymity. "They didn't know how to love in conjunction with whatever mental challenges they had. Mental illness just made for a very difficult life."

Two Eadie family members confirm Norma's story, though they refute that it was the sibling Norma sometimes named and point to another. Very little information is known, even seventy years later. An extended family member says it was a private family matter that not all family members are aware of. No one wants to talk about it further.

So it wasn't only Russell who rejected Craig. His entire paternal family did.

Rejection would soon take a back seat to a new obsession. Craig was all of twelve when he saw the films *My Little Chickadee* and *I'm No Angel*, old films from the 1930s and 1940s starring an actress he hadn't heard of before. She was the most confident and forthright woman he'd ever seen. She was feminine, just as he liked, but had an enduring, masculine strength; a "truck driver in drag with something enchanting about her." Her name was Mae West.

"Oh God," he thought. "This is someone I have to know."

Mae was a buxom blonde, with a confident swagger and a seemingly unshakable bravado and control paired with a quick wit and deadpan one-liners. She was vibrant, flirtatious, seductive, and suggestive — easily the most outwardly sexual person in Hollywood. She'd been called the "Queen of Sex" and a "Statue of Libido."

"My ego is breakin' records," she said, with her usual seductive sneer. "I see myself as a classic, you know what I mean?"

Mae was incredibly sexy for a woman in her sixties, at a time when older women, if they were seen at all, were encouraged to age quietly, with grace. In contrast, Mae wanted not only to be seen but to be lusted after. Her eyes were outlined with black makeup, and her lips were pursed and ruby red. She had buxom breasts, creamy smooth skin, and a voluptuous figure that seemed to defy what time and age did to the body. She hit all the marks of a sex symbol.

"It's better to be looked over than overlooked," she drawled.

Craig, then a preteen living in sleepy Scarborough, where everyone seemed so proper, loved this entertainer immediately. She inspired him. Who cared what anyone expected of him as a boy, what anyone thought, or how anyone else made him feel? In Mae he had found someone really compelling, someone who didn't apologize for eschewing convention and being who they were.

"Her whole image was so different than anything I'd ever seen," he recalled years later. "She had real star quality."

Craig's interest in Mae skyrocketed when she made an appearance on *The Red Skelton Show*, a variety series on CBS featuring sketch comedy and musical performances.

The show had already introduced Craig to many of the entertainers he liked. He absorbed their fashion, music, and comedy, as well as their personas, styles, and gestures. Now he was excited to find that Mae was to appear as a guest star. She had been largely absent from television and film after more than twenty years of breaking the mould as a woman in Hollywood. And true to form for her young fan, the great dame did not disappoint.

Not that there was any doubt. Mae was an actress, singer, playwright, writer, and comedian who got her start at the turn of the century. She made waves almost immediately. She got attention performing in amateur talent shows when she was under ten years old, seductively danced and sang in vaudeville through her teens, and married an older man when she was just seventeen years old, the year she first appeared on Broadway. She had many indiscretions outside of her young marriage, and the second one that followed, and was widely known for that cavalier behaviour.

In 1926 she wrote and starred in a play she daringly titled *Sex*, a word typically reserved for medical journals then. When the production opened in New York, with Mae playing a prostitute, a *New York Times* review called it "a crude, inept play, cheaply produced and poorly acted." It was later subjected to a police raid that charged its makers with "indecent performances."

Mae spent more than a week in jail for that, but unbowed, she went on to produce another play that included another controversial topic: homosexuality. Called *The Drag*, the dramatic production centred on homosexual relationships, then still illegal in the United States, and the cost of living a secret life. It was so controversial on stages in New Jersey and Connecticut that, despite its financial success, it closed after just a few weeks and was never permitted to run on Broadway.

More productions followed with much the same results. With the theatre world shaken up by the vibrant young star, Mae headed out to the film world and appeared in ten movies made in quick succession, including *She Done Him Wrong*, *Goin' to Town*, and *Belle of the Nineties* (originally titled *It Ain't No Sin*). She was so in demand, so powerful, that allegedly she commanded that her salary exceed that of a male studio head.

Her boldness spilled over into her music, too. When Judy Garland was on the charts for "Over the Rainbow" and Kate Smith was singing "God Bless America," Mae was singing songs with titles like "I Want You, I Need You," "A Guy What Takes His Time," and "My Man Friday."

Mae had a lot of talent, but the thread that wound through her work was her persona. She was dominant, provocative, and inviting. She liked her men and craved male attention but with a caveat. She treated men the way she felt they treated other women. She would never lose her position having the upper hand. Everything about how she carried herself seemed to say *want me*. And they did.

"Come up and see me some time," she'd say, with a wink and cocked hip. It was a take on a line from one of her movies. She repeated it, and others like it, often.

Censors were hot on Mae's heels as her career progressed. Her film *Klondike Annie* was to include a prostitute in the storyline, but the Motion Picture Production Code — also known as the Hays Code of acceptable moral content for movies — censored the part. Mae saw lines rewritten or altogether removed from her scripts, her wardrobe scaled back with necklines raised, and some of her material deemed not distributable.

"There were a lot of things censors wouldn't let me do in the movies that I had done on the stage," she said in 1969. "They wouldn't even let me sit on a guy's lap — and I'd been on more laps than a napkin."

It was a losing battle. She stepped away from films in 1943. Her fans still adored her. She had legend status.

"There is no other Mae West," a *New York Times* article said. "She is an institution, a living legend as much a part of American folklore as Paul Bunyan or Tom Sawyer or Babe Ruth."

Mae's 1960 appearance on *The Red Skelton Show* sealed the deal for Craig. He was more than hooked. He was obsessed. She embodied so many

Craig as a teenager, more confident with his love for Mae.

of the qualities that appealed to him: femininity, fashion and style, humour, aggression, sexual control, and above all strength and confidence. There was no stopping her. He was not attracted to her in the sense that she had intimate sexual appeal. Craig wanted to be like her. He wanted to be strong like her. He wanted to be wanted like her.

Craig set out to see, read, and learn everything he could about Mae. He saw all her movies and listened to her music, sometimes imitating her while looking in the mirror. He read her 1959 autobiography, *Goodness Had Nothing to Do with It.* He went to newspaper offices and looked for clippings in their archives. He bought posters. He repeated her jokes and quips.

Craig liked fashion and drawing, so when he learned famed wardrobe designer Edith Head at Paramount Pictures in Hollywood had worked as Mae's stylist, he sent her his sketches of ladies' fashion. Edith returned his drawings with a letter saying they were interesting. Curiously, she addressed the letter to "Miss Craig Eadie."

His family couldn't help but take notice of Craig's interest. They thought it was, in Howard Hall's words, "strange. She was old enough to be his grandmother!" But as always, they let him be with his interests.

Craig founded the Mae West Fan Club on January 13, 1962. He was fourteen. The club was really just Craig and his collection of materials and memorabilia, with self-penned newsletters about Mae's life and career. There wouldn't have been much new to report. With the exception of a few albums, Mae was a virtual recluse by then. Craig didn't care. He made things up. She was his idol and her influence made him feel more confident than he had ever been.

Mae was someone he saw as confident, strong, and wanted — all things he thought he wasn't.

Just as Craig was shaped by his obsession with Mae, he met three people who would further shape his formative years.

In 1963, when Craig was enrolled at West Hill Collegiate Institute in Scarborough, he befriended Shirley Flavell, a fellow student. She was awkward, nonconformist, more comfortable in a library or movie theatre, and as she says now, starving for meaningful conversation. They had met a few years earlier at Jesse Ketchum Junior High School when Craig was living with Norma, but they didn't really talk until one day at West Hill when he spotted her and struck up a conversation.

"I thought it was fantastic to know a guy who knows so much that most guys don't know about," she remembers.

Shirley introduced Craig to fellow student and friend Margaret Gibson who, like them, was seemingly out of sync with other teenagers. A paranoid schizophrenic, Margaret was just out of the Homewood Institute in Guelph, Ontario. She was petite, intense, and languid, with an intense gaze from her big eyes and a low, husky voice. She didn't talk much. She was an observer, a listener, and an analyzer who didn't trust people.

"To me, she was a combination of Lauren Bacall and Faye Dunaway," says Shirley. "She didn't say much, but when she said something, she was a person you could have a conversation with."

When Margaret met Craig, they were instantly the best aligned of the three of them.

"Shirley tells me that you've been in a mad house for two and a half years," Craig told her. "That's fine with me. My whole life is a mad house."

Margaret laughed and loved him immediately. There was an instant connection. Unconventional childhoods aside, the two of them shared the almost hopeless feeling of not fitting in. He was the effeminate teenage boy in love with femininity who most assumed was gay. She was the socially isolated girl who told people she was, in her lingo, mad.

"Craig was the one person who understood me, without words, and who could make me laugh," Margaret said.

She and Shirley had almost a puppy love for Craig. They wanted to be where he was, and he was equally drawn to them. Shirley noticed how he seemed closest to women, more comfortable with the intimacy shared among female friends. After his father's rejection and childhood bullying, Craig put on more armour around men.

One exception was his closeness with Phil Buckley, a British expat and fellow student at Cedarbrae Collegiate Institute, a high school with an arts program where Craig later transferred. Just realizing his own homosexuality and hopelessly shy, Phil was drawn to Craig's boldness and sense of humour. Craig was the centre of attention in a room. Appealing. Someone worth getting to know.

Craig introduced Phil to Shirley and Margaret, and the four misfits became a unit. They saw themselves as unique and different from the seemingly monolithic kids born into the growing Scarborough suburbs. They eschewed such existence and formality, fitting together when they otherwise felt out of place.

"We were like the outcasts," says Phil. "Certainly you recognize other people for being similar to yourself. We just really hit it off. We were inseparable."

It was good the friends had each other. If they were even just a few years older at the time, they could have gotten in a lot of trouble for being different or identifying as gay or lesbian. Homosexuality was so misunderstood.

As gay liberation surged forward in the early to mid-1960s, homosexuality was in the limelight as almost a curiosity. *Maclean's* magazine published a two-part series called "The Homosexual Next Door: A Sober Appraisal of a New Social Phenomenon." The *Toronto Daily Star* reported fears that after-hours clubs were opening as "hangouts for male and female homosexuals" and later published two columns that outlined medical and psychiatric treatments for people worried they might have the "homosexual problem."

The year 1964 was a big one for change: a Canadian Broadcasting Corporation (CBC) telecast led an hour-long discussion on legal, medical, and religious attitudes toward homosexuality; the first homophile organization in Canada was formed in Vancouver; filmmaker Claude Jutra brought the theme of homosexuality into French cinema; and a Catholic church panel agreed homosexuality was a sin but should not be a crime.

Legal rights and protection quickly moved to the forefront. New Democrat minister of parliament Arnold Peters prepared to introduce a private member's bill on the decriminalization of homosexual acts in the Criminal Code, but it never reached the floor in the House of Commons. The federal social hygiene committee needed time to investigate possible reforms.

In Toronto a growing gay community took shape quickly. After-hours bars ("juice bars" that went unlicensed) opened on a vibrant but seedy strip of Yonge Street, and social groups began to pop up. Soon there were so many events going on and places opening up that the weekly newspaper *Tab* featured a column called The Gay Set to report news of gay activities.

The added visibility wasn't always a good thing. Police officers frequently harassed gay men and lesbian women. They were intimidated, threatened, and sometimes beaten. More often the target, men were charged with indecency for doing as little as dancing together. Some charges stuck and others were dropped, but the social stigma of being outed stayed.

An August 5, 1964, story in the *Globe and Mail* said Toronto police were frustrated with the growing popularity of clubs for homosexuals because behaviour in them was, for the most part, proper. Police could not clear up the problem if no charges could be laid. What worried law enforcement was that the clubs were "gathering places for homosexuals and as such offer[ed] a chance for homosexuality to be spread by introduction."

Relations with police would only continue to sour.

"The overwhelming majority of gay people feel that the police are increasingly prejudice[d]," a 1967 gay community newsletter sent to the Metropolitan Toronto Police read. "The problem is not with the average police officers, but with some of you who are failing to realize that this province has changed, some of you who are failing to adapt to those changes, some of you who are failing to provide the leadership this province needs to take it into a peaceful future."

Craig, Shirley, Margaret, and Phil, who once playfully called themselves the "Four Musketeers," were aware of some of the goings-on but mostly oblivious to it. Their focus on each other and empty bank accounts made for the perfect protective bubble.

They spent their time listening to records, watching television, and going to the movies. Craig and Margaret did each other's makeup. They both had an appreciation for heavy black mascara and eyeliner. Together they'd make the boring suburban nights come alive between them.

Craig prattled on to them about Mae. He played them her records, told them about her movies, and pulled out all of his memorabilia. He proudly shared how he was the president of the official Mae West Fan Club and now they were the first members.

"He was a one-man show," says Shirley. "He did the whole deal. We got an eyeful and became well-versed in everything there was to know about her."

Growing bored, Craig said it was about time to let Mae know of "all this interest." He pulled out a phone book and wrote down a list of random names accompanied by matching signatures to signify attendance, drafted minutes for a meeting he had not had, and sent it off to Mae in Hollywood to tell her there was a growing fan club in Canada.

Mae took notice. She loved attention of any kind. She even kept the phone number to one of her homes listed in the phone book, in the hope she'd hear from fans and admirers. She was flattered to hear from this teenager and his growing club, so her secretary sent him signed lithographs for each of his members and twenty-five more for other fans she knew of who could maybe join his club, too.

Craig was thrilled. He later received a $50 cheque with 250 more names and addresses of fans who would like his newsletters. The faux fan club became real and was rebranded as the Mae West Fan Club International. He was a good leader. He advertised the club in teenage magazines to generate membership and wrote to other magazines to encourage them to write about Mae, assuring them his loyal reader base would increase their sales.

The *Toronto Daily Star* profiled Craig's efforts early on. Reporter Robert Reguly wrote how Elizabeth Taylor, Frank Sinatra, and Elvis Presley had more active careers, yet only Mae West seemed to have a fan club in Toronto. He called it "something of a freak."

Why Mae? Craig told the reporter she had "that extra something special — mainly sex. She makes it funny."

Nothing else mattered to Craig. Not the rejection from his father, fitting in at school, the bullies who were still prank calling his house, or the hostile environment in the gay community he felt pulled to. Craig was all about Mae. She gave him purpose and strength. He said she was "a connection with magic and I knew it."

Mae eventually reached out to Craig herself and encouraged him to phone her in California. He did, using his telephone with the picture of Mae taped to the centre of the rotary dial. Shirley and Phil don't remember the crux of the first conversation, but Mae was flattered by his adoration and took a liking to him. They had regular calls with updates on her activities to report in the fan club newsletter after that.

One of Craig's reports in an October 1966 newsletter reads:

> I mentioned in the September newsletter that David Mallet, whose name we all recognize as the arranger-producer of Miss West's "Way Out West" album, had telephoned with sensational news. "Miss West," he told me, "is making a new album for Christmas ... just for the fans!" ... It's exciting to be able to relate such wonderful news to all!

Craig's work wasn't limited to newsletters. He exchanged some personal correspondence with select fans across Canada and the U.S. as well. In them he wrote pleasantly and colourfully about news of Mae, peppered with details from his phone calls with her and the people in her life he was beginning to know by association.

"I spoke with Miss West last Friday night (the 21st) and she sounds wonderful," he wrote to a fan. "M.W. sends her love, and I add my warmest regards. More news soon."

Craig posed for a Toronto Star *photographer with his Mae West memorabilia.*

When Mae extended an offer to come and stay with her for a few weeks, Craig eagerly accepted. His mother, Norma, and her second husband, Eric Hurst, were perplexed but happy for him. What could they say? How many people get to go and stay with their idol? They let him go. Not that it mattered; there was no holding him back. Norma encouraged him to save his money and helped plan the trip.

It was the summer of 1965 when Craig travelled to Lotusland by bus on a trip that took three days and three nights. He said it was well worth it. He loved the California sunshine and beautiful people as much as he did Mae, with her posh lifestyle that included multiple properties, a chauffeur, maids, and a cook.

His stories of their initial first meeting had variation. In the most consistent of them, he said she met him at her Santa Monica beach house on day one looking fresh-faced and decades younger than her age, wearing a tightly fitted white miniskirt cut two inches above the knee, and holding a glamorous white chiffon scarf. Her eyelashes were alluring, her smooth skin was without imperfection, and her blonde hair — a wig — looked almost golden in the California sunshine.

"Hello, baby," she said, extending her arms to the teenage boy who said he felt pure love for her.

The hug she gave him was so tight and strong that she almost lifted Craig off the ground.

"Mae, you look great," he told her. "How do you feel?"

"Mmmm, honey, you got hands," she said, in her usual seductive tone. "You tell me."

Craig was awestruck. His idol was a splash. He wanted this life.

Mae nicknamed her live-in guest "the Kid." She took him around to her properties and favourite haunts in Beverly Hills. Her cook made up her favourite meals for him to try, and when she and Craig didn't stay in, she took him to Perino's on Wilshire Boulevard in Hollywood, one of her favourite restaurants. She entertained him by having her pet Bolivian monkeys, named Toughy and Pretty Boy, dress in bow ties, imitate her, and peel her grapes.

Craig said one of her pet monkeys bit him that summer, cutting deeply into the skin, spattering blood on the furniture, and leaving him with a scar. It was an unusual scene that ended with Mae warning him not to tell his parents and sending her pets to a local animal farm. Craig said Mae later took pleasure in driving by the farm to wave and taunt the monkeys with bananas, seemingly to remind them of their freedom and what they were missing.

It is a bizarre tale and the truth of it remains unclear. But it *is* true that Craig learned a lesson that summer that he never forgot: do not cross Mae West.

Monkey business aside, the most lasting memories for Craig involved Mae's tales of making motion pictures and records, breaking egos, and attracting men. He thought she was a true original. And just as he idolized her and fed off everything she said and did, Mae fed off the constant attention from him, too.

"I love the way you rave about me," she told him.

It was not a bad way for either of them to spend the summer.

Biographer R. Mark Desjardins notes how Mae attracted strange and unusual people, so there would be no questions asked about this guest. Of course, Mae would have a teenage fan stay over. Anything was possible. But the reality was this seventeen-year-old actually had something to offer her. Mae wanted a resurgence into the world of film and music in the growing era of rock 'n' roll. Attention from someone like Craig affirmed for her that she would have an audience.

The connection was also emotional, but all the more so for Craig. Back in Canada his mother loved and cared for him, and they certainly had a close bond when he was little, but Norma was not a soft and tender type of person. Her parenting style could be abrasive. Craig felt that Mae was more nurturing. In her, he had someone to pat his hair and treat him like a darling, sweet boy who could do no wrong.

"Craig was likely hungry for a mother figure and he saw that in Mae," Mark elaborates. "She would have never wanted to play the role of a mother but subconsciously she did in this kid who was totally devoted to her. To her, as long as you loved her, she would want you around."

And Craig wanted to stay around. After five weeks with Mae, he returned to Toronto and found himself totally dissatisfied with his life in Canada. He lost interest in school. There was no point in learning math and science if he was going to have a future in Hollywood. He believed that was where he belonged.

Craig began to act out and showed signs of outright dependence on Mae's attention. His new-found need to be with her, in her presence, bordered on extreme. One day in 1967 he called her and melodramatically told her he was about to have a nervous breakdown.

"What's today?" she asked.

"Wednesday," he replied.

"Well, honey, wouldn't it be better to wait for the weekend?" she said. "Nobody has breakdowns on Wednesdays."

She invited him back to live with her for a longer term. With a ride from Norma and Eric, savings from a job working in the family insurance business, and best wishes from his closest pals, Craig packed his bags and headed back to California.

CHAPTER THREE

FRANKIE AND JOHNNY

Craig worked as Mae West's personal secretary for about six months in 1967, though he said it was longer. He would also have a little more to say about his purpose. He said he was her "secretary-companion-slave and all-around general adorer."

Put up to live in her beach house in Santa Monica, Craig was tasked with handling Mae's phone calls, organizing and answering fan mail, helping with her writing, transcribing her dictations, and rebuffing media requests. While Mae was reclusive, she liked to appear as if she was still very much involved in Hollywood life. It fell to Craig to act as a buffer to the outside world and push the impression that Mae was just too busy to meet the barrage of requests for her time.

He quickly grew to be pretty savvy in the role. His efforts came to include working with agents, managers, and publishers. One of her biographers says Mae would eventually credit Craig with assuring she got royalties from the publishing of a previously unauthorized book on her. Working for her was a dream come true for someone so infatuated.

Craig as his beloved Mae.

Craig wasn't punching a time card, though. He simply fell in step with her life. She consumed him. Morning, afternoon, and night, his days were all about Mae, and in that dynamic he was given a key to the door that led to her private world. Few got to go there so intimately.

Mae lived separate from her beach house in an apartment building called the Ravenswood in Hollywood. The decor of her unit was as splashy as she was. The colours of her living room were white, cream, beige, gold, and pale pink, with expansive arrangements of artificial flowers, polar bear rugs, coffee tables with mirrored tops backed in gold, and ornate lamps with bare-breasted women playing lutes. The pièce de résistance was a nude statue of her likeness atop a white-and-gold piano. Her boudoir had mirrors everywhere, including on the ceiling. Why?

"I like to see how I'm doin'," Mae said.

In seeing her home life, Craig learned her tips for a healthy lifestyle, which included healthy eating, no drinking or smoking, and regular exercise, particularly in the morning. Mae was also very spiritual and believed in the supernatural and extrasensory perception. She freely shared her perspectives on both. Fifteen years before the U.S. Centers for Disease Control and Prevention first used the name acquired immune deficiency syndrome (AIDS), Mae made an eerie prediction that a "gay cancer" was coming and would take out countless homosexual men.

Craig never took to any of her beliefs and practices but, nonetheless, listened to what she had to say. She was entertaining and amusing to him. It was like she was always in persona, in character. He said she was never off for an hour in her life. He loved that. It demonstrated both strength and a means to hide behind vulnerability. It was a habit he would later adopt for his own persona.

Having Craig around more was a boost to Mae's confidence and enthusiasm, too. She took her young, adoring admirer out on the town. She introduced him to Liberace, Peter Lawford, and Peggy Lee, and told him about Cary Grant, Marlene Dietrich, Judy Garland, and Ethel Merman. Craig was dazzled. These were the entertainers he had long admired from TV and records. It was as if Mae brought him closer to them.

Mae and Craig saw each other most days when he would visit the Ravenswood or she would come out to the beach house to "take in the air." He had a lot of time alone, but he didn't complain. It gave him ample opportunity to explore the gay nightclub scene. He found the music was edgier, the entertainment was raunchier, and the boys were more open, without the threatening toxic masculinity he had encountered in high school.

It was the first time Craig was surrounded by men who seemed more like him. He was able to further explore homosexuality, and at last he began to comfortably identify as a gay man. The label would be up for debate later in his life — he would be best described as sexually fluid — but for now there was no ignoring that he was physically attracted to men. He yearned for the dominance of male love. In an environment where it felt safer to be out, he now made more gay friends than ever before; he had one of his first meaningful relationships with a man that year.

It all was very empowering, but Craig's loyalty nonetheless remained with Mae.

Mae knew that and encouraged Craig to do as he wanted with the boys. She had her own men in her life, in particular a man named Charles Krauser (born Chester Rybinski), a former marine, bodybuilder, and wrestler who fell in with Mae and was so devoted that he changed his name to Paul Novak, at her behest. To an outsider, Paul was another employee — a bodyguard and chauffeur — but within her circle it was obvious there was more to his story. Paul adored her, catered to her, and had a daily presence wherever she went. He was her lover and, as Mae said, husband in everything but name.

It was an unusual relationship for its time. Together for more than twenty-five years, the couple never formally married and, per her wishes, Mae maintained total freedom of association with other men. Paul seemed to pay no mind when Mae's attention was drawn to another man, in flirtation or otherwise, and remained accommodating to her every whim. He had security in Mae's reassurance that she gave him "special consideration."

"I believe I was put on this Earth to take care of Miss West," he said freely.

Craig had known of Paul since almost the beginning of his fan club and reported about him in multiple newsletters. In a June 1966 letter he told a fan that Paul was kind, well-mannered, and friendly. He said they talked often and shared a devotion and affection for Mae.

"With him around, she can feel secure from any kind of danger," Craig wrote.

They had regular contact now that Craig was in California. Paul never appeared displeased by Craig's closeness with Mae, even as idol and fan began to connect more on an emotional level. Mae talked extensively about her life, including sensitive details about her prizefighter father, Battlin' Jack West; her corset-model mother, Tillie; her brother, John; and her sister, Beverly, whom Craig had regular contact with. She lived at Mae's ranch in San Fernando Valley, where some thought Craig had a romance with her chauffeur.

For Mae, involvement with her family was a huge demonstration of trust in Craig. She shared her own insecurities, including the fact that she had diabetes, something she painstakingly worked to hide from others; her strained relationship with Beverly; her jealousy of actress Jayne Mansfield when she romanced actor Mickey Hargitay; and her continued grief over the death of her mother, who died in 1930. Craig knew so much about Tillie West that he once considered writing his own book about her.

He equally shared with Mae. He told her of his upbringing, including his adoption; the uncertainty of his parentage; and the rejection by his father. He shared his sensitive and emotional feelings more than he had with anyone. Mae was a good listener and came to see the real Craig, a kid in need of love and confidence, a displaced boy who yearned to belong.

It was in that closeness that Craig admitted his interest in further exploring femininity. It started quite innocently. Mae had rooms full of furs, gowns, outfits, wigs, and accessories at the beach house, and in his off time he couldn't help but explore and try a few things on, privately and alone. *No one would have to know*, he thought, but that couldn't last.

"I was spellbound," he would say later of that irresistible taste of transformation. "I wasn't Craig Eadie anymore. I was Mae West. I could walk like her. I could talk like her, and I could look like her. It all seemed like a dream but it was really happening."

Eventually, Craig confessed — his interest, not his actions — and told Mae that he would love to explore what it would be like to wear her things and impersonate her.

"Oh, you're into that, are you," Mae countered, amused and accepting.

She was all too happy to help. That very night she helped him put on a full-skirted, silk dress from one of her nightclub acts and fitted him with a wig that she later said he could keep. Feeling out his new transformation, he sang Mae's song "Easy Rider" while crudely imitating her voice and gestures as she watched. Mae got a kick out of it.

"Ya know, you're not a bad-looking chick," she said with a laugh, and they went on to enjoy many evenings with Craig dressing up and performing routines for her.

Craig felt a rush of love he hadn't felt since he was a little boy who performed and impersonated others to impress his family. But this wasn't about parental love or the novelty of playing dress-up. It also wasn't about gender identity or gender expression; Craig wanted to emulate the women entertainers he adored. He wanted to imitate them, entertain like them, perform like them, and pay tribute to them.

Impressionism was the heart of what became his craft. The art of imitation — sound, voice, mannerism, and persona — is a tool in the comedy handbook. It is not hard to get laughs with parody, especially parody of public figures. In the changing social and political climate of the 1960s, impersonation was common on television and the stage in the U.S., Canada, and Britain.

One impressionist Craig admired was Rich Little, a Canadian who had made it big south of the border with his impressions of celebrities and politicians. He got his big break doing impressions on *The Judy Garland Show*, one of Craig's favourite TV programs. Rich had a growing career in television on the variety- and talk-show circuit when Craig was living with Mae.

Craig was also aware of three other men making names for themselves as female impressionists. Jim Bailey, Charles Pierce, and Lynne Carter had growing careers in the late 1960s. Impersonating women like Phyllis Diller, Judy Garland, Bette Davis, Katharine Hepburn, and even Mae, they built careers in the gay-bar and nightclub circuits and proved what was possible for budding impressionist Craig.

Craig never lost the uncanny ability he'd had since childhood to impersonate. Performing came to him naturally. He took singing lessons in high school, but just as when he was in the church choir, he didn't like that he would have to restrict himself.

"Males did not sing with vibrato, and I knew that would blow everything I wanted to do," he said of his efforts in school. "I wanted to open it up, and they wanted me to confine it."

Back in school he admitted to his friend Lis Rock that he also felt his style of singing or entertaining made him a target for homophobic bullying. Lis, an artist herself, encouraged him anyway.

Craig didn't find the confidence to truly step into serious performing until he was with Mae. Everything about that environment felt like a safe space to explore his interests and untapped talent. He knew she was the perfect teacher. Mae was willing to open her book of tricks and secrets with him. The first lesson: if he was going to be a performer, he would have to learn about transformation.

Craig was always highly in touch with his personal grooming and self-care, but with Mae's guidance he went deeper with beautification. She taught him about hair care and how to wear and style a wig (a tricky endeavour, as most were made with low-quality synthetic fibres); how to care for his skin to make it look smoother and more supple; how to use adhesive and string to lift and change the face; and how to wear makeup to accent feminine facial features, including lips and cheekbones.

Wanting to impersonate women, Craig's interest in impressionism fit into another world, too. Drag is the centuries-old art of playing with gender for the purpose of gender expression or entertainment. Mae knew all about it. She performed as a male impersonator in the 1910s and included female impersonators in her theatre shows through the 1920s.

Mae would have known Craig's future was in the drag world, but there were no lessons about that yet. Craig needed nurturing and to build up his sense of security and confidence, so along with the lessons on beautification, Mae taught him about posture, voice, the art of carrying himself, and valuable lessons about being an entertainer and a star: how to project and control image, the art of flirtation, and how to grab the attention of an audience and make them want more.

Some of Mae's lessons were direct, in that she told him what to do, what not to do, how things were, and how to act. But more often, the lessons came from Craig's observations of her. He was a constant sponge absorbing everything she had to say, how she took care of herself, how she carried herself, and how she responded to situations. He remembered every lesson, every tip and trick, and hung on her every word.

"She taught that to be a performer, to be a star, you have to be multilayered," he said in an interview with the CBC nearly ten years later. "You have to be a little child. You have to be vulnerable. You have to be tough. You have to be silly. You have to be serious. You gotta hit all the emotions, you gotta hit it on every plane. Try to be as many things to as many people as you can. And if you're lucky, you can slip in and have fun sometimes, too."

Mae's teaching and encouragement gave him a taste of being confident and strong, feelings that at his core eluded him. She taught him how to feel in control, particularly in interactions and relationships with men. He would forever credit her for that, often quoting one of her humorous one-liners.

"Don't let a man put anything over on you unless it's an umbrella," he quipped to the curious and slightly shocked reporter during the CBC interview. "Don't take your head off with your clothes. Take it to bed with you."

Men aside, Craig felt more self-acceptance for who he was, confidence to explore his interests and needs, and a readiness to be at the wheel of his future.

"I consider that Mae West has written the script of her own life and she lives it as the title character," he said some years later. "I love her, I'll love her till the day I die."

There was insecurity under all the fun and adoration. Craig saw how Mae was not just in control of herself but also in control of those around her. Sometimes that meant cutting people off, particularly men. She did that more times than anyone could count. Who cared? There were plenty to go around. Anyone was replaceable.

"As long as they serve my purpose, they're fine," she said. "But if they take up too much of my time, I eliminate them."

Could that happen to Craig? There wasn't room in Mae's world for someone else's insecurity. That became a problem for Craig when she appeared to get close with a young man named Robert Duran, a fan who came into the picture through the fan club. According to biographer R. Mark Desjardins, Mae met Robert after Craig had him out for a tour of the beach house and was so taken with him, she invited him to live there, too.

Everything had gone along fine for a while. Robert also had an interest in cross-dressing, and together they spent hours digging into Mae's trunks, dressing up, and taking photos of each other, or rising early, putting on girdles, and running out in the warm Pacific Ocean surf at sunrise. One afternoon the two of them were hamming it up dressed as Mae, and they startled a delivery man who was ill-prepared for the sight of the two teenage males in front of him.

But as time went on, Craig felt Robert was taking not only some of his personal secretary work but also the lion's share of Mae's attention, replacing him in the life of the idol he so badly needed to love him. It was a threatening situation that Craig didn't know how to handle. He felt emotions so deeply and felt out of control regarding how to respond.

Craig tried to distract himself from those feelings by turning his attention back to having fun. He took more liberties around the beach house, including gaining access to Mae's personal files, where he said she kept news clippings and juicy notes about Hollywood's biggest stars, and dressing up more frequently in Mae's gowns, furs, and undergarments. He also went out more, sneaking away to the gay nightclub circuit after Robert had gone to sleep. Did he perhaps wear something of Mae's on such forays? No one was sure.

For Mae, Craig was walking a fine line. It was okay for him to play dress-up with her there and to impersonate her for her entertainment, but it was not okay for him to use her things without her permission. Going out using some of her things would make her angry; going out dressed up and impersonating her would have been the end of their relationship. She liked to tightly control her trademark and how she was perceived. She did not like the idea that she was possibly being mocked.

"When he was subservient to her, she was very happy," Mark says. "When he was striking out on his own, she saw it as a threat."

It didn't take long for suspicions to grow. Not only had Mae heard Paul's observations about what the boys were up to when she was not around, but Robert had also reported that he believed Craig was regularly taking money from Robert's wallet without permission. He had the IOU receipts to prove it.

It all came to a head when Paul reported to Mae that he had discovered at least one of her storage lockers had been rifled through and one of her gowns had been removed and hidden in a suitcase belonging to Craig. With the gown discreetly tucked away, the concern was that he was going out performing against her wishes or, worse, had actually planned to steal it.

This was it. The boundary was crossed. There was no going back now.

Mae confronted Craig with the allegations, told him he was expelled both from his job as a personal secretary and from her home, and gave him a cheque to cover a one-way flight to Canada. Devastated, Craig asked her if there was anything he could do.

"Forget my phone number," she said.

Craig said he was also made to sign a document that made clear he could not share specifics of anything he knew about her life. This was it for the man she once called the Kid and treated like a son. Their association was over.

It all happened so fast. He barely had time to pack and say goodbye to the friends he had made in California before he had to hop on a plane. He did manage to call his old pal Margaret Gibson. He didn't get into specifics, but with her friend in hysterics on the phone she knew something very bad had happened.

Craig was rocked. It was an abrupt separation and a bitter rejection by someone he idolized and loved. First his father rejected him, and now his beloved Mae. It was an absolute trauma for a person who was already so deeply sensitive.

Back in Toronto, Craig was a troubled young man.

He was very unhappy, sullen, and sad, and when he wasn't, he was bitter and angry. He wasn't the California sun-kissed happy teenager he had been when he came back from Mae West's house the first time. He had everything to say about Mae then, but almost nothing to say now. A mere mention of her could break his suddenly fragile emotions.

"When he went there, it was freedom and joy and going to be with his idol," says Shirley Flavell. "He thought worlds would open up. He came back kind of a broken spirit."

Craig's friends were shaken by the change. Why was he home so fast? What happened? What was wrong?

"It all seemed to happen very quickly," says Phil Buckley. "He seemed happy there. He was staying in a nice place and she seemed to treat him well. All of a sudden, he returned. As close as we all were, there were some things you knew not to ask."

Something terrible happened at Mae's house. They were sure of that. But what happened never seemed clear. Craig never told them the story about the increasingly tense environment, Robert's suspicions, Paul's allegations, and the ultimate dismissal.

The most-detailed story came from Margaret. She, not Craig, told friends that Paul Novak was a closeted bisexual who raped Craig while Mae watched through a two-way mirror. It was a deliberately orchestrated act on Mae's part, Margaret said: the action of a narcissistic sadist who wanted to punish someone who had crossed her.

It was a disturbing, awful allegation that would damage the mental health of anyone who experienced it. It would certainly be an explanation for Craig's behaviour now, if it were true. But the truth is lost in the lens of regret, shame, and decades.

Craig never spoke openly about the alleged sex assault, even to the few friends he had in Mae's circle. In a series of letters written to a friend in California in the first months after he got home, however, he shared his bitterness and heartbreak and suggested he wasn't innocent in his time there.

"So MW's lawyers are asking for the [actor Mickey] Hargitay clippings are they," he wrote on October 12, 1967. "Well my lawyer is asking for a copy of that paper I signed the night before I left. You see, nothing in it is legal or binding ... Wonder why she's afraid I'll write a book. Chuckle, chuckle ... I won't be back to California for a LONG time. There's enough to break your heart at home without traveling three thousand miles for it."

A month later, to the same friend, he followed: "When I burned bridges and went to California, it was, please believe me, for a new life.... All I wanted was to help Miss West. All I got was frustration — and you know about idle hands and mischief. There just wasn't enough mail to keep me busy. When I arrived back here, I had the feeling that six years of my life had been wasted."

But despite the bitterness, Craig wrote: "Of course I love MW very much. She will always be the number one woman around."

Mae remained a core part of Craig's heart and soul. He continued with the fan club once he was home, kept in contact with Robert, and travelled to New York to be at the premiere of her film *Myra Breckinridge*. As he later developed a career as an impressionist, Mae was one of his characters and he portrayed her exactly as he had originally seen her: a strong, vibrant, sexual, and attractive woman. He called her a true original, "the kind of woman who just doesn't come along more than once in any lifetime."

She would always be part of his act and was often part of his press. Craig and Mae's relationship was always a curiosity, and in interviews he spoke highly of her. The worst he ever said publicly was to suggest she was "as funny as [the film] *The Ten Commandments*." More often Craig's eyes would light up at the mention of her, and he not only genuinely acknowledged all that he had learned but also seemed happy to recount his affection and respect for her.

"That's why I impersonate her," he told *Toronto Life* magazine in May 1978. "I do a tribute to her because I love her."

Mae wasn't as sentimental for Craig. They never spoke again, and when Craig came up in conversation, she reiterated that she gave him the boot because he took too many liberties with her clothes, private papers, and personal effects. She never got over it. When Mae released her film *Sextette* in 1978, it was in the news at the same time as a film Craig was in. She was not pleased to share the limelight and didn't want to share a room with him when they found themselves at the same party. She ordered her entourage to keep him away from her.

After Mae died in November 1980, a will written before their fallout left $3,500 from her estate to the "Mae West Fan Club of Ontario, Canada."

Though he never ended up receiving the money because there was no longer an active fan club in Toronto, at the time Craig told the *Toronto Star* he was pleased she remembered him.

"She taught me all I know," he said. "The whole idea was to perpetuate and glorify a woman who was way ahead of her time."

And as far as he was concerned, she still had the upper hand over him, too.

"Miss West was more than a woman," he said. "She was more than a person, more than an actress. She was a dream come true."

As troubled as he was after his falling-out with Mae, Craig was able to find some healing with Shirley, Margaret, and Phil. They were family.

They picked right up where they left off with music, movies, and makeup. Shirley and Margaret were living together and their place became the hub for hangouts. There wasn't a lot of money to go around, but when the four of them got together they would "liquidate assets at the boozeteria" and get silly. Canadian Club and lemon gin were the drinks of choice.

They remained an unusual-looking group — flamboyant Craig, strong Shirley, shy Phil, and mad Margaret. Snapshots show different sides to their fun and personalities. In some they pose on an apartment balcony looking

Mad Margaret and flamboyant Craig, late 1960s.

prim and proper; in others they are half-dressed, wearing female accessories, drinks and cigarettes in hand.

"We used to look forward to weekends," says Phil. "If anybody walked in, it would have looked like a Fellini movie. It wasn't very exciting because we had no money, but it was comforting to us all at that time."

In this fun, safe atmosphere, Craig would go all the way playing dress-up. He would glamour up with cosmetics, change his hair colour, and use a bedsheet as the shawl of a dress to tease at various personas and impressions. If he wasn't working on himself, he turned the creativity on his friends, giving them complete transformations to a star of their liking. He clearly loved it.

Sometimes the four of them would go out to the gay bars of the day. One of the establishments of choice was the St. Charles Tavern, a popular place located under a distinct clock tower downtown. The club was open to men and women and had a large disco for dancing. Patrons typically entered through the back door because reception of the gay community could be hostile, but Craig, Phil, Shirley, and Margaret never felt threatened.

"I never thought that somebody was going to lurk out from the shadows and knife me," Phil says. "And Craig would never tone it down. He would be 'on' most of the time."

Craig could be quite feminine and flamboyant. He wore flashy, tight-fitting clothes, his hair was coiffed, and he wore obvious makeup, including the heavy black mascara he and Margaret liked. One would conclude he was gay. That made him a target in an environment where attacks against gays from homophobic thugs and harassment from local police were frequent.

"He could be injured or hurt," Phil says. "He would still do what Craig wanted to do."

Plenty of memories were made by the outrageous outcasts. Craig acquired an old yellow Volkswagen — he named it Mae — and would drive his friends around. They ate greasy spoon breakfasts at the Honey Dew restaurant, had memorable parties on holidays, and went to see the campy documentary *The Wild, Wild World of Jayne Mansfield*. A lot of interest in the film was generated because it was rated X and released after Mansfield died in a car wreck. Craig, Margaret, Shirley, and Phil loved the film's subject, but they laughed hysterically at the absurdity of the documentary and all that it entailed.

One December, broke but wanting a Christmas tree, the foursome took Craig's car into the expansive Mount Pleasant Cemetery and went to work cutting one down to take home. Why they chose a cemetery for the acquisition was lost in the fun of it. It was a hilarious sight, one later recreated in a movie.

"I remember Shirley falling, Margaret was probably chain-smoking, and Craig was probably doing an impersonation at the time," says Phil. "It was like a scene from *The Three Stooges* but with four of us. It was hilariously funny."

Their mission was stopped only when they caught the attention of a police car passing by. They left without the tree, but the memory would last decades.

*Phil Buckley
and Shirley
Flavell, half of
the Four
Musketeers.*

*Shirley Flavell
and Margaret
Gibson,
roommates.*

Not all memories were pleasant. Margaret was constantly struggling with her mental health through those years. Not only did she have paranoid schizophrenia, but she would later suggest she also had autism and epilepsy. She saw a psychiatrist nearly every day in those years and relied on her friends to show her the route via streetcar because she always got lost. Phil says, "She barely ate, smoked like a fiend, and liked her drinks."

She also liked writing. Margaret believed she was addicted to words. She could hammer away at her typewriter until her fingers bled. In her work she drew heavily from her own experiences, including her time in a mental hospital and some of her delusions. It would be years before she would publish a piece of writing, but that did not matter. Her motivation was simply getting the words out. It was a lifeline for her.

Margaret lived a life on the edge of sanity and insanity. On her bad days she could slip into another personality (one was named Louise) or experience a seizure-like episode. With her friends often looking on, she would shake and wail, complain of incredible physical pain, and say her bones were turning to dust. Help mostly came from Shirley and sometimes from Craig. Phil lived at home with his parents and was spared the worst of it.

Shirley says Margaret feared that in a crazed state she would be caught by authorities, taken to a mental institution, and given a frontal lobotomy. Margaret also made suicide attempts, and because it was illegal at that time, the concern was that she would be charged. It fell to her friends to protect her from the worst.

"One time she had overdosed and Craig and I foolishly thought about dealing with it like you would with a drunk," says Shirley. "We thought we'd walk around the room, fill the bathtub up with icy water.... The highs were so high and the lows were so low. Everything was so intense, so incredibly intense."

Shirley and Margaret eventually had a falling-out when, in a crazed state, Margaret threw and shattered an ashtray, cut herself with shards of glass, and wrote crazed thoughts in blood on their bathroom wall. That was enough for Shirley. She had to draw boundaries somewhere, and she kicked her mentally ill friend out.

It was then that Margaret and Craig moved in together. They had trouble getting an apartment together at first. Renting a place to a crazed woman and flamboyant man seemed like a tough sell, but they eventually found something in a new Scarborough high-rise and fell into a pattern supporting one another, working hard to make it despite their challenges.

Craig had a great coming of age in those first years. He grew up a lot. His mother, Norma Hurst, told him he had to find a career and, shunning the family insurance business, Craig went to Bruno's School for Hair Design to become a hairstylist.

With his personality and sense of style, the hair-care trade was a good fit. He worked in multiple Toronto and Scarborough salons, and while he wasn't known as the best stylist, he was known for being entertaining. Craig would impersonate, sing, and talk away about the stars when working on clients. To him it was like a rehearsal, the beginning of a show that was formulating in his head.

His impersonations began to take over his time with family and friends, too. He was always talking like the stars. People heard from "Craig" less and instead talked to Mae West, Judy Garland, Barbra Streisand, or Louis Armstrong, even in the most mundane conversations. Sometimes it was fun; other times friends say it was annoying.

"It could be very tiring just being with him," Phil recalls. "I remember saying, 'Craig, you're not on stage now — you can be yourself.' … He must have found it difficult to turn it off because it was always going through his mind."

It was a practice Craig kept up for decades. What his friends didn't realize was that he was building on his observations of Mae. She had taught him never to be off for even an hour, to always be in persona. His impressions made him feel happy and they were a place to hide. There was no place to feel and talk about sensitivities and emotions if you were doing impressions of a movie star all the time.

But Craig desired to do more than verbal impressions. He hadn't fully transformed, dressed as a woman, since his time in California. Buoyed by a confidence that came from the support of his friends, one night he teased out his reddish hair, put on careful eye and cheek makeup, and donned a black bra with chiffon stitched to it to look like a gown. All of a sudden, actress Ann-Margret was in the room. Shirley, Margaret, and Phil thought it was hysterical and fun.

It was Halloween 1970 when Craig first went out in Toronto dressed as a woman. The venue was a new place called Club Manatee, a gay dance bar opened by couple Derek Stenhouse and Rene Fortier. Female impersonators — drag queens — were regular guests and that holiday Craig was in the crowd dressed as sensational actress Tallulah Bankhead.

It is curious why he chose Tallulah over Mae. He never explained. Perhaps it was too soon after his time in California, or maybe he didn't want to bring his idol out with anything but perfection. Tallulah was a fine substitute, regardless. She had her similarities to Mae.

"People thought she drank too much, took drugs, had a scandalous sex life," he said. "Although in appearance she was physically fragile and very feminine, she always tried to be one of the boys."

Craig loved dressing up that night. It was fun and freeing. He even felt brave enough to take a few minutes on stage. He had a grand time. His transformation was put to the test when he was stopped by a police officer as he swaggered home drunk, still dressed in his gown. He said he had a pair of high heels in one hand and a martini in the other.

"What do you think you're doing?" the officer asked him.

The interaction could have resulted in trouble, but the questioning didn't threaten Craig at all. It didn't matter if the officer believed he was actually talking to Tallulah, nor did it matter what the officer would conclude about the person dressed up as her. Craig felt strong, powerful, in control. These were emotions he didn't feel as plain, sensitive Craig Eadie. He loved that feeling.

"I'm looking for the nearest Catholic church," Craig replied, mimicking Tallulah's hoarse voice and deep drawl. "I want to confess everything, darling."

CHAPTER FOUR

QUIET PLEASE, THERE'S A LADY ONSTAGE

Despite what Mae West knew, Craig didn't anticipate that his impressions and interest in entertaining would take him into the drag world. But by 1970, three years after his discreet forays dressing up around Mae's beach house, it was clear drag was a fit. If his art was the key, drag was the lock and the door was now open to his future.

Drag was rooted in theatre before it became part of gay culture. The practice of dressing in another gender's clothing can be found going back hundreds of years, extending to the festivities, fairs, and theatres of ancient Europe and Asia, where it had a place in everything from opera and ballet to cabaret and pantomime.

In the Elizabethan era, theatres — called playhouses — were rowdy places, akin more to seedy dens for vagrants where corruption thrived rather than to polite, respected institutions. The stage was a place where actors were allowed to flout rules that elsewhere they would be penalized for disregarding. That included gender norms. Boys and men almost always played women.

Productions spanned the gamut of quality, from improvised and unpolished to elaborate and professional. Some have stood the test of time. The first people to play William Shakespeare's beloved characters Ophelia, Juliet, Cleopatra, and Lady Macbeth, for example, were men. The actors who played them were called "boy actresses." That practice was widely accepted for over a century. *As You Like It* and *Twelfth Night* are routinely cast with males playing female roles, even today.

Drag even had a place in the church. Five hundred years ago when drama was used in church services to communicate with illiterate congregations, women had no part of the formalities. Choirboys played their roles. But that practice would later be edged out of public life in King Charles II's restorative era. The king required female parts be played by a "natural performer." The church and theatre worlds were cleaned up and there no longer seemed to be a place for men who dressed as women.

Drag continued in the shadows and grew as a subculture into the twentieth century when it became an established part of entertainment on a global scale. It was never at the forefront, but never out of sight, either. As entertainers used drag in the circus, ex-servicemen performed in drag in touring groups after the First and Second World Wars. Japanese director Kon Ichikawa released the film *An Actor's Revenge*, about a female impersonator's attempts to avenge the deaths of his parents, while English impersonators like Danny La Rue starred in revues called *Forces in Petticoats* and *Soldiers in Skirts*, and Jean Fredericks released a record called *Recitals Are a Drag*.

Just as it was abroad, the scene in Hollywood was not immune and people didn't see drag as being all that taboo. In the silent-film era, actor Charlie Chaplin performed in female attire in several early films, including *A Woman* in 1915. In 1959 actors Tony Curtis and Jack Lemmon played characters who dressed in drag in the film *Some Like It Hot*. The film was a hit and won an Academy Award for costume design.

That said, the practice of drag is more than entertainment for others. Some people perform drag as a means to comfort themselves or to explore their gender identity. Others may not feel they can be who they really are in public and use drag as a way to hide. The concept of gender disguise, similar to drag, is not new either and is more common than it may seem. Over the years, men and women alike have played with gender to participate in or avoid political activities like voting and military service.

Drag is "a place where illusion intersects with identity, where performance merges with personality, art with attitude." It is about confronting what is seen as normal, exaggerating and sensationalizing gender or sense of self, and provoking questions about what makes a man a man and a woman a woman. As such, it was a natural part of the sexual revolution, women's rights, and gay liberation movements. They each shared the notion that everyone should have control of their person and be able to do as they please.

"Drag is the exemplary case of challenging gender norms," says Sky Gilbert, a professional artist, actor, writer, teacher, and drag artist himself. "Drag is about gender being restrictive, and being able to play with your identity. It doesn't matter what genitals you are born with. You can dress as you like and act as you like."

Not everyone is empowered. Some see drag as a negative part of gay history and as something they have moved beyond, while others see that it brings confusion to identities, like transvestism and transsexuality. Some in the trans community are critical of drag. They see it as a blurring of the lines in a world where most have to fight for understanding.

"Most drag queens are in love with the women they portray, and they are in love with the femininity within themselves," says Sky. "It's the ultimate in confidence. It's something that makes you very brave and it makes you very strong."

In the 1960s, while drag continued to surge through the U.K., Europe, and into North America, the term *drag queen* wasn't the norm yet. Those who dressed up were more commonly called female impersonators. In Toronto they were becoming more visible in the gay bars and nightclubs of the day, including the Letros Tavern, Nile Room, Club 511, the Music Room, and La Trique. They were also appearing in mainstream venues.

One such venue was a small club called Brownings located above a space that later became the famed restaurant Bistro 990. Brownings started as a straight discotheque, but before long it was floundering and the owners introduced a drag night to liven things up and get more customers in the door. Things were going well and as their audience danced away one night a week, drag also popped up literally across the street.

The Global Village Theatre, the brainchild of accomplished artists Elizabeth Szathmary and Robert Swerdlow, opened behind the Sutton Place Hotel in 1969. Elizabeth and Robert were known for being provocative and avant-garde in their work, so it was little surprise when they included drag artist Sacha MacKenzie in their first production, a play about the downfall of America after the Vietnam War called *Blue S.A.*

What was surprising was the interest around Sacha, biologically male, performing as Marilyn Monroe. In one scene he played the still-beloved star in her final moments, taking her own life as she was gripped with a mental illness no one seemed to know or care about. Sacha was very talented and his performance touched hearts, but it was more than that. People were simply fascinated to see such a talented man wearing women's clothing. That was not common in Toronto theatre, a city still mired in the "Toronto the Good" moral stiffness implied by the straight-laced, "anti-vice, anti-gambling, anti-liquor, Bible-thumping" former mayor William Howland.

"It was magic," Robert says, nearly fifty years later. "It was revolutionary to have a female impersonator as Marilyn Monroe.... He was unbelievable."

Drag seemed to have a lot of potential, not just for audiences but for business. A Toronto man named Michael Oscars, who grew up in England in a culture that, he says, revered drag as a comic device, recognized an opportunity. Seeing that the Global Village and Brownings needed a push to get to the next level, he encouraged the bars' owners to pay attention.

They did. Brownings quickly rebranded as a "discreet, but comfortable" gay club called Oscars, named after poet and playwright Oscar Wilde, and introduced a regular drag show that included Sacha and other female impersonators from across the city. It was a gamble, but the *Blue S.A.* reaction couldn't be ignored. Michael was right. Their efforts were an instant success.

As Oscars flourished, the Global Village was running into trouble. Their open mics and Andy Warhol movie nights got the attention of authorities, and questions were raised about whether the operation was running above board with its licensing and standards. Even its operating hours seemed cause for suspicion. People wondered what patrons were doing in the club all night. Were they selling drugs?

"This was all very new to Toronto," Robert says. "They tried to close us down…. We never got fined. We never broke one rule, one law."

The answer to change perceptions was more drag. In hand with Michael from Oscars, the Global Village threw itself into a full-length gay musical revue for the mainstream public. Six entertainers came together and the end result was a show called *Façad*, cleverly named to indicate, as the *Toronto Daily Star* reported, "that things are not what they seem."

"They were the most talented group of guys you'd ever seen," Robert says. "It was so funny. There were times the audience was in tears laughing … It could have been an off-Broadway show. It was that good, that professionally done."

Every show was packed, with all three hundred seats sold out. Michael calls it nothing short of a sensation.

Local businessmen "Honest" Ed Mirvish and Bill De Laurentis saw the show and, wanting to get in on the fun, split the production into two. *Façad* wrapped at the Global Village and went on to a run at Mirvish's Royal Alexandra Theatre, while a new show called *She-Rade*, produced and directed by Michael, went on at De Laurentis's Theatre in the Dell, a dinner theatre that hosted cabaret-style shows above the Dell Restaurant and Tavern.

Both were pieces of respectable theatre. *She-Rade*, including Sacha and female impersonators Riki-Tick, Anita, and Crystal, had two acts and supporting crew including stage manager and costume designers for male and female attire. The head of public relations for the Royal York Hotel handled publicity, and the audience was for the most part straight, prim, and proper, buying tickets for good theatre and a need to feed a curiosity about the art form.

"The art of female impersonation is not new to Toronto," the program read. "For many years it has survived as almost an underground movement hidden from the eyes of the general public. In Europe impersonation is looked up as an art form to be enjoyed as any other form of art. Unfortunately in North America female impersonation is connected with such words as *perverted* and *homosexual*. We ask you to relax and enjoy what is in our eyes a superb form of entertainment."

Offstage, amid all the excitement of preparations and parties, was Craig. He caught on to Toronto's drag community, the female impersonators, and the buzz at the Dell. He didn't sign up to perform, but he showed up many nights and befriended the artists. Michael remembers him with a notepad, going from person to person and peppering them with questions. Where did you get your dress? Where did you get your shoes?

"I remember somebody approached him and asked if he was reviewing the show," says Michael. "He said, 'No, no, no. I'm just taking notes.... I am a female impersonator.' But he hadn't performed yet."

A key friendship Craig made at that time was with female impersonator Anita Mode. Born Russell Alldread, Anita had been doing drag for the better part of a decade and had plenty of advice. A shoe salesperson, she was known to help male performers get women's shoes in men's sizes and connect them with seamstresses willing to make dresses that would fit the male frame.

Once a Guinness World Record holder for being the world's oldest performing drag queen, Anita is now known as Michelle DuBarry. Michelle says she saw Craig's talent and potential right from the start. He was in it for more than dress-up. Michelle knew what to look for. She was a trained singer and dancer, performed in the *Façad* and *She-Rade* shows, and had travelled with theatre and drag touring groups.

Michelle was later part of a group of artists called the Great Imposters, which travelled across Ontario to perform a drag revue of their own design in hotels and small clubs. In places like Hearst, a tiny, primarily francophone town in northern Ontario near Cochrane, they were a curious sight — four men dressed as glamorous women. It seemed like a recipe for disaster, or maybe even danger, away from their seemingly more tolerant urban roots, but Michelle says they had no trouble.

"To them, when we arrived in small towns ... people would wonder where the girls were," she says. "We'd say they were coming later."

Michelle and the others felt comfortable being out of character and out on the town in their blue jeans and jackets during the day, shopping for the show at women's clothing and cosmetic shops. There was no harassment, no homophobia. Michelle says there was a division. While they were part of the gay community at home, no one in the towns they visited considered they might be gay themselves or even talked about it. They were accepted and respected as the entertainers they were.

For budding impressionist Craig, Michelle's career demonstrated what might be possible. Becoming a female impersonator would be his ticket. He was inspired and motivated, and he fit right in with Michelle and the other impersonators at Club Manatee that Halloween in 1970. In December he took things further when at last he stepped on the Manatee stage to perform officially.

Craig left Tallulah at home for this, his first official show. This was Mae's time to shine. It was a role he'd been preparing for since he was twelve years old.

Craig looked great as his idol. He still had wardrobe materials she had given him, and, with all his practise doing impressions for family and friends, he was pretty good performing in front of strangers as the aging, sexual star. The scene itself wasn't all that inspired: the stage was small and bare, the sound system merely passable, and he had neither props nor prepared music. He only had his look and his dead-on impression.

"I feel like a million tonight," he quipped as Mae, with her low voice and slow moan. "One at a time."

Craig was so good you could hear a pin drop. He was happy with his performance, too. This was even better than going out as Tallulah. He liked his impression, the atmosphere, and the audience reception. He officially had an act, his first venue, and pretty soon a stage name: Craig Russell, his legal first and middle names in reverse.

There was no time for Craig Eadie and his problems anymore. He thought less about his dad, less about California, less about his feelings. Working by day as a hairdresser, he spent all of his nights and weekends practising impressions and preparing for his next show. His goal was to unveil a new impression every month.

Choosing impressions for his act was easy. He just looked to the Hollywood women from the movies and records he had loved since childhood and pulled out everything he had absorbed about them — their personas, fashion, style, gestures, music, quotes, and humour. He was also keenly in tune with their quirks, oddities, and sensitivities.

He took a liking to conveying an impression of a woman at her most fragile. The best example of that was Judy Garland. The real Judy was at her best in her younger years, singing in *The Wizard of Oz, Meet Me in St. Louis,* and *A Star Is Born*. But Craig preferred to shape his impression and perform as Judy in her later years, addicted to booze and pills, yet valiant and strong when singing her songs for her beloved audience. He wanted to show Judy finding the victory she never found in life.

Craig did Marlene Dietrich because he liked her sensuality and thought she was the ultimate personification of glamour, while at the same time possessing a persona that reached "the point of self-parody." He called her a mistress of illusions and once wrote that "although her youth has disappeared, it has been replaced by tremendous strength and endurance ... [she is] in total command of herself."

His Bette Davis impression was based on her character Margo Channing in the film *All About Eve*. He liked to perform her commentary more than her singing, gesturing with a cigarette and acting half-drunk. As he did with Mae, he admired her seeming control over men.

Craig's impression of Carol Channing was a lot of fun. He followed her career closely and liked how her feminine self was exaggerated and over the top. She seemed in touch with her masculinity as much as her femininity. There was a hope in her, too. He said her wide-eyed awareness made audiences believe "there is no unpleasantness, no lasting evil in the world."

He said he did Barbra Streisand because she represented that anybody "can be beautiful if they develop their talent to the ultimate degree." She was "an inspiration for people who look different but sound great." He was drawn to craft his Bette Midler impression for similar reasons. He thought she was genuine and "as outrageous as any female impersonator." At her best, she was probably the most like the real Craig — loud, fun, and a little abrasive.

Craig never created an original character. He said he was "more of the 'monkey see, monkey do' school." To create someone was too much responsibility. He cared only to do the ladies he loved and to emulate their strength. That made sense. It is what had attracted him to Mae West years before. She, too, maintained a place in his act.

"I'm dealing with classics, not stereotypes," he said in 1979. "The whole message is stars, it's all about stars. Before it gets too outdated. Before they all die ... I find it much more interesting to be somebody else."

Things were simple at first. Drag is expensive and Craig didn't have a lot of money. He was paid as little as $15 per show. His early transformations

Craig as Marlene Dietrich, singing "Lili Marlene."

included borrowed makeup from sample counters and as little as a loose sheet draped around his shoulders. Over time he saved his money and bought gowns, shoes, wigs, and accessories. He spent hours perfecting his makeup, with particular attention to his lips, eyes, and contour from the temples to the cheekbones to define and enhance his face to look feminine.

Slowly but surely, Craig refined his impressions of each of the women he now called "his ladies." Just as he put in constant work on his physical transformation, he made an equal effort on personification; practising the personas, the singing, the jokes and quips, and how it all was delivered. His impressions remained solid, and it wasn't long before he developed a following of people who wanted to see the latest lady Craig Russell had to deliver.

He stretched his muscles mostly at the Manatee. Michael was by then working for the club's owners, and he gave Craig direction and encouragement to branch out, polish, and experiment. In that spirit Craig did some group shows with other female impersonators. They had fun, but he didn't like it much. He preferred to be alone and wanted to sing live, whereas most of the other performers did pantomime.

Taking Michael's direction, Craig experimented with making his characters interact with one another. This meant making up one half of his face to look like one person, such as Bette Davis, and the other half of his face to look like another, such as Tallulah Bankhead. He would then flip back and forth to give the impression they were talking to each other.

"Unfortunately, some things look great on paper, but in execution ..." Michael says with a laugh. "He got confused as to who he was doing."

The idea flopped but, nonetheless, Craig was working hard to bring something new to the act. He soon concluded he didn't want a writer or a director; he thought they got in his hair. He just wanted to do his own thing.

Craig kept doing his act his way, performing full shows of his impressions at multiple Toronto venues, including gay bars Club 511 and the August Club, as well as at small, forgettable hotels near Toronto's airport and at lounges along Yonge Street. He also made appearances at the Parkside Tavern and the Quest. He cared little about the calibre or profile of the venue, and he channelled frustration from the places that wouldn't book him into making the act better.

The Great Imposters had Craig out with them on the road for several shows. He performed his impressions between their three acts. They all liked him. Just as he turned to them for some of his wardrobe supplies, he became their go-to hair and wig guy, showing them how it was best to use low heat on the synthetic Dynel wigs they wore. There can be a sisterhood in the drag circuit and that existed among them.

Craig stood out among his peers as the most versatile performer in Toronto. The impersonators of the day were typically known for their look, their comedy, or one particular impression. Craig not only had a list of impressions he brought to the stage and an ability to toggle between them all in one show, but he also sang live with an impressive vocal range that went from as deep as Louis Armstrong to as high as Carol Channing. He sang to tracks at first, but in no time proved he could sing with live accompaniment. That was almost unheard of in the Canadian drag scene.

His growing profile also helped him grow relationships with club managers and potential agents. One of them was colourful impresario Gino Empry, a public relations man who worked primarily as a booking agent for the glamorous Imperial Room at the Royal York Hotel. They were friends at first — Gino had a huge soft spot for Craig — but their relationship would eventually be vital to Craig's career.

Gino was not only very well connected, he was beloved by the stars who came in contact with him. He treated them like royalty. He respected and appreciated anyone who came through his venues, assuring they got anything they needed, and in turn, they answered his calls when he needed something. But Gino stressed he was not in it for favours. He was driven to be of service and he took that responsibility seriously.

"God gives everyone certain talents and he gave me this gift," he wrote in his autobiography *I Belong to the Stars: Adventures in Public Relations*. "I automatically put the needs of people I work for and with first. They entertain the public. I consider it my job to make sure they don't have to climb mountains to do just that."

Gino had an impressive Rolodex of contacts from Tony Bennett to Anne Murray. Now his list of talented artists included Craig. They crossed paths frequently through those first years, but Craig wasn't high profile enough for them to work together that closely then. That would come with time.

Craig started to venture out of Toronto to perform on his own in 1971 and 1972. He was booked between exotic dancers at Hanrahan's Tavern in Hamilton, played for tourists at the Hotel Fort Erie in Fort Erie, and he spent a week performing in the lounge at a London hotel. He took on private work doing shows at corporate parties — once performing a party full of insurance agents, the family business — and performed at a convention in front of hundreds of queens.

One show would have as many as sixteen impressions, including Mae, Tallulah, Marlene, Judy, Carol, Barbra, Peggy, Jayne Mansfield, Eartha Kitt, Pearl Bailey, and Shirley Temple.

Publicity photo of Craig as Peggy Lee.

"[The] Channing takeoff is the best of what I heard from him," a May 1972 *London Free Press* review said. "The whole performance is a strangely captivating experience, a big dash of nostalgia with an even bigger dash of show business."

A reporter for the *St. Catharines Standard* gave him a glowing review after a performance in the Cameo Royale Lounge at the New Murray Hotel.

"This has got to be one of the best acts ever brought into the Garden City," it read. "We've had female impersonators in St. Catharines before … none of them could handle the big ladies of the stage so well."

One person often in the crowd was Craig's mother, Norma Hurst. He made no secret in the Hall family of his hobby-turned-career. His Eadie family knew about it, too, but Russell Eadie by no means supported it and never saw his son perform. Norma was different. She saw what using his talent did for him and concluded it was better to support him and have him in her life than to have him go on without her.

"I didn't want to lose him, that's about it," she told a documentary crew decades later. "From what I learned meeting the other boys, not only his friends but other ones at the shows, was how desperately they needed somebody. They thought I was wonderful because I would go and see him."

Norma opened her home to the friends Craig was beginning to make. She saw how many were alienated or rejected from their families because of their sexuality. Some had nowhere to go, and she was more than happy to give people a place to belong outside of a bar or club. Anyone Craig wanted to bring along was welcome at her house or even the family cottage (which Norma called "Craighurst," her son's name and married name put together). Even the entire Great Imposters troupe went out one weekend.

Back in the clubs, it wasn't uncommon to have sweet, grey-haired Norma alongside the young and hip gay and lesbian crowd out for a good time at a drag show. It was certainly an experience out of her comfort zone. Norma was a conservative woman. She didn't approve of the smoking, drinking, or drug use she saw. But she never preached, ignored what she didn't like, and focused on what she did. Her husband, Eric, and sister Cathryn even joined her sometimes. They all had a great time.

Shirley Flavell, Margaret Gibson, and Phil Buckley also went to see

Craig perform. They were thoroughly supportive and admired him for his bravado. He helped them break out of their shells, too.

Shirley remembers one night when Craig gave her a makeover to look like German actress Marlene Dietrich in the film *Golden Earrings*. His efforts were so good, Shirley says, that she didn't recognize herself. She understood then why someone would want to transform.

"I totally got what getting into drag was like," she says. "It was such a trick. It gave you power, control and joy."

Another night, Craig and Shirley dressed up for a night on the town, with Craig looking very feminine and Shirley looking very butch. As they sauntered down Yonge Street toward the clubs, a police car started to trail them. Worried they would be stopped and questioned, they ran home, ripped off their clothes, and jumped into bed together so they would look like any straight couple if the police got as far as their door.

It was a humorous tale, but there was volatility and danger in the community around them. The first Halloween when Craig stepped out as Tallulah at Club Manatee, crowds of spectators, most of them homophobic, came out in droves to watch and taunt LGBTQ2S patrons outside the St. Charles Tavern. That was somewhat of an annual tradition and, as years went by, bricks eventually replaced the insults, eggs, and ink that were thrown at people.

Female impersonators made an easy target, and they complained of frequent harassment and intimidation. There were physical and sexual assaults, most of which went unreported. Police were little help. Some say police would pick the men up and drop them off down at the cold and dark Cherry Beach on the shore of Lake Ontario, where they were left alone, out of sight and out of mind.

Craig was never afraid. He was buoyed by a strength that came from finally doing what he felt he was meant to do. He believed he could use his biting humour to talk his way out of anything to defend himself.

"I can get away with a lot more dressed as Tallulah Bankhead than I can dressed as little Craig from Toronto," he said.

On the outside he was absolutely unstoppable, but inside his feelings and emotions were far from airtight. He was still deeply sensitive. Michelle says she and the other Great Imposters could see the soft side of Craig, but no one saw it more than Margaret. They continued living together as his performing career got off the ground. She had a front-row seat as her friend honed his impressions, before he took them into the clubs and came home to report how everything went.

With Margaret, Craig revealed his worries and insecurities from everything about his show to the men he met. Always in search of love and affection, he had almost constant boyfriends. He was also sensitive to criticism. Even practical advice from his mother hurt his feelings and could leave him devastated.

Margaret was an excellent listener, but her mental health remained unstable. She needed Craig just as much as he needed her. In tune with how polarizing her condition could be, one day she was shaken after observing a mentally unwell person in a restaurant, dishevelled, struggling, isolated, and worst of all, alone. Margaret feared that would be her future — alienated from others and disconnected in her madness.

"Cheer up, Marg!" Craig told her when she confided in him. "Last year it was fashionable to take a Black to lunch. Next year it will be chic to take a faggot to lunch. And in no time at all they'll be taking crazy people to lunch. Your time will come!"

Craig was pretty good at breaking Margaret from her depressing thoughts and making her laugh. Overall, he seemed capable of handling the bad days, but as Shirley would later describe her, Margaret was "a 24-7 girl." She could wear her friends out.

Friend Steve Postal recalled an episode when Craig called him in a panic. Margaret had tried to kill herself again and Craig said he could not handle it alone this time.

"Margaret had slit her wrists and she was bleeding all over the place," he said. "I carried Margaret to my van and we took her to Toronto General Hospital. Craig was hysterical. He was crying … [there was] a lot of very powerful love there on both sides."

But just as there were bad days, there were good days. They got closer as they struggled to make it, he as a performer, and she as a writer. As Craig worked on his art in the bathroom mirror, Margaret hammered away at a typewriter in their small kitchen, her cat Garbo not far away. They often shared a bed and suggested they had also been sexually intimate.

They never talked about becoming a couple, and it seemed inevitable one day they would be separated, with Craig off performing and Margaret off to a marriage. That seemed more likely as time went on. While she had always shunned conformity, Margaret now wanted marriage and motherhood. Those traits, she said, would prove she was functional.

Steve said Craig encouraged him to marry Margaret, but he said her mental health would be too much for him. It was then that Stuart Gilboord entered the picture. Stuart and Margaret met when they were eighteen and reconnected in 1971 when she looked him up and gave him a call. Stuart says he found her distinctive, intriguing, and easy to talk to.

As their relationship progressed, Stuart saw Margaret's closeness with Craig. Everyone needs a gay friend, he reasoned at the time, but a mutual dependency was also apparent. Margaret told him she and Craig had a suicide pact to kill themselves together if they were alone at the age of forty. It was a morbid idea, but less of a concern now. Her sights were set on her new suitor. Before long Margaret and Stuart got married.

Craig and Margaret's time living together was over. Like their mutual friends Shirley and Phil, Craig was also supportive of the marriage and believed Stuart was the right man to take care of Margaret. He stabilized her.

If Craig was relieved to not be a caregiver anymore, he didn't say so. Others assume that while sad to separate, he may have also been somewhat relieved.

"You've got a performer who's on most of the time and a lady who's not always very well," says Phil. "It was a hard go, very stressful.... She zapped all your energy because she was very intense. It sounds very selfish, but sometimes you have to make that choice."

Still needing to share the bills, Craig invited a friend named Helen Phillips to move in with him. They had met a few years earlier at Bruno's and bonded from the start, two dynamic, alternative people in a group of linear people. Helen easily folded in with Craig's high school group and eventually got to know Norma and Eric.

There were nights out to the clubs and some memorable parties — "everything was always so dynamic and dramatic," she remembers — including a notable New Year's gathering. At that party they tenderly posed

Craig with close friend Helen Phillips.

for a photo together, hippy Craig with his loose-fitting long black vest and no shirt, his blond hair coiffed, and his arm tightly around Helen, who posed next to him with a big smile.

"There was as much trust there as there could be," Helen says of their bond. "He was such an unusual person. I loved him, there's no question about that. He was wonderful.... We had a very good relationship."

Together Helen and Craig shared an apartment with a trans woman named Jean who was in the process of transitioning and also dabbled in drag. They were close friends and made a few memories, sharing a pet bird and chasing some of the same boys, but if anything, Craig loosened ties to friends and went even deeper with his act. He had not lost his unwavering focus.

Craig made no secret that his future was in the entertainment world. He wanted to keep going, play in bigger venues with bigger audiences, and have more of an ability to make a name for himself as Craig Russell. He bemoaned that Canada didn't seem to have "a star system." The great entertainers didn't seem to come from Toronto.

"Canadians don't have stars, apart from hockey players and politicians," he said six years later. "It's about time that they realized they've got one right here."

He got a big break when an agent approached him in the fall of 1972, when Craig was performing in, of all places, a hotel lounge in small-town Galt, Ontario. They agreed that with the calibre of his show, the timing was right for Craig to head back to California and work in clubs there. An agent and manager could represent him and assure his career kept going in the right direction.

The invite would be Craig's big chance. The best opportunities for any of the arts seemed to be in the U.S. The limits in Canada were obvious, and not just in female impersonation. Some of Canada's best entertainers, from stage to television to radio to film, regularly made the pilgrimage to take their careers to the next level.

"Canadians are more embraced in the States, especially if you are nuts," says Hart Pomerantz, who in the early 1970s was an entertainer working on a television variety show called *The Hart and Lorne Terrific Hour* with a young actor and comedian named Lorne Michaels.

Hart saw first-hand how the likes of Canadian artists like John Candy, Eugene Levy, Martin Short, Andrea Martin, and Catherine O'Hara would build up a career in Canada only to go south to keep growing. American artists who once came to Canada for work — think Joe Flaherty and Gilda Radner — did the same thing. Even Lorne, Hart's performing partner in the *Terrific Hour* project, left and went to New York to start a show with a similar format. Lorne called it *NBC's Saturday Night*, or as it was later known, *Saturday Night Live*.

"People only really seemed to have longevity in Canadian entertainment if they looked like an old bank teller," Hart says, with a laugh. He eventually abandoned entertaining and went on to practise law.

All that said, an opportunity to go to California was very welcome news for Craig. He did all but jump on the next plane. He quit hairdressing, stepped away from the clubs, and started packing his bags.

Sharing his excitement with his mother, Craig's news was met with caution more than excitement. Norma was forever practical. She had been more than supportive of his act but wondered if his efforts and talents were enough to make a lifetime career.

"I don't think that is the place for you to go," she said. "I don't think there is any real future in it for you."

She had a point. A sustainable career in female impersonation, let alone in film, television, music, or anything in entertainment, can be fleeting. The challenges and potential rejection could be hurtful to her sensitive son. She wanted him to be reasonable and logical. His ladies were a fine hobby to pursue in his free time, but maybe there was a different, more traditional path for him to take with his career.

Craig would not be dissuaded.

"Give me five years," he told her. "I'm going to be a movie star."

CHAPTER FIVE
STARMAN

When Lori Jenkins was born on September 28, 1957, three months premature and weighing three pounds, her father said the delivery doctor took him aside and told him he could flush the tiny, sickly baby down the toilet to save the cost of a funeral.

Eddie Jenkins recounted the story to his daughter often and added, "So Lor, every time I flush, I think of you."

He would laugh and Lori would laugh right along with him. She loved her dad's humour. He was an outgoing man with a large presence and a laugh that could fill a room. Lori had a special place in his big heart. She was the second of three kids in the span of three years with his then girlfriend, Hazel Westman. Paul came first, then Lori, then Dena. They eventually married to make the family official. Brothers Eric and Marc came along after that.

Eddie and Hazel raised their kids mostly in Etobicoke and west Toronto, moving often. Eddie was a car salesman, loved baseball, and treated anybody he met like a new best friend. Money was often tight, but the kids were provided for, and when he wanted to impress them, Eddie went all out. He would whip up big breakfasts with all the fixings, and he occasionally took his family out for flashy dinners at fancy Toronto restaurants.

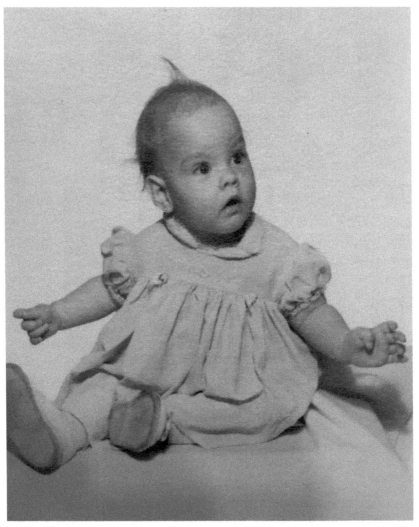

Baby Lori Jenkins, wide-eyed and ready.

Discipline fell to the kids' mother, Hazel. She was well-suited for the role. She could be tough and mean, and she did not hesitate to discipline Paul, Dena, Eric, and Marc. But when it came to Lori, she paid little attention to her sensitive daughter. When she did, the attention was not friendly.

"You're going to get my five brothers!" Hazel would bark, waving her hand to threaten another spanking.

The first three Jenkins kids: Paul, Lori, and Dena.

Sweetly calling Dena by her name, Hazel nicknamed Lori "Josephine" and hissed the name in disdain and resentment. She held her eldest daughter in constant contempt, mocked her for her glasses, and said she had worms for brains. Lori was blamed for almost everything that got broken or messy in the family home. As punishment she would be forced to kneel in a corner until she felt dizzy, or she would be spanked until her skin burned.

When young Lori slurped soup, Hazel made her eat it under the table without utensils like an animal. When she was seen holding hands with another female friend, Hazel seethed, yanked Lori into the family car, and called her a lesbian, asking what the neighbours would think. When she poured a glass of milk a bit too full, Hazel poured it all down the sink, calling her daughter wasteful and greedy.

The attention grew to unthinkable abuse, including totally unprovoked physical attacks. Lori said Hazel once lifted her off the ground and threw her against a wall for no reason at all. Another time Hazel hit Lori over the head with a cast iron frying pan. After blood splattered onto the wall and down Lori's head, Hazel yanked her into a bathroom, forced her head under a faucet, and blamed her for the mess.

"To survive our upbringing, you really had to be tough," says Paul. "My mother would beat the shit out of her and then she'd make us clean up the blood so my dad wouldn't see it."

Eddie was not around much and didn't seem to know the extent of the abuse. Hazel wasn't overly nice to him, either. She mocked his cleft palate. When Eddie was around, he'd entertain the kids with trips to the Sam the Record Man music store, the ballpark, or the track. He knew enough to know Lori needed a little more love from him than his other kids did. Lori adored him.

But still, Lori grew to be scared of her own shadow and afraid to talk. An elementary school teacher once described her as "too quiet for normal." She was soft-spoken, not wanting to draw attention to herself or to be thought of as having started a confrontation. Other things triggered her traumas. Breakfasts reminded her of interactions with Hazel, so later in life she avoided the meal altogether if she could.

Yet Hazel's abuse made Lori physically tough and resilient, characteristics that served her well. When she was just four years old, a car hit her as she crossed a busy city street at a crosswalk. Paul saw it happen. He says her collarbone was broken and one of her arms was nearly severed. It was repaired in emergency surgery at Scarborough General Hospital, where she stayed for weeks in a cast from her neck to her waist.

Her emotions, already fragile, were tested further over time. The biggest blow came when her brother Eric died in an accidental hanging while playing with a friend outside. Hazel seethed at her daughter for crying at his funeral, so Lori toughened up and worked hard to keep her sensitive emotions to herself. She became an excellent compartmentalizer and kept her tears private.

Lori never questioned her mother's behaviour. She never referred to herself as someone who had suffered abuse, and throughout her adulthood she persisted in trying to maintain a relationship with Hazel. Lori not only thought it was just a part of life, she thought she deserved the treatment somehow. She almost never stood up for herself and rarely questioned when someone mistreated her.

"My family was the classic definition of the dysfunctional family in every way, shape and form," Paul says, noting how he left home at fifteen to get away from it all. He harboured guilt for years for leaving his siblings to fend for themselves.

In 1970 Hazel and Eddie separated. Lori was devastated to be separated from her father, and she contemplated suicide. She walked to a nearby rail line, lay down across the tracks, and waited for a train. One never came, so she walked home and got on with her life. She was a budding teenager, figuring out what mattered to her and growing into the person she would become, a "weird blend of driven, innocent victim and triumphant, creative person," her sister-in-law said years later.

Lori's creative side became apparent when she was thirteen and she tried out for the lead in the school production of *Oliver!* She had never sung in public before and was painfully shy, so when her voice cracked at tryouts, she ran out crying and hid in a washroom. She came back for a second attempt and sang a solo with so much emotion that she cried again. Her effort earned her the part of understudy for the lead character. Lori was proud of that.

Lori had more capacity to explore her interest in the arts after she, Dena, and Marc went to live with Eddie in a working-class neighbourhood of Toronto's east end, where he worked for Robertson Motors on the Danforth. Away from her mother, she got more into movies and music as she prepared to enter high school.

She couldn't have found a better place to go. Riverdale Collegiate Institute is known for great courses and extracurricular art programs. Lori took full advantage of the opportunities. Pictures of her are peppered through the school yearbooks. Her 1974 school portrait shows a happy, well-rounded-looking girl with a big smile. In another photo she appears reserved, but with lips pursed and eyebrows perked and sly, she looks like the cat that caught the canary, someone intriguing and worth getting to know.

Lori's style was initially quite feminine, with pretty skirts and blouses, but by her third year of high school, she adopted a more androgynous look with T-shirts and loose-fitting collared shirts over jeans or overalls, along with a colourful accessory. She was taller and a little more masculine than other girls. Her brown hair was long and straight at first; she later had it

Lori, initially shy, pensive, and curious, at Riverdale.

permed and teased it out. She didn't wear cosmetics and her eyes were hidden behind thick tinted glasses. Some might have described her as bohemian, but Lori avoided labels and convention.

Style aside, Lori was studious. If she was interested in a class, she was dedicated and would go the extra mile. She respected her teachers — Lori called them professors — and the people around her. She listened more than she spoke. She was naive and innocent, yet she liked a good joke and showed some raunchy humour now and then. No one ever said anything bad about her. One teacher says she "stood out for the right reasons."

Lori was mostly below average in terms of her grades, but she wasn't stupid. She simply liked to spend her time in clubs and groups more than she liked going to class. She was manager of the girls' volleyball team and joined the junior basketball team in her first year before she went on to be secretary and editor of the yearbook. In her editor's message for the 1975–76 edition, she sounds like any outgoing teenager.

"Riverdale, I hope that when you look back on this book in years to come, treasured memories will be revived once more," she wrote.

But it was when Lori joined the drama club that she found the outlet that gave her the most satisfaction and joy. Riverdale was known for its drama department, described as being "geared toward excellence." The club provided an opportunity to produce good theatre and a safe place for students to step forward and be themselves. That certainly applied to Lori. When she was preparing for a production, the shy, coy teenage girl stepped out of her comfort zone to show a driven, organized, enthusiastic, and passionate woman who made things happen. The experience changed her.

She preferred taking on a supporting role backstage to being the star and centre of attention. She started in Grade 10 as a decoration assistant for the comedic play *You Can't Take It with You* and took the set design reins the next year for *Not with a Whimper, But a Bang*, a take on the T.S. Eliot poem "The Hollow Men." The yearbook describes the play as a "potpourri of pandemonium, conceived in horror, nurtured by guilt, and presented with a sincere concern for the future of humanity."

Lori thought it was brilliant. For the production she designed and built a large cyclorama of a spiderweb made of thick, heavy-duty rope. On it she placed a macramé spider, slightly off-centre and illuminated with lights from different angles for various effects. The whole thing was made in such a way that it was transportable from the school to Hart House at the University of Toronto for the district competition, the St. Lawrence Centre theatre for the provincial competition, and finally to Victoria, British Columbia, where the group took second place in a theatre festival and got a standing ovation.

She took on two plays the following year. She was stage manager for one of the two plays, a production called *Two Sides of Madness*, about eight mad women in an insane asylum. Lori was so prepared for her half of the show that she had all of the lines memorized and was ready to go on when another student fell sick and couldn't perform. Teacher Ian Waldron says Lori was very good in the role, but he could tell she was not happy to get the attention.

She was back behind the curtain for the next semester's production of *The Rook*, a play about a chess game. As the stage manager, she had to understand the script, the actors, and the characters and keep control of the flow of the performance. She kept a master script with notes in the margins for all of her cues, using them to call out requests to the crew for changes to set decor, sound, and lighting. When they took the show to Hart House, Lori was named Outstanding Stage Manager in the same theatre where her grandfather was once a house manager. She was pleased with that.

All of the students involved in the drama club and classes were theatre junkies. Teachers like Ian treated students as equals. They often joined him at a coffee shop after class or went with him to see shows. They did that a lot through the 1975 teachers' strike that stretched on for two months. Lori got along with everyone and made friendships with both students and teachers, with whom she kept in varied contact over the next decades.

"I knew she was different," says Alex Bostock, one of her teachers. "She was an old soul in a sense.… She spent most of her teenage years avoiding going home. Riverdale was her whole life."

Lori's best friend at Riverdale was Tom Veitch. Born and raised in downtown Toronto, Tom knew the theatre scene and venues like the Opera House and the Colonial Tavern long before other kids did. He met many artists and had plenty to talk about when he met Lori. The first thing they had in common was a love of French-Canadian writer Michel Tremblay's

1973 play *Hosanna*. It was about a conflicted transvestite and her relation-ship with an aging homosexual biker.

Tom calls them kindred spirits. He was one of the few people who knew about the trauma in Lori's family life. Other people only knew she had a cool older brother who worked downtown, and that she was close with her younger sister, Dena, who also went to Riverdale. Lori was more apt to talk about the latest entertainer she was into. She loved Richard Monette as the lead in *Hosanna* when it came to the Tarragon Theatre, and she went to see Maggie Smith in multiple roles at Stratford. She adored David Bowie and kept a poster from his film *The Man Who Fell to Earth* above her bed.

By 1975, the year she turned eighteen, Lori started to venture down-town to feel out the cinemas, theatres, and dance clubs. She tagged along with her sister, Dena, at first, but it wasn't long before she headed out on her own. She could lose herself in a movie storyline, a stage production, or a crowded dance floor. The experiences all fed her fascination with people who were different. She had a particular preference for gay-friendly bars. She felt safer and more anonymous in them.

Great political change and unrest remained in the gay community since the likes of Craig and his friends had been through. A man named John Damien went to the Ontario Human Rights Commission after he was fired from the Ontario Racing Commission for being gay. Demonstrations were held for multiple incidents, including a public "kiss in" to support two men charged with indecency for kissing in public. The United Steelworkers of America affirmed their support of the Ontario New Democratic Party's supportive stand on gay civil rights, and the United Church of Canada publicly supported the inclusion of sexual orientation in the Ontario Human Rights Code.

Nevertheless, danger remained prevalent. As police executed numerous bathhouse raids and charged countless people, gangs attacked gay men in parks believed to be cruising spots. Several men who frequented the St. Charles Tavern and the Parkside Tavern were found viciously and violently murdered. They were frequently called "homosexual murders," not "mur-ders," and some cases remained unsolved. Was a serial killer in their midst? There were no answers.

Many in the LGBTQ2S identifying community began to question others they had once believed were allies. A backlash hit the gay community in the summer of 1977 when a twelve-year-old boy named Emanuel Jaques was sexually assaulted and murdered by men believed to be gay. Many questioned the conduct of homosexual men after that and called for a cleanup of the Yonge Street blocks that included gay and lesbian establishments.

Media hysteria did not help. Anti-gay reporters like *Toronto Sun* columnist Claire Hoy routinely wrote about the threat of gay people.

"Homosexuals want to spread their message, to sign up converts, to get into the school system and preach," one of his columns said.

Another warned that "our taxes help homosexuals promote abuse of children."

Anti-gay types were also making the news. One of them was Anita Bryant, an American singer, activist, and, as an opponent of gay rights, part of a coalition called Save Our Children. Her sensational talking points gave her an almost regular spot in media through the late 1970s. In May 1977 she would be quoted as saying that "sperm is the most concentrated form of blood. The homosexual is eating life."

Lori never said she was impacted by any of it. Most news items involved men anyway. It seemed she was a little safer because she was a woman. She continued her routines, safe in her naïveté, and felt stronger than ever. She did not see herself as a target, but in reality she was very vulnerable, and it was only a matter of time before danger caught up to her, too.

It happened on a cold January night in 1976 when she was eighteen. Lori had been out watching a drag show when she decided to hitchhike home. She usually made the two-hour walk no matter what the hour, but she was tired and wanted to make it to school in the morning. She found a ride quickly and, as was her way, made small talk with the stranger behind the wheel. But the man would not be a new friend. He sexually assaulted her.

It happened quickly. After some pleasant introductions the driver offered Lori a joint. When she declined, he got angry and amplified his aggression.

"Have you ever fucked a man?" he asked.

Lori was embarrassed by the question — she was still a virgin — and tried to dissuade his interest. It didn't work. The driver pulled into a

Lori in 1976, androgynous and stronger after finding creative outlets.

parking lot a few blocks from the family apartment, forced her down across the front seats, climbed on top of her, tore her pants open, and raped her.

Lori was paralyzed with fear. She shut her eyes tight and waited for him to finish. She did not fight him off. It was like this was just another form of abuse that she somehow thought was inevitable for her. She didn't know how else to respond.

When it was over, her rapist drove her home. Watching him drive away, Lori felt ashamed, violated, and like so many victims of sexual assault, that it was all her fault and no one would believe her if she told them what happened. She thought she shouldn't have been out on a school night; she shouldn't have been hitchhiking.

Lori told no one. She became even more shy and withdrawn. She attended even fewer classes and turned all of her attention to nightlife downtown.

"Thinking that the real world wasn't so hot, I retreated into the world of make-believe," she wrote years later. "Every chance I had was spent in movie theatres, or, better yet … live theatre! I felt a sense of peace watching theatre from a distance. All the while, secretly wanting to be a part of that world, where everything was magic and wonderful."

Almost as soon as the plane touched down in California, Craig got to work.

It was the fall of 1972 and he was ready for the next phase of his career, the start of the chapter that would make him a star. His first move was a good one. He partnered with Bud Haas, a professional talent agent working out of North Hollywood who, with help from manager Richard Kerr, put together a publicity package to sell the emerging star.

"CRAIG RUSSELL, at the age of 24, is one of the world's foremost impressionists of famous ladies," it declared. "His exciting and unusual show presents completely live the illusion of many top stars appearing 'in person,' and the extremely versatile entertainer captures the authentic vocal and visual trademarks of each."

The package is certainly impressive. Its seven pages include biographical information, a listing of twenty-four impressions, and glowing reviews. Featured ads from previous bookings noted he was "the ultimate impressionist" and "one of the world's best female entertainers."

Bud's efforts worked. Craig had no problems getting booked. He played at popular Hollywood-area nightclubs, including PJ's, Tony's, the Red Fox, and the Millionaire's Club, and walked away from all new venues with positive write-ups. He was a hot ticket and it didn't take long for his work, including his impression of Mae, to get back to her. Mae was livid and threatened to take things legal for "stealin' my material." Craig never answered her threats and kept going.

Instead, Craig kept in touch with family and friends in Toronto and proudly shared his accomplishments with them. He sent along the ads, reviews, lithographs, and other materials to his mother, Norma, and his aunt Cathryn, who started a scrapbook about her nephew that she maintained for decades. Craig also kept PR man Gino Empry apprised of his successes.

The person Craig talked to the most was Margaret Gibson. They exchanged letters frequently as she also underwent a life change. Margaret was now a mother to a son, Aaron Dane Gilboord. He was born in November 1972. Her husband, Stuart, continued to be a strong guide in her life, but Margaret arguably drew the most strength for motherhood and mental illness from correspondence with her old pal.

Another person whom Craig kept in contact with was his Toronto roommate Helen Phillips. They maintained their close friendship, even after Helen declined his invitation to move to California with him. Now, going into the new year, they had something important to talk about — their daughter. Susan Allison Phillips was born on January 6, 1973.

Craig and Helen were never a couple. Helen thought he was amazing, charming, talented, and good-looking, but with his career and his boyfriends, the idea of a relationship was never on the table. Helen is a dynamic, strong woman, and because she always wanted to be a mother, a surprise pregnancy after a night with Craig was welcome news.

This was new territory for Craig. Fatherhood and parenting are life changing for anyone. He never planned on either, but he wondered for a while if he and Helen could make it work together. Should he keep his time in California short and come back to support them? Or should he stay, make a little money, and ask them to come out to live with him? He was okay with that, too.

In the end, Craig's being in the baby's life was not meant to be. Helen wanted to stay in Toronto and raise Allison on her own. On one hand, she knew it was the best way to have stability for her child when the father of her child was not stable, but on the other, it was just as important that Craig have total freedom.

"It was very important to me that he have his career and that he fulfill his dream," Helen says. "He was so good. The whole idea was to support his dream.... I never wanted [a bigger life], I just wanted my baby."

Craig got word of his daughter's birth two days after she was born. Phil Buckley called and told him the news. He was close with Helen, too, so close that he became the baby's godfather.

Craig's response to Allison's birth was to write Helen a letter.

"Phil called to give me the news and I hope you're both well," he wrote on personalized stationery femininely branded *Craig Russell.* "Great to get that load off your … mind?!"

Jokes aside, he got serious. He was sensitive to the situation, how she was feeling, and her choice to stay in Toronto alone.

"You must have been through an experience no male can really understand — psychologically, physically and emotion [*sic*]," he wrote. "I did receive your last letter and didn't reply. Couldn't think of what to say. Your decisions are yours and what can anyone say. I never listened to much advice either, and don't regret it."

He didn't say it directly but between the lines a mutual understanding was clear. Craig was free of obligations.

If Craig was disappointed by Helen's decision, he didn't speak about it. He didn't celebrate the reality, either. It just was what it was. Few knew he was a father at all, other than his mother and his high school friends Margaret, Phil, and Shirley. He kept it to himself. That is telling for an expressive person like him. Protecting the privacy of Helen and his daughter was sacred.

Craig kept in touch with Helen over the years, but he kept both Allison and his feelings about her private. He had distractions. There were plenty more shows in California, and it wasn't long before he took his act on the road, too. In 1973 he did more than a week of shows in Chicago and made his first appearance in Provincetown, Massachusetts. He went to perform there almost every year for the next eight years.

The atmosphere in Provincetown is open, family-friendly, and liberal. Female impersonators, later more commonly referred to as drag queens, have long held a place on its stages. Craig felt he could relax there and not worry about being too feminine or over the top in public.

"Everyone there has a happy, tourist look and they dress and act to please themselves," he said. "You see all kinds of people … and they all seem to blend together … You feel comfortable colliding with other people."

Performing in Provincetown was another step into the mainstream big leagues. Comedian Lily Tomlin, actress Bette Davis, and actor Richard Gere spent part of their careers there, and as Craig stepped on the stage in the fine Massachusetts summer, he got to meet female impressionists who had big careers in theatre and television, like Lynne Carter, Arthur Blake, and Charles Pierce. Around the constant stream of performers were managers, producers, directors, agents, bookers, and writers. Being there meant more visibility and the opening of doors.

That was appealing to him. Craig's audience was changing, and where he felt he fit into the entertainment world was changing. He was moving away from being associated with drag. When people drew parallels between him and drag queens, he bristled. He was an impressionist. Drag was tacky.

"To me, technically, a female impersonator is a man who impersonates a female, whereas an impressionist does an impression of a particular female," he said in 1979. "A drag queen just wants to get in drag to fulfil their need for dressing."

He was more direct in other interviews.

"Drag queens are the lowest on the totem pole," he said flatly, on more than one occasion.

These were harsh comments considering where he got his start and the friends he made. But there was no changing his mind. Drag was an art he now diminished. He even began to chafe at working in gay clubs. He wanted to be taken seriously as an artist and that didn't seem part of the deal with those people in those places. Craig not only felt like an artist in places like Provincetown, he also felt like it was the type of environment where he was supposed to be.

Craig spent most of July 1974 in New York City. He said he performed his solo show at the famed club Rocco's and was featured in a revue called the *Manhattan Follies*. The latter was a great opportunity. It was produced by impresario Robert Stigwood, who worked with bands like Cream and the Bee Gees and staged productions like *Hair* and *Jesus Christ Superstar*, with some help from producer and manager Allan Carr, who had managed the likes of Tony Curtis, Peter Sellers, and Rosalind Russell. Stigwood and Carr previously worked together on the rock opera *Tommy* and would go on to co-produce the musical comedy film *Grease*.

Staged at the posh Persian Room cocktail lounge in the Plaza Hotel, and far different from the likes of Club Manatee and the August Club in Toronto, Craig's audience now included musician Eric Clapton, artist Andy Warhol, and singer/actress Lorna Luft. He opened the show with his Carol Channing impression, which the *Hollywood Reporter* said was "the best performance of Channing since Channing." The reporter wasn't alone in thinking that. Carol and her husband, Charles Lowe, saw Craig perform that month and introduced themselves.

"I don't think you look like me at all," Carol told Craig. "I think you look like some idiotic blonde woman who doesn't know where she is."

Hearing this, Charles gently reminded her that is exactly who the real Carol was. The three of them had a good laugh. Carol nonetheless followed with some advice.

"You're much too feminine when you're impersonating me," she said. "Work on your male identity.... You can't live off the ladies forever."

That was good advice for Craig, but he didn't take it. He didn't give much consideration to his life out of costume at all. Being and performing his impressions — his ladies — consumed him. Craig took every gig he was offered, and stayed in character when he wasn't working. He was always in stage mode.

The habit was becoming obsessive. If he didn't speak as one of his ladies, he would refer to his impressions in the third person. In conversations with friends, fans, and even interviewers, he'd say things about his show like, "Peggy really freaked out there because of the lights, but Judy got turned on," as if the women lived through him and he was not in control of what they said or did. The *Toronto Star*'s Martin Knelman picked up on it. He called the split-personality routine creepy.

Craig wasn't oblivious to that impression. He knew what he was doing, how he perplexed people, and he admitted it took away from time to just be himself.

"In researching their lives, I think I neglected my own a little bit," he said in one interview. "But you can't have everything."

The tendency certainly was good for practise and good theatrics, but it always had another purpose. His ladies were still a place to hide from being Craig Eadie. Living the path he was meant to follow, Craig had every reason

The Poop Deck Presents
In the "LOWER DECK"
"The Craig Russell Show"

CAROL CHANNING—CRAIG RUSSELL

Direct from New York—opening Sunday, Feb. 2 through Saturday, Feb. 8th. Two different shows each night at 8:30 & Midnight. Price of admission good for one or both shows plus disco until closing—all for $3.00 advance ticket sales at the Poop Deck—your double decker restaurant Bar, disco & show room on Lauderdale Beach.
523-6551

An ad from a 1975 show in Florida.

Craig as Judy Garland at Toronto's Theatre in the Dell. Every return to Canada had a step up in venue.

to be happy and fulfilled. But he couldn't avoid his emotions. He was still deeply sensitive, needy, and emotional, and the demands and pressure of his growing career exacerbated them. Staying in character was his way to cope.

All of these changes in Craig — his show, persona, commitment, audience, and the depth of his talent — were becoming apparent in his professional relationships. Michael Oscars saw it. They crossed paths several times between 1973 and 1974. They met up in San Francisco, where Craig was performing at a bar called the City, and then later in Provincetown, where Craig was performing at the Crown & Anchor, an inn with a bar that offered live entertainment.

Michael was happy for him. He always believed Craig had talent, but exactly how much of a true artist he was hit home on a night they spent together in Toronto. Craig was in town to perform at a small venue called the Upstairs Sidedoor and on the same visit, he'd been asked to appear as Mae at a party. Michael went along as "Mae's" date because the real Mae never travelled without a male companion.

"I remember knocking on the door, and the door opening.... It wasn't Craig [at the door], it was Mae West," Michael remembers. "He was in full, full character. And he stayed in character, which kind of freaked me out."

The trick continued on their limo ride and at the party, where Craig entered the room as a surprise guest. Michael remembers the moment doors opened, in walked Craig, and for an instant, as far as anyone knew, the great Mae had joined them. Craig was totally convincing in his impression. It was an absolute riot, made more so when he performed a mini show for everyone.

It was a memorable night, not just for the surprise, but for the clear transition that Craig had made. He was no longer the budding, innocent kid honing his skills as an impressionist masked as a drag queen in gay clubs. This entertainer had star power. He was going places.

Margaret's star was on the rise at the same time as Craig's.

She was still writing intensely. She was so determined she said she got physical pain in her hands if she didn't get the words out. Her efforts finally paid off in 1976 with the release of her first book.

Called *The Butterfly Ward*, the book is a series of powerful and wrenching short stories. They, like her life, walk the line between sanity and insanity, serene peace and crippling madness. The first story, "Ada," is about a woman locked in a mental ward. The third story, "Considering Her Condition," is about a woman who takes her own life after the birth of her child. The fifth story, "Making It," is an exchange of letters between a pregnant and mentally unwell woman and her best friend, a gay hairdresser trying to make it in show business as a female impersonator.

Margaret never admitted that "Making It," or any of the other stories that followed, were autobiographical or at least based on her own experiences. She merely teased that she felt "all people are material for fiction." Craig took a more pragmatic approach and shrugged off comparisons.

"I call it fiction based on fact," he said of "Making It." "Margaret has an incredible imagination. She made a sad story out of a happy one."

Fiction or not, Margaret got accolades for *The Butterfly Ward*. The literary editor of the *Globe and Mail* described her as "an accomplished explorer of hidden caves of the mind." *Chatelaine* magazine said she had "controlled passion and impressive skill." The *Montreal Gazette* said there was "no mistaking her huge potential." A year after its release Margaret shared the Toronto Book Prize with author Margaret Atwood.

At first the story "Ada" generated the most interest. French filmmaker Claude Jutra made it into a TV movie for the CBC. The project got some buzz and the attention of a writer named Richard ("Dick") Benner, whose own work was turned into a TV drama called *Friday Night Adventure*. It was about a man's first experience in a gay bar and the one-night stand with a male patron that followed.

Gay themes were still largely avoided in media in the 1970s, so Dick's work was a bit of a talking point. He wanted his next project to keep him on that track. That was when he read the original short story "Ada" in *The Butterfly Ward* and latched onto "Making It." He approached Margaret, bought the rights, and went to work on a screenplay.

There were many elements to the story that made it attractive as a project. Dick, himself a gay man, understood sexual identity and was known for an appreciation of drag. He also said he had long had an interest in love between incompatible people. *Friday Night Adventure* was about love between men. This would be about love between a gay man and a mentally ill woman, both taboo subjects then uncommon in Canadian television and film.

The final script came together in as little as six weeks. *Animal Crackers* was one of its first titles. Dick planned to direct it, and coincidentally, Michael Oscars was one of the people he shared his work and intentions with. They agreed it had great potential.

Before the cameras started rolling, an early review of his writing noted it, too.

"It's in [the screenplay] that Benner's vision of the gay culture as a valuable part of modern society is most maturely explored," reads a September 1976 profile by writer Jon Redfern in *Mandate* magazine. "Set in Toronto's gay world, it re-examines Benner's thesis that strange loves and even stranger identities must be accepted and cherished."

Redfern's story highlights that "multi-talented Craig Russell" would play the film's lead role of Robin.

The full story of how Craig got the part remains unclear. It's most likely that Craig's name came up in Dick's frequent chats with Margaret. Neither explicitly said so, but Dick confirmed he knew about Craig before the script was written and told Craig himself that Robin was written with him in mind.

When Dick officially approached Craig about taking the part, the two of them butted heads at first. The would-be actor said he was unsure about the opportunity and treated this writer-turned-potential-director with skepticism. He asked Dick what, if anything, he had directed before.

"And what have you starred in before?" Dick charged back, insulted.

A mutually challenging relationship was born.

"Craig's fans are really going to be jolted to see that his talent for acting goes a lot deeper than makeup, wigs, and glitter gowns," Dick told the magazine feature writer.

The article also mentioned a new name for the pending movie. It was no longer called *Animal Crackers*. It would be called *Outrageous!*

CHAPTER SIX
OUTRAGEOUS

Outrageous! seemed destined for history before cameras started rolling.

It all came together so quickly and easily — the short story, the rights, the script, the talent. Next came the need for a producer, someone who could develop the project further, coordinate all the moving parts, and arrange financing so filming could begin. A producer can raise or sink a project, making Dick Benner's next move a crucial one.

As with all the moves that came before, Dick made the right one now, too. With help from a mutual friend, he got his script in front of Bill Marshall, a Scottish-born Canadian with an eye for good books and cinema. He worked by day as the right-hand man to Toronto mayor David Crombie, where he started an office for film production. By night Bill worked in the entertainment world, notably forming a production company called the Film Consortium of Canada with business associate Henk Van der Kolk.

Bill and Henk had one other project on the go in 1976: Toronto's first film festival. Called the Festival of Festivals, it included a week of films screening at a handful of theatres packed with an international crowd of critics, filmmakers, and movie lovers. It was a hit when it launched that October, and after a few lessons learned, it would continue year after year and morph into the Toronto International Film Festival, an annual celebration of the best in global filmmaking.

Bill and Henk were festival coordinators, project managers, and businessmen. They had minimal experience in filmmaking, but through that entire first festival, they believed making a full-length feature film was their next step. And now *Outrageous!* landed in their laps.

Bill wasn't sure of the script's topic at first but was sold on it later that same day when, by happenstance, he saw Craig interviewed on an episode of Brian Linehan's show *City Lights*. He thought Craig was outstanding, a new performer totally different from others he knew. He knew this was a tale that needed to be told.

Bill called Henk, told him to watch the last few minutes of Linehan's show, and sold him on Craig's act. Henk admits he was very tempted by the opportunity, both to work with the very talented Craig and to bring this particular script to life. Themes in Dick's writing had been on his mind for a long time. Henk didn't understand the seeming separation of heterosexual and homosexuals in Canada, how gays and lesbians were segregated, and how they were absent from most media.

"I came from Holland where they didn't have all this arbitrary separation of the sexes," he says. "It appealed to me to do a film on something with a gay subject to try and bridge that stuff. That was in a time when [police] were still raiding the various bathhouses and the like, picking up gay people and arresting them.... I thought it would be really great to get a good script and see what we could do."

Bill saw that separation, too, and felt film was a medium where LGBTQ2S life could be explored so people could understand and relate. He and Henk agreed the script fit the bill for the kind of film they were looking to do. The script also got in front of a young filmmaker named Peter O'Brian who also saw a new world in its pages.

"It was a beautiful script about a gay man who did this performance and had his own difficulties; it was unknown territory to people like me," he says. "That's what was special. [Craig's character] was someone I didn't know. I read the screenplay and did know the person. The film worked that way."

In addition, the film worked in portraying a character with mental illness. Just as in Margaret Gibson's short story "Making It," the character

Robin Turner is a struggling drag queen trying to find his footing in his career while subsequently juggling his friendship with Liza Connors, a woman with paranoid schizophrenia who finds herself pregnant. Liza is both understandable and relatable despite her alienating condition — a character whom viewers can root for. Through Robin and Liza's shared effort to make it, they share a need for belonging, acceptance, and love. They find it together and liberate each other.

The characters in *Outrageous!* reflected young people in Canada living a grittier reality than what had been depicted before. Dick's deep understanding of Robin and Liza, a homosexual man and a woman with mental illness, was unique and beautiful. It not only made for a great partnership on a project, it also made for great filmmaking.

Motivated by their "naiveté [and] lack of exposure to the world," the men assumed their roles. Bill and Henk agreed to be co-producers. Bill was the marketing guy and promoter. Henk was the nuts and bolts. Peter joined them as an associate producer, and Dick was confirmed to move from writer to director.

Another man named Murray "Dusty" Cohl came into the pre-production fold for a while. Dusty, a "charming salesman, shrewd deal maker and cultural ambassador," was a film lover with deeply rooted movie industry connections who had worked with them on the film festival. He helped the team make some connections for financing and later was looped back in to secure distribution. Bill and Henk gave him a spot in the credits for that. His title? "Accomplice."

The budget was written on a just a few sheets of paper. The financing, requested in $5,000 increments for each investment, came from various stakeholders and a grant from the Canadian Film Development Corporation, then a relatively untapped resource because so few people were making films in Canada.

"We were [some] of the few people that actually ever took [the government] up on that capital cost allowance deal," Henk says. "It's the only reason we were able to do the film."

With their combined grant and investments, the producers had $165,000 to start. It wasn't much, mere pennies in comparison to film budgets today, so everyone had to get creative to make it work. Bill and

Henk kicked in their fees, sought cheap office space in the Harbour Castle hotel, agreed to film with 16 mm film instead of the more expensive 35 mm theatres use, and auditioned local talent from the drag queen community instead of bringing anyone in.

The decision was also made to hire more inexperienced production staff to save money. They weren't hard to find. There were passionate film types in the city who wanted to work. People took time off from what they were doing or juggled their duties on-set with their day jobs. Where the producers couldn't hire, they relied on family and friends. Henk's wife, Yanka, would go to work on the set, stand in as an extra, and help with makeup, while Henk's brother Willem took care of publicity photographs. Even Dick offered some labour. His boyfriend, Bruce Calnan, took on the job of stage dresser.

What was important to Henk and Bill was that the people were passionate about making a film, rather than making a dollar, and that the film set would be seen as inclusive.

"I tried as much as possible to get all the functions filled by gay people," Henk says. "I figured we should try and make it an environment where everybody was going to be very comfortable.… There was such a separation, a misapprehension, about what gay people were like."

As director, it fell to Dick to work with all of the cast ahead of filming. He spent the most time with Craig, who in his first acting role was concerned about doing a good job. Craig wanted his role as Robin to celebrate his craft, not make a mockery of it. The film was partly comedic, and he did not want his tributes to be seen as farcical.

"[Dick gave] Craig the confidence that he would look good in this film, that it would show his act the way he wanted it to look and that it wasn't any kind of a joke, that it was artful and about the craft," says Peter. "They worked great together."

One person Dick had trouble working well with was Margaret Gibson. While Dick reportedly had regular contact with Margaret while he wrote the screenplay, details of her payment and the promised level of involvement beyond that remain unclear. That was between them. Margaret certainly thought she was to be involved beyond selling the rights to her story. She was "inflamed with artistic license." Who could blame her? The fictional story mirrored her own relationship with Craig. It was impossible not to take it personally.

But in Dick's world Margaret's interest in some creative control and plans for her involvement in the production stage were not part of their arrangement. She would not get to have a say in all that was portrayed in the lives of the characters she created. That led to consternation between the two of them. Dick was frustrated. Margaret was pissed off.

Peter says though it may have been hard for Margaret to accept, as the director, Dick would have to back away from good-faith agreements and sometimes take a hard stance for what would happen and what would not, both in the script and in production. He was in the best position to

Bill Marshall (left) and Henk Van der Kolk in their "office" at Cannes.

know what worked and what he could make happen, more than the original writer with more budding creative ideas.

"Artists initially are all going to say they are in a group and going to stay together," Peter explains. "When the actual contracts kick in, and you have the money interests making demands, you have time making demands, the cast making demands, those sort of promises between friends are harder to keep. At a certain point, Dick had to say, 'No, we are doing this.' She said, 'How can you say that?' You know what, 'I've rewritten the scene and I have no time to talk to you about it.'"

Dick barred Margaret from the *Outrageous!* set before anything even started. She never met the film's producers and didn't watch one frame of the picture until it was in theatres for all to see. Though she was paid enough to upgrade her apartment and be recognized in the film's credits, she was forever bitter about how the process turned out. She felt abandoned and left out in the cold.

Craig knew how Margaret felt, but his focus was on *Outrageous!* and doing the best job he could. He was staying in character as he usually did, but he was in control, focused, and able to temper his usual manic excitement to be ready for the task at hand. The idea of being in a film was his dream, and larger than anything he knew. That humbled him.

"When we had a meeting and it was him just in jeans, with no makeup, and he was just himself, I thought he was a nice guy, he was professional," Peter says. "He knew that there was no money, but I don't think he understood that there was *that* much no money."

As soon as the first Festival of Festivals wrapped in October 1976, *Outrageous!* moved forward on "a prayer and a song." Cameras started rolling in January 1977.

Outrageous! *opens with Craig as Robin, an attractive and seemingly reserved gay man with aspirations of being a female impersonator. He is enjoying a drink with a friend in a gay club and together they are watching a drag queen rehearse her act.*

"You're just dying to get up on that stage," the friend says.

"I'm not that desperate," Robin replies. "Not yet."

The movie then cuts to a scene of a slightly harried and crazed-looking woman running through Toronto's slushy streets. She is wearing a bathrobe and clutching a book in which she has a hand-drawn map to get herself to Robin's apartment.

She meets him there, disrupting him as he is practising his female impressions; he is wearing a wig and lipstick as he watches himself in the bathroom mirror. The woman's unexpected and unannounced arrival has surprised Robin but there is an understanding between them about her condition and where she came from.

"I was so afraid you weren't going to be home," she says. "I escaped."

"You are going to make the doctors real mad," Robin replies.

"I can stay, can't I, Robin?" she asks. "I'll get my own place soon, really. I'm not crazy like they say. They only make me crazier. Please?"

Liza has just escaped from a mental institution. Her relationship with her family is strained. She is terrified of doctors and the idea of returning to hospital. She wants to prove she can make it on her own. She struggles with her "craziness," and the demon that torments her, whom she calls "the Bone Crusher." It is Robin, seemingly her only friend, who she turns to.

He puts his arm around her, guides her into his apartment, makes her comfortable, and holds onto her hands to warm them. He has the means to take care of her and protect her.

"I'm better already," she says. "Really, I am."

This is the introduction to Robin and Liza.

Craig, of course, played Robin, a role that was tailored for him. Liza was played by Hollis McLaren, a professionally trained actress who had a handful of previous film roles. She was likeable, friendly, and believable in the role of a mentally ill woman. Hollis was totally consumed by her character, described as "either a brilliantly skittish performer or an authentic nervous wreck."

It was almost an opportunity missed. Bill originally wanted actress Kim Cattrall for the part, long before Cattrall became known for her role as sex-crazed PR woman Samantha Jones in the HBO series *Sex and the City*. But Dick nixed the idea of casting Cattrall because it was obvious Hollis had the best chemistry with Craig.

Key to that chemistry was how Hollis's understated presence as Liza made for a perfect balance to Craig's dominant presence as Robin. Liza is not a total waif, though. Her strength comes out when Robin withdraws and admits to feeling depressed. Craig and Hollis were able to see that and toggle their characters' strengths and vulnerabilities as the film continues with this shifting dynamic — Robin, the struggling female impersonator, is there for Liza, and Liza, the schizophrenic, is there for Robin. What could become of characters like this?

Other characters were as equally well cast, though some admitted to skepticism going into their roles. Actor Richert Easley, a friend of Dick's from graduate school, played Robin and Liza's mutual friend, an affable character named Perry who is also trying his hand in female impersonation. The part was written specifically for Richert, but he had reservations — the opportunity and subject matter felt risky.

"I had great confidence in Dick as a writer; I didn't have confidence in the film itself," Richert says, explaining how he felt that *Outrageous!* was not a common kind of film. "I never imagined it would be the success it was, given primarily that the lead character was a drag queen hairdresser."

Still, Richert went forward. It was work, and the comfortable dynamic working with Craig and Hollis was apparent from the start. He says one of the first scenes he shot was in a doughnut shop, where his character talks about his plan to go out for Halloween dressed as actress Karen Black in the film *Airport 1975*. In the scene, Robin seems jealous as Perry shares his attire that he had just purchased with his friends.

"I was really nervous," Richert says of his feelings when they started filming. "It was sort of like we were all in this together and shooting on the fly."

That was a good way to describe the philosophy of the whole production schedule. On their small budget, Henk, Dick, and the cast and crew filmed as much as they could in a day. One of the scenes with Robin in drag was done in one take. There wasn't a lot of time to strategize or stand back and do a reshoot. Time was money they didn't have.

They filmed up and down parts of Yonge Street, in front of Union Station, on a Toronto streetcar, in a dilapidated space behind Dick's downtown loft, in the theatre at the Harbour Castle, in a Yorkville hair salon, and at Club Manatee. The latter location was a homecoming of sorts for Craig. It had been six years since he began his performing career there, and now it seemed his past was joining him. Local drag queens Rusty Ryan and Jackie Loren, as well as Manatee co-owner Rene Fortier, got small parts in the film.

With them, in addition to Craig, Hollis, and Richert, were some pretty notable names. Allan Moyle, a writer and actor of a handful of movies who later directed the films *Pump Up the Volume* and *Empire Records*, played Liza's crazed friend Martin. Actress Helen Shaver, who later had parts in *The Color of Money* and *The Craft*, played an antagonistic character named Jo.

A lot of time was spent on the third floor of a house that was the set for the apartment Robin and Liza shared. The space was small and hot with everyone crammed in. Initially, it didn't look fitting as a space for the set, but with some creativity on their shoestring budget, a designer brought in used drapes and fabrics and bought lampshades that were dyed with tea bags to looked aged.

One person who constantly seemed to be part of the action was Bruce, Dick's boyfriend. Credited as a set dresser, Allan remembers him as always seeming to be part of the authority keeping everything together and everyone in line.

"It didn't take long to figure out he was deeply involved in everything that was going on," Allan says, calling Bruce a grey eminence, a powerful decision maker operating behind the scenes in an unofficial capacity. "Dick depended on him. He was kind of like an enforcer. He was the person who would take you aside and make sure you're okay, but with a look that said you better be okay.… It was not a very comfortable dynamic."

Production continued, relying on the experience of a few to balance the inexperience of the whole. Peter probably had the biggest resumé for movie-making, including a producing credit for the film *Love at First Sight* with actor Dan Aykroyd. He was professional and organized, the right man to "make the trains run on time." Pauline Harlow, who had experience working on numerous films in the U.K., was the continuity person. Not only could she time the actors, she could walk onto a set and point out what wasn't working with just a quick glance. Almost everyone else was relatively new to the process. Mistakes were made, but they had to keep going.

"[Dick] Benner also didn't know what he was doing," Henk says. "But he had the sensibility, the sensitivity for it."

Allan remembers Dick for his intensity.

"He made me nervous, he was so intense," he says. "I could see from the set of his jaw that he carried quite a bit of anger. He was militant, which is fine. I didn't blame him. I didn't suffer from it. I just knew he was super intense ... like he was carrying a river of anger underneath him."

Certainly, everything was happening because of Dick's original interest in drag and the homosexual life subtext, and his efforts to find Margaret and write the screenplay. Everyone there owed a lot to him, but that played on Dick's rapport with people after a while. He could be stubborn, difficult, and inflamed, and it only got worse as he sparred with Bill.

Bill and Dick had an adversarial relationship, particularly when Bill questioned the creative direction. He questioned everything from the weight given to Liza's character to Dick's choice of cameraman. On one occasion Bill insisted that a whole scene they had filmed that included homophobic violence be cut from the final product.

In the commentary that later appeared on the *Outrageous!* DVD, Bill said Dick would seemingly act out when they disagreed on something. On his time off Dick would shut off communication, head into an editing studio and tailor what was filmed to make "something absolutely unintelligible."

"The thing dragged on for two and a half hours of sad stories," Bill said. "We got George Appleby, who was our editor — and a great editor — to come back. I got in there with the scissors with him and we turned it into a short, funny movie, and a life-affirming movie, which I think was the point."

It was safe to say that director and co-producer did not like each other.

"Dick was very moody," Henk says, noting there was some mutual understanding that Dick's life, being homosexual himself and trying to push boundaries in his work, could not have been easy. That brought tremendous pressure. He was also relatively young as a director, putting on some bravado behind feelings of insecurity. "He did a terrific script.... We were all learning on the job."

Henk loved the process, though, and maintained patience as everything chugged along. He admits that he, too, was learning. He would later rely on George, the film's editor, to cover up mistakes in timing and framing.

"[Bill and Henk] were not sophisticated producers," says Helga Stephenson, then a rising communications professional with a love of film who later took the reins of the beloved Festival of Festivals. "It was everybody's first everything, but they just went out and did it."

One of the best decisions the producers made was to bring in Paul Hoffert as musical director. Paul was a jazz musician with experience in TV and off-Broadway theatre, in addition to four years with the Canadian rock band Lighthouse. His wife, Brenda, was a singer, lyricist, and writer. Through their separate working relationships with Bill, they read the script and jumped at the chance to participate.

Their contributions include original songs "Step Out" and "It Ain't Easy," the latter being the film's theme song. Brenda sang it for one scene, and sang "Ave Maria" in another. They had a terrific time, got a deal to record the film's score, and won a Canadian Film Award (later known as a Genie Award) for their work. They also chummed along well with Craig, a relationship that blossomed when filming was over.

"Craig introduced us to the gay club scene, including the drag club scene, which was super fun," Paul says, still seemingly amused by the experience. "I was pretty amazed that there was this vibrant underground club scene in Toronto right in front of everyone's noses ... I remember not wanting to appear too naive, but trying to figure out the vernacular."

While Bill, Henk, Peter, and Dick went to great lengths to film as much as they could in Toronto to save money, some filming still had to be done in New York City. Peter put the plan together, which took some creativity. New York has strict rules for filming, with a lot of red tape, permits, and costs — all things the *Outrageous!* crew couldn't wade into. They instead planned to film as much as they could until they were told not to.

They filmed over one day, keeping to a small section of Manhattan with a skeleton crew, trying hard to get every scene done in one take to save time. They were down to the last scene when an official finally intervened and asked for their non-existent permits. That could have stopped everything, but after some jovial conversation, they were given permission to finish without getting hit with a costly ticket.

Along the way they had a brush with history. One of the film's scenes was shot on Christopher Street in Greenwich Village, a popular hub with bars for LGBTQ2S people and gay-friendly businesses. One of them was the Stonewall Inn, the tavern where the Stonewall gay rights riots took place less than a decade before, events widely considered to be the start of the gay liberation movement.

Their day's work complete, the men celebrated at Mineshaft, a notorious Manhattan club known for catering to gay men who were into bondage, discipline, sadism, and masochism (BDSM). Richert says it was Dick who insisted they go. Dick was very much into the scene and had a great time, while everyone else was mortified by this very new, very different world that was far more outrageous than their movie.

Craig did well during the film shoot. He was very focused and gracious, and he brought personal touches to his character and impressions. His biggest opportunity for improvement was his timing, but with help from Pauline, he got better. His co-star Allan appreciated that he was low maintenance and able to go with the flow on such a minimal budget where there was bound to be challenges.

"He was fabulous," Allan says. "Making a movie is a lot harder than just recording him performing. Dick had a real problem in that without time, you don't have the ability to get rid of a small problem quickly. You are always fighting little accidents and problems. The fact that Craig didn't [get difficult] is to his credit. He was rough and ready to go."

The crew could see how hard he was trying. He was friendly, sweet, and unpretentious — anything but a difficult star. He even chipped in to help with some of the makeup. But on top of all of that, even with his minimal experience compared to his co-stars, he also was just a very good actor.

"During filming I never saw him off," Richert says. "I remember thinking, watching the opening scenes with Craig and Hollis, how completely real and natural he was. I was really, really impressed. Whether he was trying hard or not, I just accepted him on set when we worked as an actor. He was just so easy to work with."

Hollis echoed the sentiment.

"I found Craig very generous to work with," she told a reporter. "What he does is amazing; he's a genius."

The most negative thing anyone could say about Craig was that some days he was a little tired and unprepared to film some scenes after he and

Hollis McLaren and Craig pose during filming of the final scene in Outrageous!

some members of the cast and crew over-partied and overconsumed during off-hours. The drug of choice then was "poppers," a slang term for alkyl nitrites that are inhaled to get a rush.

"There were a couple of days when they were worried about him," Peter says with a bit of a laugh, noting "there was a lot of coffee involved and stuff like that" to bring their lead star around.

Nevertheless, Craig nailed his character. He totally captured Robin's uncertainty and insecurity, his motivation and his finesse at female impersonation, performing on camera as Tallulah Bankhead, Bette Davis, Barbra Streisand, Mae West, Carol Channing, Ethel Merman, Bette

Dick Benner and his boyfriend Bruce Calnan clad in leather at the Outrageous! *cast party.*

Midler, and Judy Garland. His emphasis was on his ladies, not that he was a gay character, something that Bill and Henk wanted to portray right from the very beginning.

"He did what he did with total confidence and with tremendous talent," Henk says. "He is so totally believable as a human being. The gay part was incidental to that ... He was a very genuine actor."

Two of the more touching scenes they filmed became the final scenes of the picture. The first scene starts with Robin performing as Peggy Lee and singing Brenda's song "It Ain't Easy." The song is testament that life is hard and one can't do it without the support of close friends, loving each other.

"It ain't easy in this crazy world," Yanka says, looking back on filming day. "We were crying our eyes out. It was so poignant."

The second scene sees Robin and Liza in a dressing room after the song. Liza has just delivered a stillborn baby and moved to New York City to live with Robin. She still fears "the Bone Crusher" and confesses that she believes she is dead inside.

"You are not dead," Robin says, still dressed as Peggy. "You are alive and sick and living in New York like eight million other people. Listen, you're Liza…. You'll never be normal, but you're special and you can have a hell of a good time."

Liza listens and begins to relax her defences.

"You know, there's only one thing," Robin continues. "You're mad as a hatter, darling. But that's alright because so am I. So am I. I've never known anyone worth knowing who wasn't a positive fruitcake. We are all nuts. You and me are here to love and look after each other. You're not dead, you just have a healthy case of craziness."

"Craziness," Liza affirms.

"Yes, make it work for you," Robin concludes.

Robin and Liza laugh together and head out to the crowd to dance the night away.

Outrageous! worked for all the stakeholders involved. It wrapped after about four weeks of filming. The final cost was $171,126 — only $6,126 over its original budget, with every dollar recorded and reported to their investors.

Altogether, with what could have been a nightmare with budget and inexperience, everyone had a charmed time. There was a magic through it all. The participants did not do the film to get lavishly paid or be part of a big blockbuster production, but because they believed in the story and had a love of filmmaking. They were proud of the final product. They didn't even know what would come of it, if anything at all. Some figured it would be a late-night movie at most. All that counted was that they made something genuine and special.

Richert Easley, pleased as punch, and Craig, struggling and sad, at the Outrageous! *cast party.*

Now it was time for a celebration. Henk and Yanka hosted a wrap party for the cast and crew at their apartment in Harbour Square on Toronto's waterfront. The cognac and cigars came out, Henk and Yanka's teenage son poured the drinks, and everyone seemed to relax a little bit, including their intense director, Dick. He arrived clad in leather and chains with his "startlingly good-looking" boyfriend, Bruce, wearing a leather jockstrap with chain collar and nothing else.

"It was a hell of a party, quite fun," Henk remembers.

Craig went dressed as actress Raquel Welch. He looked great but something in him seemed to change. He wasn't friendly and humble as he had been on set. He was abrasive and snarky, totally disconnected and cold to his colleagues and friends. It was like he was a different person.

"I was stunned," Richert says. "It was almost like a weird betrayal of our friendship. He was not friendly to me at all. He'd been so terrific and warm during the shoot. I just didn't know who this person was.… It was a shock to me."

Richert and the others were right; Craig was not himself. What they didn't realize was that Craig wasn't deliberately rude to everyone. He was hurting and trying to hide his sensitive emotions. He was overwhelmed by the fact that the experience was over. It had been so gratifying to him as an artist, and it felt so rewarding to make good on his promise to his practical mother that he could make a place for himself in the world of entertainment.

"I gave myself five years to really make it," Craig said later. "I played Vegas and Provincetown and the Persian Room in New York. But that wasn't making it. Then I did this movie, and I told Margaret, this is it."

It didn't take long into the evening before Craig got outwardly emotional and rushed to a bathroom to try to compose himself. Yanka went to his aid, comforting him, making him laugh, drying his eyes, and reapplying his makeup.

"Oh, gorgeous, darling, thank you," Craig told Yanka. "Thank you for being such a good mother to me."

Craig cleaned himself up and went back to the party. It went unsaid, but those who observed him that night had an insight into who Craig was deep down. He wasn't necessarily the happy entertainer. He was hiding emotions and his behaviour that night was a foreboding of the troubles festering in him that would bubble outrageously to the surface in ways no one could anticipate.

"I remember Dick saying, 'I think he is really an unhappy person,'" Richert says. "He channels all of this turmoil into these ladies when he does them."

CHAPTER SEVEN

FEVER

Bill Marshall and Henk Van der Kolk went big with the first promotion for *Outrageous!* Before it screened anywhere or even had an ad in a newspaper, they took it to the Cannes Film Festival in France.

That was a very brazen move for two young filmmakers — Cannes brings together the best of the best in film — but it was a formula that had worked before. Cannes was where they drummed up interest in a Toronto-based film festival when most people in the North American market would have panned that as a silly idea. Their first festival was a hit; now it was time to make a hit out of their first film.

With them was Dusty Cohl. Dusty hadn't been involved with the *Outrageous!* production, but as a long-standing Cannes patron, it made sense to have him with them. If anyone could get them visibility, it was Dusty. He was not a man who blended in with a crowd. His usual attire around the prim and proper set of Cannes was faded jeans and an aged T-shirt, with a black stetson cowboy hat that had a star pinned to it. He was a "schmoozer" and could pull any two people together for a conversation, no matter who they were or where they came from.

Toronto mayor David Crombie (left) stopped by the Cannes efforts with Murray "Dusty" Cohl and Yanka Van der Kolk.

The men put $25,000 into the Cannes idea. Just as they had through filming, their strengths balanced each other and covered all the bases. Bill had the media-savvy rapport and the face to market it, Henk was the Dutch pragmatist and a producer at heart with the vision, and Dusty had his Rolodex of contacts and a philosophy to "swear you'll turn up or you'll hear nothing about it."

They had quite the entourage with them. Henk's wife, Yanka, who had done so much on the film's set, was there, as was Dusty's wife, Joan. Dick Benner came along. He was in his element, rubbing shoulders with some of the best directors in the world who were there. Popular Toronto

Outrageous! *director Dick Benner (left) and entertainment journalist George Anthony.*

mayor David Crombie and his wife, Shirley, were with them, as was Hollis McLaren; although, she was turned off by media attention and shied away from the spotlight as much as she could.

Outrageous! wasn't there for competition; it was there to generate buzz. To do that, Henk, Bill, and Dusty set up office on the terraces and beaches around Cannes to loop in anyone who came by — think the likes of prominent film critics Rex Reed and Charles Champlin — into conversation. They also pushed swag into the hands of anyone who would take it. That choice was particularly smart. Before anyone knew it, *Outrageous!*-branded bags and windbreakers were in sight everywhere, and they were getting attention.

"When all the movers and shakers at Cannes saw Roger Ebert, Peter Noble and Rex Reed wearing the windbreakers, they became the must-have rainwear for the Croisette," Bill would write later in his book *Film Festival Confidential.*

They even managed to get a few screenings in a small theatre. That didn't come cheap. Because the movie was shot in 16 mm, the film had to be sent to New York in advance of their trip to be "blown out" to 35 mm so it would work in theatre projectors. No studio in Canada could do it at that time, and it wasn't cheap. Henk says it cost $35,000.

The rain poured in Cannes through the festival that May, but the heat was on for *Outrageous!* David Perlmutter, president of the Canadian Association of Motion Picture Producers, credited Bill, Henk, and Dusty with doing "a great job with the pizzazz … just what Canadian movies need." Robert Kaufman, a Hollywood screenwriter followed, "You'd think these guys had made *Gone with the Wind.*"

The film about the drag queen and the mentally unwell woman was all the talk. *Outrageous!* is perhaps better remembered than the film that won the Palme d'Or that year, *Padre Padrone* by Italian film directors Paolo and Vittorio Taviani.

"We turned Cannes outrageous," Henk recalls.

The next question was where to open *Outrageous!* in the North American market. Despite the warm reception with film elite, the characters and topic matter still made it something of a gamble, so Bill and Henk made the decision to bring the film to New York first. If it flopped with audiences there, the scent of failure seemed less likely to follow the filmmakers over the border to Toronto.

Bill and company got the film in front of Donald Rugoff, a seminal figure in the independent film world and president of the Cinema V movie theatre franchise. As Bill recounted, they set up a private screening for Donald at New York's Rivoli Theatre, only to have Donald fall asleep ten minutes into the film. That was concerning, but Donald nonetheless roused himself in the end credits with an offer to screen it. No one could believe they'd gotten a deal.

Outrageous! opened on July 31, 1977, at Donald's Cinema II theatre in New York's Upper East Side. It was like an unbelievable miracle, an end result of riding the coattails of hard work and luck. It was just six months after they finished filming and eight weeks after they got home from Cannes. They had zero money in the bank. All they had now was a basic marquee with simple words: *Outrageous "This one is a gem" – Reed.*

The latter phrasing came from a highly complimentary review from Rex Reed, the film critic they befriended in Cannes, who wrote that the "touching, vibrant film adventure" was "a marvelous, fresh touching film with heart-tugging insight and compassion, and most definitely the season's major, unheralded surprise." Bill and Henk were so thankful for Rex's words and support, they included his copy in their media booklet and on some of their posters.

Vote of confidence in hand, they were ready for everyday moviegoers to see *Outrageous!* The first screening, on a quiet Sunday afternoon, had only a few people in the theatre. That spelled trouble, but then something happened. Word got around. People were talking. There were lineups down the street for the second, third, and fourth screenings, seemingly out of nowhere.

The film was having an immediate impact.

"It was so impressive to see people coming out, humming the music and being in such a terrific mood, because that's what the picture did for you," Henk says. "It put you in a terrific mood. I thought, 'This is my kind of world.' From there on, it went everywhere."

Richert Easley felt the same way and saw that it wasn't just one crowd who enjoyed it. Screening after screening, audiences had the same warm, receptive reaction.

"I never dreamed for an instant that it would become the success that it did," he says. "I loved stopping into the theatres and listening to the audience reaction. It was so consistent from time of day to time of night that you went, it was always consistent. It was, to me, a real surprise and a real phenomenon."

Outrageous! went viral. It had rave reviews — the *L.A. Times* called it "original, alive and ribaldly funny" — and it became a cult phenomenon with fans. They had viewing parties, costume parties, and dance parties. It had the potential to be a blockbuster hit with international presence and recognition, but in the haze of early excitement, mistakes were made, including a decision to decline an offer from Cinema V to buy the total rights for $500,000 U.S.

The only marketing Outrageous! *had in New York at first was this marquee. Left to right: Henk, Billy "Silver Dollar" Baxter, and Bill (looking undeniably Canadian) pose underneath.*

The eventual U.S. distribution deal, made in a meeting organized by Dusty and observed by film critic Roger Ebert, went to film producer Billy "Silver Dollar" Baxter and his partner Herbert Steinmann. Roger documented the meeting between the men in his book *Two Weeks in the Midday Sun.*

"I'm a guy who is new to this," Dusty reportedly said. "I'm feeling my way, I'm learning as I go along, I appreciate the opportunity to talk with you gentlemen, and maybe we can make a deal that will make everyone happy."

"Cut the crap," Billy replied. "You got a film here about a Canadian pricksickle aficionado, and nobody wants it.... How much you want for this movie?"

Billy didn't like *Outrageous!*, but after hearing all the talk among critics, he thought the film was an opportunity he couldn't ignore.

"There's got to be something to this," he said, looking back on it. "We got the film pretty cheap."

Details of the figures from the deal are murky (Roger wasn't allowed to disclose the numbers in his book), as was the actual distribution plan. Henk says the film stayed in theatres mostly in the east, hampering its growth across the market and dampening its reach. It was all kind of a bummer for its filmmakers. More mistakes followed, including a choice to take a market-by-market approach. In the end they felt they essentially gave the film away for free.

"We just got stolen from," Bill said. "We didn't know anything about the distribution business."

Henk says he brokered one of their best deals in Germany. It wasn't just about money. It was that it was so widely embraced and accepted. That made sense. The country, and Berlin in particular, was known for a thriving gay community and arts scene. It was too bad that not all deals would go as well as that one did.

"We should have kept much more control over how everything was going to happen," Henk says now. "I'm so sorry we didn't get the picture out to a much larger audience. But you know what? We packed the damn halls all the time. One place in the U.S. had *Outrageous!* for almost sixty weeks.... [But] in the end, nobody made a lot of money."

Called "baby producers" in terms of the world, Bill and Henk still retained enough control to continue screening the film themselves. The next stop was their home country — Canada — but still a little apprehensive, they chose to take it to the "cozy little Ottawa FilmExpo" before their own Festival of Festivals in Toronto. They still weren't totally comfortable, even there.

As Bill wrote in his book: "Could a singing gay hairdresser and his nut bar buddy be too much for federal bureaucrats on a Friday night? We agreed it might turn out to be a nightmare."

Bill hid in the back of the theatre at the first screening, and handed introductions of the film on the stage to Henk and Wayne Clarkson of the Canadian Film Institute, who compared *Outrageous!* to being "like Mary Poppins ... sort of." Bill need not have worried. The reception mirrored what they experienced in Cannes. He said that first audience giggled, laughed, and "clapped till their hands bled." Bill wrote that he hugged Wayne with such relief it was like they were "shipwreck survivors."

At last they took *Outrageous!* to the 1977 Festival of Festivals in September. It was in good company. Other films screened that year included director Frank Capra's *It's a Wonderful Life* (1946) and writer Arthur Miller's *The Misfits* (1961). Running the second night of the festival, *Outrageous!* was just as enthusiastically received in Toronto as it was in Cannes, New York, and Ottawa, singing gay hairdresser and all.

"We screened it and at the end, the audience sat in stunned silence," Bill remembered. "And then Donald Sutherland got up in the middle of the audience, and he's a fairly big presence, and screamed out 'Bravo!' and started clapping, and everybody was up cheering and carrying on."

Audiences were singing and dancing out of their seats. Bill and Henk, plus the film's lead stars Craig and Hollis, were all the talk. It was a relief.

"When you are shooting a film, you don't do it with everyone filling up with laughter," Peter O'Brian says. "The laughing came later. It was hilarious. It was wonderful. The feeling of life, joy and happiness, and just fun in it all, was not something I had seen while filming it.... People loved it, right away."

Audiences were all about Robin and Liza. They danced around conservative eyes and reached people. They opened a door to places where people dared not tread in Canadian film. The media gobbled it up. *Globe and Mail* reporter Robert Martin wrote that *Outrageous!* was "a charming and arresting film ... Richard Benner has written a touching and generally realistic asexual love story."

But in fairness, its strength was in its story and acting, not in its moviemaking. The thin budget and slim resumé of the filmmakers were apparent to trained eyes.

"I liked it to a certain extent," *Toronto Sun* columnist Sylvia Train would later say. "I personally thought it was shot badly, cutting off people's heads and things."

Critics wrote how the image was grainy from the transition to 35 mm from 16 mm, there were "awkwardly staged and loosely structured sequences that go on too long," and the cutting from scene to scene lacked flow. All told, it was "an understatement to say that *Outrageous!* is not exactly a cinematic masterpiece," critic Martin Knelman wrote.

Even Bill and Henk thought so. Henk says it can be considered "a piece of shit as a production." But whatever it missed in production, its sincerity and authenticity made up for it. Audiences connected with the message that we are all human, we all have problems, and we are all the same. Anyone could relate to Robin and Liza's yearning to find a place to belong.

"*Outrageous!* is not a plea for understanding for either homosexuals, like *A Taste of Honey*, or mental patients, like the recent *I Never Promised You a Rose Garden*," the *Globe and Mail* review said. "[Richard] Benner, who also directed the film, simply presents in a blunt fashion the concept that schizophrenics or gays are no more sick or aberrant than so-called normal people, that they need no special consideration and that they can live 'normal' lives. After all, these days, what is normal?"

The timing to tell the story was perfect. Definitions of *normal* were changing everywhere. The release of *Outrageous!* fell in lockstep with the rise of feminism, the sexual revolution, and gay liberation, all of which shared the sentiment of having the freedom to make one's own choices. The little film from Canada encompassed the spirit of social change and represented so much to so many people.

"It showed [a] drag queen as a real person," says Sky Gilbert, who was then two years away from co-founding Buddies in Bad Times Theatre, dedicated to the promotion of queer theatrical expression. "He was a hairdresser, he was effeminate, he had a boyfriend, he had problems. He was just a person. This was about Craig Russell as a leading character, who was a drag queen and a highly effeminate male, who walked around looking like a girly boy all the time. That was groundbreaking. That was a gender milestone."

Henk sums it up more simply.

"The picture had some kind of profound social impact," he says. "I really believe that."

Outrageous! had implications for the film world, too. Not only could Toronto hold festivals for film, it was a great place to make them. The market saw a rise in workforce and movie sets after that, and more hands reaching for funds available from the Canadian Film Development Corporation, which had just increased its budget to $25 million. *Outrageous!* would eventually be credited as being a "pivotal moment in Canadian film history" that "set the stage for much of what we have here now."

"Only in Canada would that movie get funded," Allan Moyle says, considering the film's subjects and storylines. "I thought it was amazing it was being made.… It was a good time. It was a moment in North American culture where there were no impossibilities."

Outrageous! was a point of national pride that demonstrated our skill in filmmaking and the diversity of our population.

"I remember it being a real Canadian celebration," Richert says of the *Outrageous!* premiere in Canada. "It felt like for the first time maybe something had come along that was Canadian-made that was different and was going to have people talking. The response had been so great."

Bill and Henk were grateful. They took an ad in a nationally distributed newspaper to thank everyone from the actors to the distributors for their support of *Outrageous!*

"Everybody was always giving us shit for having too many Americans involved all the time," Henk says. "So, we put this in to get to all these critics and to thank everybody in Canada to put a point on it."

Craig was grateful, too. Critics praised both his dramatic acting and his comedic timing as Robin. They also made note of his excellent impersonations and suggested that *Outrageous!* was the turning point of his career, the start of the stardom he longed to find.

"Watching Russell, we feel the excitement that has been merely faked in scores of backstage movies," Knelman wrote. "This time we can see that a star really is being born."

The spotlight was on Craig and he could feel it. He just could not feel it up close. Craig was absent from all premieres, screenings, and promotions. There were multiple reasons for that. Funds were tight to send anyone out to Cannes, New York, or elsewhere, and it made sense that the filmmakers and businessmen go ahead of him. They were also testing waters with their storyline. A film about a drag queen was fine, but having an actual female impersonator on hand may have been too radical as they felt out how people were responding.

Craig also had his stage act to attend to. Demands for his show had not slowed down, and he had already lost money being away for filming. Now things were ramping up. He had some big gigs on the books, including a handful of shows at Toronto's Theatre in the Dell and another season at Provincetown. No one, least of all Craig, could have expected the reception *Outrageous!* got. He hadn't anticipated the need to keep himself free.

In the end Craig's continued performing and touring had a remarkable benefit: it was free *Outrageous!* promotion. With the film in movie theatres, its lead star was out on stages simultaneously selling the movie, his act, and his brand. That strategy had worked for other artists and projects in the past, like the Beatles with *A Hard Day's Night* and the Monkees with their television show. It was a marketing ploy that they didn't even have to think of.

Craig did a few interviews when he could, including a long interview that ran as a feature in *Canadian* magazine and an appearance on the CBC game show *Front Page Challenge,* where looking warm, engaging, and proud, he chatted with a panel of notable Canadians: broadcaster Betty Kennedy, journalist Gordon Sinclair, writer Pierre Berton, and actress Barbara Hamilton. He said he was thankful for the reception *Outrageous!* got and his opportunity to be part of it.

"I hope it is going to put Canada on the map as one of the major filmmaking countries in the world," he said. "I am grateful to Bill Marshall, Henk Van der Kolk for putting up the money, and I'm grateful to Dick Benner for getting good performances out of all of us."

Craig and the panellists talked about his background. "My father always wanted Carol Channing for a son," he teased, and went on to discuss his time with Mae and the fan club. He said his act was as much a service to fans as it was performing tributes to ladies he loved.

"I love these women so much and I feel the public misses them and they want them," he said. "I went to Australia last year and the reaction for Judy Garland, you would have thought that she was there."

Perhaps it wasn't all easy. He said that in female impersonation "you're fighting a lot of odds," but he still obliged a request for impromptu impersonations of Marilyn Monroe, Bette Davis, Judy Garland, Joan

Crawford, and Katharine Hepburn on the show. Sinclair clapped with glee at Craig's talent.

Craig also said it had been hard to get jobs in Canada even though he was well received in places like Los Angeles, Las Vegas, and San Francisco. After years being told Toronto was not ready for his type of act, it seemed that now he had a place. Doors were opened thanks to his talents and *Outrageous!*

Closing the program, host Fred Davis gave credit where it was due. "We are deeply indebted to you for a number of things," he told Craig. "The performances for one thing, and along with your colleagues, what you've done for Canadian films. Congratulations on *Outrageous!*"

Lori would never graduate from Riverdale Collegiate. She missed too many classes. But getting her high school diploma didn't matter to her. She was at Riverdale to experience life; even her teachers saw that. She simply stopped going when she thought she had all the education she needed.

Buoyed by the confidence she found watching an empowering one-woman show, Lori eventually moved out on her own and into a tiny one-room, $27-per-week flat in Rosedale, an affluent neighbourhood. The location made sense because it was between her father's apartment and her downtown haunts. In addition, Rosedale was home to some of Toronto's elite and she indulged the idea that she might get to meet some of them. It didn't matter that her apartments were in rooming houses or small units in attics or garages.

She wasn't home much anyway. Lori had living to do. The entertainment world was at her doorstep, ready for her to be a part of it. With classes behind her and a home of her own established, she worked a part-time job and ramped up her time downtown.

Lori loved the movies and if she paid to see one, she'd see three. She saw *Superman* with her sister, Dena, and brother Marc at the Imperial Six (later the Ed Mirvish Theatre) on Yonge Street and went to screenings presented by film archivist Reg Hartt. She got work as an extra on the film *Metal Messiah*, amused by the idea of dressing in a corset with fishnet stockings and high heels only to be stabbed to death in the middle of a scene that was nothing short of anarchy. She later was an extra in a film remake of the 1955 movie *Blackboard Jungle*.

The disco scene was booming and Lori was dancing right along with it. Lori's taste for disco came from frequenting Club David's. Open for less than three years and mere steps from the gay bars of the Yonge Street strip, the club was one of the posher venues of the time, with couches, red carpets, mirrored walls, and a billiards room. A larger-than-life statue of a well-endowed David stood predominantly between two winding staircases that led down to a dance floor. At a time when many bars were segregated by gender or sexuality, the venue was open to anyone.

"We open our doors to those who are open-minded," the welcome policy read. "There are no strangers at David's, just friends you haven't met yet."

Lori loved it there and often brought someone with her, usually Dena or her Riverdale friend Tom Veitch. Lori laughed when Tom, who resembled the very attractive French pop icon René Simard, was cruised by gay men in the club. On a rare night out with his sister, Paul couldn't help but notice how comfortable Lori seemed at Club David's. What happened to the shy, diminutive girl he knew?

She could literally dance for days. Lori once entered a dance marathon and danced from 7:00 p.m. on Friday to 9:00 p.m. on Sunday, stopping only for five-minute breaks every hour and a thirty-minute meal break every twelve hours. She went to Fran's restaurant for her meals and gobbled up platefuls of eggs and bacon or hamburgers and fries while she chatted up the drag queens that hung out there. Lori came in second in the contest.

After a mysterious fire closed the doors at Club David's, Lori and Dena moved on to clubs like Sugar's and Mrs. Knights. She also frequented places like Stages, a glamorous discotheque that was inspired by the famed New York City hot spot Studio 54; Fly By Night, a bar for lesbian, bisexual, and queer women that opened behind a strip club and offered live music; and Studio II, a club that had not only multiple dance floors, but also a library, restaurant, and theatre. The cover at Studio II was $3, a significant sum for that era.

"You, a friend, friends, or a large group, plus the small cover charge are the correct combination to a timeless experience you won't easily forget — because you will want to return again and again," a newsletter from the club read.

Lori was in her element. As she partied, she dabbled with drugs. She smoked pot when it was offered, and experimented with acid. She had one memorable trip on that drug, and while she laughed it off, it was enough to scare her out of doing anymore. She was still a little naive and, deep down, fearful and afraid.

But above everything theatre was at the centre of Lori's heart. She loved most going to cabaret-style shows at Café des Copains near the Flatiron Building and the St. Lawrence Market, and Toronto Workshop Productions Theatre, in a space near the Gay Village that later became Buddies in Bad Times Theatre. She loved dramas, musicals, anything cheeky. She was quite amused to bring a few unsuspecting family members to a play with five male characters who, smoking cigars in top hats and tails, were played by women.

Lori called herself a "theatre-a-holic," and she liked aligning closely with artists in that world. She got to know singer Peter Donato and art dealer Jack Pollock, impressed herself upon entertainer Quentin Crisp, saw fellow Riverdale classmate Brenda Donohue perform in a production of playwright Michel Tremblay's play *Sainte-Carmen of the Main*, and saw future Tony Award–winning actor Brent Carver in a production of *Rocky Horror Picture Show*. She took classes in dance and pantomime from artist Lindsay Kemp. She saw some of his shows as many as thirteen times and joined in with his dance company when a festival of mime was held at Nathan Phillips Square.

Lori continued to follow Richard Monette's career, saw him everywhere from the theatres of Stratford to the Glenn Gould Studio at the CBC's broadcast centre in Toronto, and once gave him a bottle of Johnnie Walker scotch after he performed in a one-man play even though she didn't know him personally. He was touched by her generosity. What he didn't know was how once she got it in her head that she liked an artist or entertainer, she became a total adoring fan.

"If she liked you, she attached herself to you," says former teacher and friend Alex Bostock. "She was a delicate, ethereal butterfly that attached herself to people and didn't let go."

Why she was like that is rooted in her upbringing. Lori found solace and escape in theatres when things were bad in her life, and when she found that safety, Lori found a deep love. That love only got stronger when

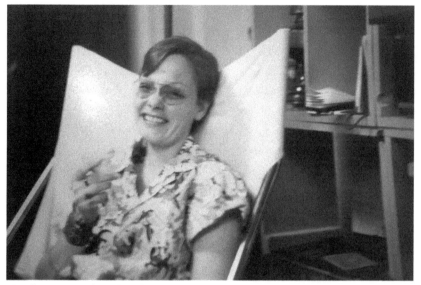

One happy Lori, fangirl and "theatre-a-holic."

someone was kind to her, and she expressed it with giving. She didn't give to make someone like her; she gave to thank them for treating her like a human being. Generosity became her hallmark. She would live a life giving everything she had.

Her adoration could turn intense. One example was a chanteuse Dorothy Poste, a theatre actress who starred in productions of *Hair* and *Jesus Christ Superstar,* and who had a tribute show to French singer Édith Piaf. She was a popular draw when she performed in Toronto.

Lori went for twenty-six straight nights to see Dorothy when she performed at Café des Copains. Ordering the same blue cheese salad and white wine each night, Lori would lose herself in Dorothy's torch songs, "mesmerized by those melodic tunes," she wrote. Some would move her to tears, particularly a cover of Peter Allen's "Don't Cry Out Loud." Lori would lay a red rose on the stage for Dorothy every time she saw her.

Dorothy herself couldn't help but take notice of Lori, her loyal attendance, her gestures, and her behaviour. At the opening night party, she fell into conversation with her new fan, who had snagged an invite to the private affair.

"You're so sensitive," Dorothy said. "How do you exist?"

"Good question!" Lori said with a laugh.

Her new-found adoration was no secret to her friends, including her high school theatre teachers. They believed she fantasized about having a life with someone like Dorothy, or the next artist she got hooked on at the café, a cabaret singer named Samantha Samuels. Lori was attracted to expressive, theatrical, and talented people.

Some believed Lori identified as gay. Her family did. They gave her a cake shaped like breasts for her sixteenth birthday. Lori loved it but never came out or publicly identified. A few people assumed she was androgynous, which was a rising counterculture in the era of Davie Bowie, Freddie Mercury, Mick Jagger, and even John Travolta. But Lori did not seem to conform to anything. No one asked her about her sexual identity and she wasn't telling, if she even could have described it herself.

"You wouldn't be able to find the label," says Ian Waldron, another teacher whom she now called a friend.

There was, perhaps, one exception. Lori had many heart-to-heart conversations with friend Wayne Legere from the Riverdale drama crowd. He says one day she told him she was a lesbian. She was as excited as she was nervous to admit this revelation of her sexual identity. But she told few others and was later romantically involved with men. Was she bisexual? She didn't comfortably say that either. No label stuck with her.

Alex says she simply "beat to her own drum and mostly did it alone. She was a total individual and never apologized for it."

When her adoration for Dorothy and Samantha faded, Lori turned to Craig Russell. She read about him, loved drag, loved the same entertainers he impersonated, and loved everything he seemed to stand for. She saw *Outrageous!* more than thirty times. With Craig away touring the U.S., Europe, and Australia, her adoration would have to be from afar, at least for now. But she was smitten.

Lori immersed herself in his craft. It was a natural fit. Drag embodied so many elements of the arts that she liked — stage presence, music, dancing, fashion, and humour. Bending gender norms, teasing at sexual identity, and playing by one's own rules were concepts she could relate to. Before long she was a regular at the Toronto gay bars of the day that allowed women.

This was "a world where I made new friends; Chris became Christine, Jack became Joan and Angelo became Angela," she would write whimsically two decades later.

She wasn't afraid to spend a little money and time on this new interest, either. Lori paid top dollar to see Danny La Rue, the British-born entertainer known for cross-dressing, at the O'Keefe Centre. She later waited ninety minutes after the show to get his autograph and was thrilled to run into his backup dancers later that night at Fran's. They were her kind of people and she felt like she fit right in.

She was not alone in that sentiment. The theatre and gay club scene were havens for people in the constantly changing and often volatile times when it was safer to keep sexual identities private.

"You didn't want to get in front of police, you didn't want employers to know," remembers Frances Share, a friend of Lori's. "Once you got into the clubs it was amazing. It was incredible.... When you went to the [Gay] Village, you were free."

The scene was Lori's life, and she had jobs rather than a career. Her work was just the means to pay for her small apartments, tickets to shows, and entry fees to theatres, clubs, and cinemas. She first worked at the post office, but after she was fired for missing too much work, she started working as a clerk at Elliott Research, a market research company. It was a good job and they were good to her, but it was almost temporary.

On St. Patrick's Day in 1980, Lori was on a break from work and dressed in green for the holiday when she was hit by a van passing a bus stopped at a crosswalk. She was thrown one hundred feet through the air, landed on her head, and broke her pelvis.

She spent weeks confined to complete bedrest, followed by rehabilitation at Riverdale Hospital. She was twenty-two years old and had to learn to walk again. Her days were spent working with physiotherapists and doing exercises she had learned in Lindsay Kemp's class. At night, she would wheel herself down to the lobby to call in requests to host Peggy Graham on CKFM Radio so she could still hear her favourite music.

The pain was excruciating for her. Craig was her absolute favourite entertainer, and when he was in town that March, she had to miss his show as she continued to recover. She did, however, make sure to get clippings from the *Toronto Sun*, the *Toronto Star*, and the *Globe and Mail* newspapers. Her scrapbook with clippings about his career could not be neglected.

When Lori was finally released from the hospital in June, she was still so stiff and sore that it took her forty-five minutes to climb the one flight of stairs up to her second-floor apartment. Still, despite her pain and what became lifelong physical impairment, she was determined for everything to get back to normal. She would not be stopped.

Lori took up active cycling as means for continued physiotherapy. She liked to go to the Toronto Islands, where she would cycle from Hanlan's Point to Ward's Island. The views were pretty and the repetitive movement felt good. She was out on her bike on a sunny afternoon when, colliding with another cyclist who came into her path as she zoomed along, she was thrown off her bike and into the air toward a tree. She landed on her arm, breaking it. It was the fourth time she had broken her arm in her short life and just three months after her major accident.

Lori shrugged off the new setback. She got a cast for her arm, accepted modified job duties at Elliott Research as she healed, and was back in the theatres in her off-hours.

It was a lot of physical trauma for one person to endure, but conditioned from years of abuse at the hands of her mother, and a sexual assault by a stranger she blindly trusted, Lori seemed to have grown somewhat immune. And when it came to emotions, she was still a great compartmentalizer. It was as if she turned off the switch marked *pain* in her brain and carried on no matter what came her way.

Lori did that for the rest of her life.

CHAPTER EIGHT

HELLO, DOLLY

Before *Outrageous!* was even officially released, its success was driving Craig's career forward.

With Craig's resumé now capped with a feature film, Bud Haas, Craig's agent and manager, could seek bigger venues with bigger audiences in bigger cities; Craig could generate more publicity and collect bigger paycheques. But bigger expectations came with all of that, so Paul and Brenda Hoffert were asked to go with him.

Paul and Brenda were accomplished musicians in their own right who could join the bill and raise the profile of the show. They also provided grounding to give Craig structure and guide him through the craziness. Craig knew he had a good thing going with the Hofferts, and just as he didn't want to disappoint his audiences, he didn't want to disappoint them either.

Part of that had to do with their careers and the potential their talents brought to his act, but also Paul and Brenda were more low-key, traditional people. He wanted to be like them. Even with seven years performing his act and a successful movie in theatres, Craig was starting to wonder if he should stop it all in favour of a more traditional life. He could work in hairdressing or insurance, like his parents. He could lead a life more aligned with how he was raised and be loved as Craig Eadie, the person, not Craig Russell, the entertainer. It was a struggle he shared with few people.

Paul teases that Craig yearned to be "a Don Mills housewife."

"Craig Russell the person should have been able to be pretty confident," he says. "Despite his success, Craig would think maybe Norma's right — 'I should become an insurance salesman.'"

Paul and Brenda were a salvation for Craig. They had two young boys and welcomed him into their family. He was a regular presence in their house, where he was able to leave the performer at the door and relax a little bit out of character. He rarely did that elsewhere because he didn't feel comfortable and relied on his characters to mask his emotions and any probing questions.

"We made him a part of our family," Brenda says. "He acted like he was happy with that because he had some estrangement issues with his own family."

Their relationship was a nurturing dynamic amid his growing doubts and the insecurity he tried to ignore as the *Outrageous!* machine moved him forward.

Craig, at his best, as Carol Channing. He said she made audiences believe "there is no unpleasantness, no lasting evil in the world."

Back onstage as a team, Paul and Craig worked together to make the show better. They got on, as Henk Van der Kolk says, "like a house on fire." There was no stopping them. Paul built out the band, expanded their repertoire, and massaged the flow of the act. Craig worked on the wigs and gowns for his impressions and rethought some of his jokes. He nixed some of the bad humour and foul language.

"I stopped doing put-downs and started doing send-ups," he told an interviewer. "The important thing is that the ladies I send up know that I really dig them."

After playing together in London and Toronto, Craig and his new entourage were back in his beloved Provincetown, Massachusetts, for a summer of shows at the Crown & Anchor. It certainly was an impressive return. He had been mostly on his own the previous summers, and now here he was with a full band led by an accomplished, respected musician.

While they were there, buzz continued for *Outrageous!* with premieres in North America and Europe. It all went on without him, so when it premiered in Provincetown and Craig could go, his mother, Norma, and his stepfather, Eric Hurst, flew in, as did old pal Phil Buckley.

Phil remembers the night well. He and Craig sat together at the back of the theatre through the screening, watching what was to be a fictional movie that in fact mirrored their experiences with Shirley Flavell and Margaret Gibson.

"It was kind of weird to see [but] it was impactful to a lot of people," Phil says. "When you've lived some of it, it's a strange feeling. Craig being Craig just relished it all."

When the Crown & Anchor gig wrapped for the season, Craig was off to New York for a full schedule of shows booked through October. By November the buzz was that Craig might be offered a residency in Las Vegas, and by December the act landed on the stages of Key West, Florida, for a few weeks.

By all accounts, Craig was a very talented musician. He had minimal formal training, but after all this time doing his act, he had matured musically. His singing was at its best. He could toggle from the deep drawl of a Louis Armstrong ballad to the high-pitched vocal jazz of Ella Fitzgerald's scat singing, a fast-paced style of improvised words and sounds forming a melody and rhythm.

"The first thing that impressed me about Craig and the reason I stayed with him … was that he was a fantastic musician," Paul told a documentary crew. "Craig could, and would, when he was in character be able to emulate the expertise that [each character] brought to their singing."

Craig could point out the key each instrument in the band was playing in and he could keep tempo, change, and adapt at the drop of a hat. His repertoire was expansive and he played with countless successful musicians. He earned the respect of even the most hardened people who would have once put their noses up to play with someone they would have ignorantly regarded as a run-of-the-mill drag queen.

"He could hear shit that always astonished me," says musician Alan Ett, who played with Craig on and off for five years starting in 1978. "He knew what he wanted and he knew how to get it. It was quite remarkable…. Amazing jazz musicians in New York, Europe would walk away and [say], 'Holy shit. That guy was amazing.'"

Craig was respected as an actor, too. In November, he was up for the best actor prize at the Canadian Film Awards, the leading awards for acting by Canadian talent, for his role as Robin Turner. He was excited, but he lost to actor Len Cariou, star of thriller film *One Man*. That was all right. That same weekend he was named Best Male and Best Female Performance of the Year at the Virgin Islands Film Festival. It was two awards for the price of one.

A few months later, Craig won the Silver Bear award for Best Actor at the twenty-eighth Berlin International Film Festival. The award was a plum. Robin was only his first acting role, and here Craig was being recognized alongside experienced actress Gena Rowlands and film-maker John Cassavetes. Henk and Yanka Van der Kolk were in town for the event. The attention helped Henk score German distribution for *Outrageous!* where, like in the U.S. and Canada, it would become a cult classic.

Craig's wins were always part of his press, but awards didn't matter much to him. He gave the Silver Bear to a friend as a gesture of thanks for support and friendship. He was more grateful for his fans.

"After all, they made me what I am today," he told one reporter. "A broken-down, alcoholic transvestite."

Craig as his still beloved Mae West.

* * *

Craig turned thirty on January 10, 1978. The mark came with excitement for the year ahead as he continued to ride the *Outrageous!* wave.

"My roaring twenties are over and I'm coming into my best ten years, when I'll be most productive," he said. "In 1972, I told my mother I'd give myself five years to make it as a female impersonator. In 1977, it happened. I'm psychic."

The year kicked off with what was probably the best news yet. Craig was booked for an eleven-night engagement at the Imperial Room in Toronto's Royal York Hotel.

The five hundred–seat space was regarded as one of Canada's premiere theatres and nightclubs. Presidents and prime ministers held events there and the greats performed on its stage, including Ray Charles, Duke Ellington, and Tony Bennett. Craig was thrilled, excited, and more than ready. He knew he could deliver the calibre of performance only a star could give. He called it a dream come true.

"It's the room when I was growing up that was the most elegant in Toronto," he said. "That's where people went to see Marlene Dietrich, Ella Fitzgerald, and Peggy Lee — all the ladies I love."

But Craig wasn't too humble. He also thought he belonged there.

"I'm going to be in my proper element to do people like Mae West," he said.

He arrived to fanfare. Toronto's daily newspapers and TV stations from across southern Ontario covered the news leading up to the show. The gay community was abuzz with continued support for their hero gone mainstream. The general manager of the Royal York sent him a personal welcome letter, and entertainment moguls Ed and Anne Mirvish invited him to dinner. They had one caveat: Craig would have to wear a suit. He couldn't promise that.

Gary Dunford of the *Toronto Sun* reported that Craig's "daring week-long booking" was "already sold out for much of its two-show-a-night run. … [Russell has] grown from being a teenage weirdo to an on-the-brink, one-of-a-kind star … the gig at the city's top-of-the-line nightclub is the payoff to a lot of hard times."

His mother, Norma, acknowledged the significance of the show, too. She was on hand with her sister Cathryn when Craig moved into a suite at the Royal York to prepare, and reporters were booked for interviews. They happily answered questions about Craig's success.

"This is IT for Craig," Norma told reporter Bruce Kirkland. "Just as with some kids in hockey whose dream it is to play in the big leagues. Well, the big league is the Imperial Room for Craig. This is IT."

The show came off without a hitch. With Paul still leading the band, Craig sang "All of Me" and "Frankie and Johnny" as Mae West (purring

Craig dazzled in his debut at the Royal York Hotel's Imperial Room.

"I only like two kinds of men — foreign and domestic!"); "Hello Dolly" as Carol Channing; "Lili Marlene" as Marlene Dietrich; and "Is That All There Is?" and "Fever" as Peggy Lee. In between, he quipped as Bette Davis, Billie Holiday, and Anita Bryant. He closed the show as Judy Garland singing "Over the Rainbow," sitting on the edge of the stage while reaching out in tribute to Judy herself. The audience responded with a standing ovation.

"What one remembers most is a succession of famous ladies from Hollywood and New York ... not some former hairdresser from Toronto the Good," read the *Globe and Mail* on February 28, 1978.

Another review said he "conquered the Imperial Room in a dazzling one-man, dozen-woman show that left customers yelling for more." It was a "hypnotic tour de force" that had no equal.

Craig conquered more than the Imperial Room. He conquered his hometown, reputation, history, and everything he came from.

But there was one person Craig did not do well by, and that was friend Michael Oscars. Michael was now a talent agent, and even though he didn't work directly with Craig in his day-to-day career, he did a lot of work for Theatre in the Dell and produced Craig's shows there in 1977. While Craig had misbehaved over those weeks — caught up in his growing popularity he was partying too much, showing up minutes before showtime, staying up all hours, and generally being an unpredictable wild card — he had put on fantastic, profitable shows, so Michael got him in on a contract that stipulated Craig was to perform in another theatre Michael was working with and not to perform in other local venues in the city without permission. The Imperial Room gig may have generated a great reaction, but it put the glowing star in breach of contract.

"Craig's booking harmed us irreparably," Michael says, noting how Craig phoned him, angry that Michael had a problem with his plans. "I told Craig, 'I do not not want you to play the Imperial Room but not under these circumstances. You have to honour your commitment.' It became a huge fight."

Michael was not at all pleased. He reached out to Gino Empry at the Imperial Room and agent Bud Haas in California, informed them of the situation, and told them he could pursue legal action against Craig and the Imperial Room should their show continue. It was a terrible predicament. It took Gino offering a generous deal to settle the waters.

Even though Craig was legally in the wrong, he was furious. He swore he would never work with Michael again and tore Michael to shreds so badly in an interview with television reporter Brian Linehan that Brian said the footage could not be aired on television. Craig would not see that he was in the wrong.

His professional relationship and friendship with Michael were over. If he was sentimental about it, he didn't tell anyone. Nor was he concerned about how Bud and Gino had covered for him and were also rightfully upset. In fact, after the Imperial Room show, he said he was pleased as punch at how people reacted to the show.

"Being respected for a change is great, having people happy to see me," he said to the *Toronto Star*. "It never happened before, especially when I was an insurance salesman."

Respect was very important to Craig and he was very sensitive to criticism. He was still riding a high from the Imperial Room stay when he performed for a sold-out crowd at Montreal's austere three thousand–seat Salle Wilfrid-Pelletier in Place des Arts in April. The show met his usual standards, but the local reviews were lukewarm. They said he was too sentimental and described the show as a clumsy, chaotic revue. Craig cried when he read that the next day and was still weepy when he gave an interview to a reporter.

Craig was beginning to show signs of being tired and overwhelmed more and more. He was to have appearances at both the ACTRA Awards and the Juno Awards that spring but missed both due to exhaustion. He was reported to be "unable to walk on" at the ACTRAs and outright collapsed at rehearsals for the Junos. No one suspected anything was wrong or questioned his workload.

Gino told the *Toronto Star* that Craig had "a million dollars worth of talent but he hasn't learned discipline."

"I know he has problems," Gino said, dismissing concerns. "But we've all got problems."

Still, Craig and his entourage surged forward with an almost dizzying schedule. He was back in Toronto that July for a high-profile screening of *Outrageous!* at the New Yorker Theatre. After that he was again off to Provincetown for the rest of the summer months and on to his first European tour in September. The shows were great, the audiences packed.

Craig and Paul had a good schedule down. As a booking approached, Craig would fly out in advance and do a few days of media interviews. Paul would fly in later and train the local musicians on all the music before a three-hour rehearsal. Craig would eventually join in onstage most days, and everyone would run through the whole show.

They would break for dinner before dressing (the band in tuxes and suits, Craig in his first gown) as the house filled and everyone took their places. Paul would come first, jazz up the band, and introduce "the one and only Craig Russell." The opening number was often "Hello, Dolly." It was the most uplifting number.

They'd do it all again the next day, before moving on to a new venue somewhere else. City after city, the show grew and got even better. Eventually Paul had the music ready for an eighteen-piece orchestra as Craig and his manager worked harder to find a residency somewhere in the U.S., perhaps San Francisco, Hollywood, or Key West, if not Las Vegas.

But first, New York. Craig performed at Carnegie Hall in New York City on October 13, 1978. While the Imperial Room show had been sentimental and top of the pops for the Canadian arts scene, being booked at Carnegie Hall was another universe. It was the world stage.

Craig threw everything into making sure the show came off perfectly. He spent days in preparations, including seven hours just on his wigs, gowns, and makeup for the one-night-only, two-hour performance. He considered it an honour to appear where so many of the entertainers he idolized and impersonated had performed. He was focused and gave no indication that he was nervous. He didn't have to be.

"He did his homework," says Phil. "Once he got onstage, and was getting reactions from the audience, he had them and off he'd go."

Norma and Eric went to New York for the show, as did a handful of members of the Hall family. Phil also went with his partner, Dennis Wood. Phil says Craig was brilliant, as expected. The music sounded great; the audience applauded and laughed as if on cue; and Craig's gowns and accessories were just right. It was the perfect performance.

"I get chills because I remember it vividly," Phil says. "We don't always recognize [a special time] but when we do, and you're living it, it really is special."

"It was beyond fabulous," says Brenda. "The audience went wild. Craig was brilliant and the orchestra was extraordinary."

That December Craig made an appearance on the CBC late-night comedy and variety talk show *Canada After Dark*, said he was in talks for an extended stay at the Royal Alexandra Theatre, and did numerous interviews. A broadcast piece for the program *Newshour* was particularly insightful about his feelings and how far he had come.

"I didn't have enough self-confidence in myself as a male figure, that's why I went into working in drag," he said. "I went through a very bad transitional period because you're so used to handling failure, you don't know how to handle success. I'm learning, though … I used to be ashamed of the way I lived, put it that way. I didn't reform. I just got over being ashamed."

Craig was at his best. When he performed to a packed house at Massey Hall on December 1, he got a standing ovation for his Judy Garland impression, and his efforts to slip in some Canadian content with impressions of singers Anne Murray and Paul Anka were well received. His reference to Margaret Trudeau, estranged wife of then prime minister Pierre Trudeau, had people in hysterics.

"She says she has the best bum in Canada," he quipped. "I think I voted for him."

When a heckler in the audience asked Craig onstage what his sign was, Craig replied that it was "full speed ahead." The show was so good that it was recorded, and plans were in motion to have it released as a live album, a first for a Canadian drag performer.

"We may go with Bomb [Records]," he told the *Globe and Mail*. "Story of my life."

The year seemed to go by in a flash, and 1979 continued with much of the same — performances, appearances, charity events, endless touring. He also added in some TV and film work. Craig had a small part in the comedy film *Nothing Personal* with actors Donald Sutherland, David Steinberg, and Suzanne Somers, and a script was in the making for another film with Craig in the starring role. There were also talks for a follow-up to *Outrageous!*

Craig, the Hofferts, and their entourage spent a lot of time in the U.S. and overseas as Craig grew a following in the U.K., Europe, and Australia. He was more than well received.

"Sold out all the way through, sweetie," he purred to a reporter. "I don't want to play nightclubs anymore. When you can fill concert halls of two thousand to twenty-five hundred people, you just get in and get out and collect all that money."

He felt adored, especially in Europe. Two of his shows — one in Hamburg, Germany, and another in Amsterdam, Netherlands — were recorded and distributed.

At his performance at the Royal Theatre Carré in Amsterdam, Craig gave his all, impersonating, singing, and telling jokes for a delighted audience. In a show titled *The Craig Russell Show*, he opened as Carol Channing singing "Hello, Dolly" in a hot red gown speckled with jewels and big red feathers. He sang the number mostly as Carol, but with interludes as Ethel Merman and Louis Armstrong. He followed that as Marlene Dietrich in a glittery gold gown and full-length white fur coat.

"It has not been an easy career for me," Craig said as Marlene. "I started as a waitress at the Last Supper."

He then broke into a rendition of her song "Lili Marlene" that was so perfect, you'd think the faded German actress and singer were on the stage herself. He followed with Mae West, Peggy Lee, Bette Midler (in a purple-and-black corset with fringe tutu), and finally Tallulah Bankhead. As Tallulah, he pranced around with a cocktail and cigarette in hand.

"I'm not really a singer, you know," he quipped. "I'm a dancer. Choreography by Ray Charles."

Before the show was over, he was Bette Davis as Margot Channing in *All About Eve*; sang as Barbra Streisand and Elvis Presley, and preached an antihomosexual message as Anita Bryant before finishing as Judy Garland singing, "Battle Hymn of the Republic" and "Over the Rainbow." He came back for his encore as Shirley Bassey and Liza Minnelli. The audience thanked him with bouquets thrown onto the stage. He pulled them apart and threw individual flowers back into the crowd. They applauded and cheered.

When he was overseas, Dutch magazine *Nieuwe Revu* interviewed him — and took a photo of Craig in a bathtub at the Amstel Hotel that they used on the front cover — and published a thoughtful feature on the "*Canadese travestiet*" (Canadian transvestite). The writer described Craig as

Craig as Tallulah Bankhead with a cocktail, a cigarette, and an attitude.

someone friendly and full of jokes who stands out from ordinary transvestites because he wants to be a star so badly.

"The old Hollywood with the star system is dead," the article concluded. "But Craig Russell revives it again."

Craig was a darling in that interview, but away from the press and the stage he was still very tired, and in that state his behaviour was more and more unstable. Sometimes he'd be lonely and needy for attention; other times he scoffed at all the people around him and the relentless schedule. He was increasingly belligerent, would deliberately mess up at rehearsals, or might push people's buttons with crude jokes and remarks. He was also drinking heavily.

And it was all caught on film. Toronto photographer David Street joined Craig on the road to document life onstage and off. His photos show Craig dressed as his ladies onstage, hamming it up in hotel rooms with his materials scattered everywhere, and looking exhausted in planes and cabs. He looks happiest and most relaxed in photos that were taken in his off time in Provincetown and Los Angeles. David packaged the exclusive photos with text written by Craig in a book. *Craig Russell and His Ladies* was released in October 1979.

"I believe that the desire to write a book, make a record, paint something beautiful or star in a film, is the desire for immortality," Craig wrote. "None of us want to get lost in that big world out there. Everybody secretly wants to be a 'star' even if it's only to one person. I guess my life has taken a certain path because I just don't think one person is enough."

Craig dedicated the book "to everyone who has ever made a dream come true." It is a rare package that gives insight into Craig's thoughts and feelings after ten years performing and touring. He wrote that when it came to travel, eventually there was no thrill left. He didn't even have a home of his own because he was spending so much time away. He gave up his permanent address. His life was a series of airplanes, taxis, theatres, and hotels, repeated day after day.

"I know that I am constantly fighting with reality — always putting more red paint on the old fire engine," he wrote.

Old fire engine? Craig was thirty-one years old. He was depressed. He admitted to Paul and Brenda that a doctor told him he was bipolar or manic-depressive. The diagnosis made sense. When Craig was up, he was very up. He was hyperactive. When he was depressed, he was incredibly low. He was filled with sorrow. Many nights alone were spent crying. The mood swings were incredible, and if he had any kind of stress or pressure, he would act out again.

Craig's doctor prescribed downers. It was an answer and a solution, but not one Craig would accept. An energetic performer deliberately brought down? Craig had seen this before. Margaret juggled the need to take pills for her mental health, but it took the wind out of her creative sails. Her writing was her purpose. Impressions were his. Craig had to be up.

"The drugs [would get you] better but at that time, they put this cap on your very being," Brenda says. "[People] would say that they don't feel alive."

Craig felt he couldn't be medicated for depression and maintain his career. He needed the edge. He would find his own way for what to do. He said it was an easy decision. The answer was cocaine.

Craig not only believed cocaine would help him be up and energized, he also believed it helped him focus on his performance. He could zero in on his impressions and be better than ever. It wouldn't hurt if he were a little strung out sometimes. One of his best impressions was Judy Garland in her later years, addicted and struggling for a life on the other side of the rainbow.

Craig's drug use was no secret. He had always been a recreational drug user. He partied hard through the making of *Outrageous!* But now he was ramping it up. Big time. Everyone knew. There was cocaine in his hotel rooms, in limos on the way to the venue, in his dressing rooms, and between acts. Some people partook with him; others didn't. But it was understood to just leave him be. He could perform. He would come through. No one was worried it could turn to addiction.

"[His] psychological condition would exacerbate his drug or alcohol use," says Paul. "If he was in an OK state of mind, he could have a drink and be fine.... He could also have a joint [or] a line of coke, but as his mental illness progressed so did his [substance use]."

He also was losing some passion in his work and there were times he found himself less than fulfilled. He still wanted to perform and be an entertainer, but as early as February 1978 he told the *Globe and Mail* that he had no intention to "live off the ladies" forever, just as Carol Channing advised.

Craig wanted his art to grow. He wanted to sing, he wanted to perform, and he wanted to act. He didn't want to be seen as the guy who dresses as a woman all the time. He wanted to be seen as an artist but felt his audience had expectations of him and he was somewhat stuck.

Even his management at the time didn't seem to understand. Over the years he rebuffed some promising offers if he felt typecast, including an acting role in what became a major production, where he would have played the part of a flamboyant gay man.

"When he was made that offer, he went ballistic at his manager," Alan says. "Craig went ballistic at him [and said], 'So what do you think, all I can get is these fag roles?'"

Craig wanted acknowledgement as an artist, and as he didn't get it the way he wanted, he continued to unravel. The partying got harder, and more people — hangers-on — seemed to be around him. As a star he opened doors to the best bars, the best parties, and the best hotels with seemingly endless tabs for alcohol and an endless supply of drugs. They were using him, taking from him, and enabling his own consumption.

Craig liked the attention and liked having more people around, even if things got ugly at times. There were fights in bars late at night with patrons, band members, and club owners, and the trashing of hotel rooms, all incidents fuelled by alcohol and drugs and started by his hangers-on. He knew he was being taken advantage of, but who cared? In the moment everyone was having fun. Paul and Brenda noticed, with raised eyebrows. They thought he was getting more depressed and more unpredictable than he already was.

Craig's unpredictability spread to the stage. Each show had a set list with a planned order of what impression he would bring, but more and more he was going off plan. You couldn't count on who he would be when he came out onstage. It was almost like an improvised show.

"That kind of thing was a regular occurrence," says Alan. "The show was supposed to start with Carol coming out and there were nights when he would come out as Mae West first, or Bette Davis, and everybody would (scramble) to try to find the right music to be playing. In his mind, it was just like, 'This is who I feel like being tonight.'"

Craig paid no heed to concerns for his increasingly erratic behaviour and his destructive lifestyle, nor to any impacts to his career and reputation.

If he wasn't going to be seen as an artist, he might as well have fun. He cared less about people, and his care for what people thought of him was buried under the growing chaos of his own making. He was cocky, untouchable.

"Once you've established yourself in the world as a homosexual hairdresser turned female impersonator, what are they going to accuse you of — smoking too much?" he told a reporter in October 1979. "I've established the fact that I'm the best in the world."

The world would see him very differently just three months later.

On January 31, 1980, Craig was again on the bill at Carnegie Hall in New York.

It may have been his second time on its stage, but nothing about it was old hat. There was incredible pressure, more than the first performance. It really said something to be back so soon after his October 1978 appearance. Eyes were on him, and with them were opportunities. All he had to do was deliver another showstopper.

Unfortunately, after almost ten years working his act and growing his reputation, Craig simply could no longer handle the pressure. The haze from self-medicating with alcohol and cocaine did not help either. Red flags were raised before it even began.

Craig met up with Paul, Brenda, and the band in New York in a totally manic state. His behaviour was all over the place. One minute he would rave about how wonderful the show was going to be, and the next minute he'd be all over Paul telling him that he would make him proud. Craig couldn't focus on a task or even a conversation.

He had been drinking early that day. When rehearsal came around, he was falling down drunk. Paul and Brenda worked around him, managing the venue staff and the band. Alan was there, as was Craig's makeup artist, Paul Raymond. They told themselves Craig would pull through. He'd get his game face on and do the show. He always had before.

The show had to go on.

At showtime, Paul took his seat at the piano, ramped up the band, and with the same great fanfare as he did at the beginning of every show, he introduced the show's star. Craig came onstage to the usual hyped-up applause from the crowd. They were excited, but his band and crew were alarmed. Something was very wrong.

As usual, Craig was to start as Carol Channing. But he walked onstage dressed up and impersonating a discombobulated and drugged out Judy Garland. Or maybe not. Others thought he was trying to be Billie Holiday. You couldn't tell.

Okay, everyone thought. *We will improvise. Follow his lead.*

Craig greeted the crowd as he always did, but instead of approaching his mic stand and launching into "Hello, Dolly," he crawled under the grand piano and started singing something else. Paul and the band tried to keep up.

There wasn't much to it. High on cocaine and drunk, Craig stayed under the piano as he continued singing, badly. Everything was off plan. He had no stage presence. He delivered few jokes. He launched into songs totally off the planned set list with Paul at the helm of the twenty-five–piece orchestra trying to find where he was and catch up. The audience grew quickly agitated.

"You let us down," a fan yelled to him as they headed for the door.

"Well, you brought me up," Craig yelled back, still under the piano.

It was the most pathetic scene in the grandest venue Craig ever performed in.

"People were throwing things; it was terrible," says Paul.

Actor and director Allan Moyle, an *Outrageous!* co-star, was there to see his old friend and found himself both shocked and dismayed.

"It was a trip because this wasn't the Craig I knew," he says. "I remember thinking 'This ain't right.' I felt disappointed. I felt sorry for him."

By intermission, Craig's behaviour was totally off the rails — "way out there" was how one of his band members described it — and guests were sneaking out, asking for their money back.

"I just remember a lot of people leaving the audience," Alan says. "It was not a happy time."

The show was a flop.

Paul calls it the worst professional experience of his life. And when it came to Craig, it was a personal betrayal. They had an unwritten, unspoken, but understood code between them — do what you want with your life, be it drugs, drinking, partying, whatever, but don't let it affect the show. Craig had now betrayed that and embarrassed everyone in the process.

"The audience has paid for tickets, and you have a responsibility," Paul explains. "It's not about us, it's about them. As we were sneaking out the stage door, the promoter came by. I said that I [was] so embarrassed and ashamed."

Everyone packed up, snuck out the stage door, and went home. The media coverage was heavy. It even reached Canada. Headlines called it "the Craig Russell disaster." Upcoming gigs were cancelled. Worse, anything left on his schedule wouldn't have Paul and Brenda. Their relationship with this falling star was over.

Craig initially laughed the whole incident off and returned to the hangers-on who cared nothing for the show and were down to keep partying. They were shallow, empty relationships but enough of a distraction for Craig as all that was good for him and his career had come undone.

"Success doesn't change you," he said. "It changes the people around you."

It wasn't until the next week when he went back to California alone that he had time to think and acknowledge what he had done. What happened? How had he gotten here? Could he make it better? At the very least he could sober up. He told the *Toronto Star* in April that he had checked himself into hospital for "a drying-out period."

"To live up to the title of *Outrageous!*, to be amusing all the time, is very tiring," he said. "I've found that I can be amusing when I'm sober."

His later manager, Gene Mascardelli, sums up the whole failure this way: "What he did at Carnegie Hall was a combination of fear of failure and trying to come up with something that was so novel, it would take Mr. Outrageous to the next level…. That, of course, was a tragic failure where he let everybody down."

Craig never apologized to Paul and Brenda, the venue, or the musicians they were working with. Internally, he was devastated and embarrassed. He knew he had damaged his relationship with the Hofferts, two people who had brought continuity and stability to his crazy, outrageous life. He was more alone now.

That was more of a crushing blow than the impact to his professional reputation.

CHAPTER NINE

IT AIN'T EASY

Lenore Zann remembers the moment she met Craig. It was March 1980, almost two months after the Carnegie Hall flop, and Craig was at the Royal Alexandra Theatre in Toronto for an appearance at the first Genie Awards.

Lenore was an actress who performed as Marilyn Monroe in a rock opera called *Hey Marilyn!* The Nova Scotia–born, York University–trained singer was awfully good as the sexy American actress and had been generating a lot of attention. She, too, was set for an appearance at the Genies, and knowing Craig would be there, she was looking forward to meeting him.

A fan of *Outrageous!* — she says she "loved him immediately" — Lenore was at the Royal Alex for rehearsal and just called to the stage when she heard Craig screech out from somewhere in the waiting crowd.

"Oh, my God!" he hollered, sounding defensive. "I've got to meet this woman who apparently can play Marilyn Monroe better than I can!"

As Lenore headed for the stage, Craig met her halfway.

"He was ready to hate my guts," Lenore remembers. "He met me, and was sizing me up. I looked him in the eyes and said, 'Craig Russell, you have the most beautiful eyes I have ever seen.' And then he dropped his defences."

Entertainers can be critical of each other and threatened, especially by another's success. Vibrant and engaging, Lenore wasn't about that. She told Craig she admired him and that he was even more beautiful in person. Craig relaxed and they fell into conversation. By showtime, the thirty-two-year-old established entertainer and twenty-year-old newbie chanteuse were friends. They shared a love for old Hollywood and an appreciation for impressionism, and both played larger-than-life entertainers.

"We felt emotions deeply," she says. "We wanted to please people. We wanted to entertain people. And we were both very lonely deep down, too."

Lenore and Craig hung out that weekend in Toronto, and Craig later invited her to California to stay at his new apartment. Lenore likened the invitation to a flip of roles; now he was the entertainer inviting a fan out to Hollywood to see the stars.

Craig took Lenore under his wing for a few weeks. Wearing matching fur coats, they went around Los Angeles by limousine, and he showed her small bars in the city's underbelly, popular gay community hot spots, and clubs where he performed. He dyed his hair blond to match hers and told everyone she was his daughter. Some nights he performed in a club while Lenore watched on with pride. Other nights they'd take in a show together and party late into the night.

"He treated me with respect; he treated me with kindness, as if I was somebody who was worthy of admiration," she says. "For a young actress who is trying to make her way in the world ... he was a great teacher that way."

It was a fun and outrageous experience, but Lenore is an old soul. She knew under the showmanship there was an increasingly troubled man who was struggling and needed her there. Craig couldn't hide it.

After a show one night, Lenore went backstage to Craig's dressing room to congratulate him and celebrate another outstanding show. His impressions were totally on, the audience loved him. His dressing room was filled with bouquets of flowers from fans. But Lenore found Craig alone and in tears. She tried to console him, reminding him how much the audience loved him.

"They don't love me," Craig told her, adamant and exasperated. "They love my characters."

Her efforts were no help.

"He showed me where he was really coming from," she says. "He did not at all feel self-love."

Lenore saw what the Hofferts had seen. Craig was insecure, doubting himself, and despite the fan adulation and caring friends like her, he did not feel loved.

As time went on, he was more expressive about that struggle. He told some interviewers that he felt he had neglected his own life in focusing on being not one, but more than thirty other people all the time. One interviewer asked him if he had difficulty living with his characters.

"A little," he said. "At my expense."

But he had to keep working. He had plenty of shows and some TV work through 1980 and into 1981. He appeared on the TV shows *The Love Boat* and *Trapper John, M.D.*, did a television special with impressionist Rich Little, travelled to Australia for two appearances with Oscar Peterson, and had a ten-day run in the Imperial Room in Toronto's Royal York Hotel.

The media was still hungry for him and PR man Gino Empry kept a full schedule for Craig between shows. One day he had phone interviews with seven different stations, a meeting to arrange a television appearance, two sit-down interviews for magazine features with reporters from *Maclean's* and *TV Times*, and another sit-down interview with a *Toronto Star* reporter for a retrospective story about his Mae West Fan Club. The next day he made an appearance on *Canada AM*, was picked up and driven to CFRB Radio for an interview with Gordon Sinclair and Betty Kennedy, and then joined a parade and reception to benefit the Canadian Cancer Society in the afternoon. At night he appeared at the St. Lawrence Market for an ArtsCanada benefit draw.

He still wasn't always behaved. Newspapers reported that he was banned from actor Alan Thicke's talk show after advising female viewers that "if you can't sing, dance or act, you'd better marry a politician." The target of the comment was Margaret Trudeau, someone he increasingly referred to when he was in Canada. She was backstage at the time, heard it all, and allegedly slapped him in the face afterward.

Craig didn't care much and wondered what the big deal was. He was just trying to be funny, trying to push his outrageous profile. Isn't that what his audience wanted from him? He needed to do something. His show was

A poster signed by Craig. He used this poster to promote his show for years.

beginning to grow stale. Some venues, including those in Provincetown, had hosted him multiple times and when he returned, he had the same impressions, songs, and jokes. There was little change or variation.

"He was coasting," musician Bill King says. Bill had just taken over the show's music and saw that Craig was unhappy, bored, and needing to push things to a new level. "In an act like that you need to modulate, find more stories and things to talk about. He needed to expand artists."

That wasn't an option though. To truly take on a "lady," to adopt a new persona and all the things that entailed, Craig had to love the entertainer. They had to be fabulous, glamorous, sexual, eccentric, and strong yet also play on their vulnerabilities and have a persona, a caricature, that is built on that. That was what he was so good at. He didn't have the heart to throw himself into an impression of someone he didn't care about.

"You can't imitate Diane Keaton, Joanne Woodward," he told an interviewer a few years before. "They don't paint up into an illusion. I'm into doing illusions. It's like reproducing a classical painting."

Instead of new artists, Craig abandoned his decree to be more positive and came up with awkward antics onstage, including crawling around on the floor through his Judy Garland routine or using biting humour toward people in the room. Sometimes his targets were notable people in the audience, including playwright Tennessee Williams, comedian Rusty Warren, and jazz musician Johnnie Ray. One night he tried to grope a press person from the *Village Voice* in the middle of the act.

Reviews of his work picked up on that. They suggested that instead of presenting new characters or new songs, Craig was working hard to find new outrageous antics to build out the characters and the act. Audiences expected it of him.

"The basic problem with Russell's latest show is that the noted female impersonator has to work so very hard at maintaining his sense of the outrageous," reporter Alan Niester wrote in a March 1981 review that ran in the *Globe and Mail*. "Russell's audiences are now somewhat jaded. They've seen it all. How can Russell keep them laughing when most of the audience are as familiar with his routines as he is?"

Craig had work to do on his act, but more work was the last thing on his mind. His moods were still manic, but he was down more than he was up. He was self-deprecating and talked openly about having depression. He also seemed constantly on the hunt for love and attention. He had a series of boyfriends. None lasted more than a few weeks.

In that state, Craig's sensitivity was heightened. Any bit of criticism would always get him down but now it seemed to take a lot to rise above it. Bill remembers one night when Craig arrived at his home dressed as Tallulah Bankhead. His humorous presence in drag had Bill's preteen son and a friend in hysterics, but Craig took it offensively. He left hurt and in tears, all from the innocent laughter of children.

Incidents and reactions like that got Craig thinking. As he thought about love, and he thought about his profile as a female impressionist, he was also thinking about himself as a man. How could people think of him differently? How can he be more than a man in drag? How could he break free? How could he feel love?

The struggle was apparent in March 1981 when he was in Toronto for another series of shows at the Imperial Room. Lenore met up with him and they picked up where they left off with their fun and fabulous banter, but something was different. Lenore took notice that Craig was trying to change. He was turning off performer mode, and had traded in his more flamboyant clothes and makeup in favour of shirts and ties in an attempt to look more masculine.

"I didn't ask him to or anything like that, he just started doing that," she says. "He wanted to show people that he was not like they think he is all the time."

Lenore says they shared a love — they wanted to "look out for each other and care for each other" — and she wondered if Craig wanted the two of them to be a couple. He invited her to stay with him at the Royal York and introduced her to his mother, stepfather, other members of the Hall family, and some of his friends, including Lady Iris Mountbatten, the eccentric English actress who was a great-grandchild of Queen Victoria.

It was clear Craig was trying to get away from his Craig Russell persona and endless impressions of women. He was tired of his act, bored. He knew how his audiences were beginning to feel, and the truth was, he felt the same way. He wanted new material, but outside of the dress. He still had an interest in more acting, but despite his hopes for parts away from being his ladies, any possibilities seemed to fall through.

"Once you've done a movie called *Outrageous!*, you don't have that much of a desire to be outrageous anymore," he bemoaned. "I'd love to grow a beard like everybody else, or have a mustache."

Cathryn Hall kept a detailed scrapbook with articles and pamphlets from Craig's shows.

His dissatisfaction fed his overconsumption. There was no shortage of parties. The drinking continued and the hangers-on were there to get what they could from the star. Cocaine was still very much part of the picture and Craig showed no limits.

"One night he came to the door and he was like Judy Garland with his Mae West wig on crooked with makeup peeling off of his face, like a grotesque clown in a circus," Lenore says. "He had this big bag of cocaine and long red fingernails, dipping his fingernail in the bag and putting it in my face."

Lenore was growing uncomfortable. She didn't like the overconsumption or the people around him. They enabled the drinking and drug use and kept him from any sense of normalcy. He was lonely, taking chances, and desperate for more attention.

One example was Craig's boyfriend that spring. Lenore doesn't remember his name but remembers he was just out of jail, broke, and on the hunt for a place to live when he latched onto Craig. He stayed for weeks and seemingly took her friend for all he had to offer until he simply left without a care or concern when Craig had nothing more to give.

Craig didn't say if that bothered him. His sights were likely set on some career progress. In May 1981 he was hired for his first role in a theatre production. Scheduled at the Onstage '81 Toronto Theatre Festival, *Hogtown* was a musical comedy set in Toronto in 1885, in an era of "Toronto the Good" with puritans sweeping into office to clean up everything sinful. Craig played the madam of a bordello who leads the charge against turning Toronto into a place "fit for a Christian and hell for everybody else."

Produced by Peter Peroff and directed by Brian Macdonald, there was hope the production at the Bayview Playhouse Theatre would make it to Broadway in New York. The potential seemed to be there. Preview performances were nearly sold out before the play opened officially.

For Craig, the job was an opportunity to stretch his acting chops, even if he was still playing a woman. It was a scripted part with an ensemble cast in a theatre production, something he hadn't done before. It was also a chance to get back in Paul Hoffert's good graces. Paul and Craig hadn't worked together since the Carnegie Hall incident almost a year and a half before, and now they were together again with Paul involved in the show's music.

"He knew that we were really upset with him ... I didn't want to work with Craig because of the disappointment," Paul says. "But we met with Craig and he promised he would be good and it would work out."

Craig went into the play very excited. A friend remembers him being totally silly on opening night, stuffing a bunch of grapes down his leotards to look like testicles. It was hilarious to some but made others nervous. He was like an unruly child, always playing and being unpredictable.

Hogtown was good but did not get the best reviews. Acknowledging the show seemed tailored for him, critic Peter Goddard wrote that Craig was "larger than life and larger than the play." He overshadowed the whole performance. The show struggled to become "yet another Craig Russell one-person extravaganza."

Craig deserved some of the kickback. He was very funny as Belle.

"There are people who'd like to see this place closed down," he said in character. "Thank God the critics are all at the Shaw Festival."

The audience roared.

"Toronto was really straight-laced in those days," says Gloria Martin, then a popular broadcaster and entertainment reporter. "He was a breath of fresh air."

The power struggle was real, onstage and off. Craig did not get along with the producer or the director through the production, and he took to misbehaving. Unhappy, he started to act out first in rehearsals and later during the live show. It was just like what Paul had seen when Craig was in a manic state or hyped up on cocaine.

"Everybody would be up onstage on their cues and he would start making up lines just [to change] the show," Paul said. "He started talking about the producer having an affair ... To say the least, it was unprofessional."

There were other problems, too. The *Globe and Mail* reported there were questions about rights and shaky good-faith agreements, and there were rumours of potential legal action against the producer. A separate story said the production relied too much "on the staples of American musicals" and described Brian's direction as "not too inspired."

Craig said the producer "made it possible for me to go legitimate and keep a legitimate theatre half-empty eight times a week."

Hogtown would not make it to Broadway. The show closed after less than three weeks, and regardless of other factors, Craig took most of the blame. Another blow came when a plan for him to perform in the title role of Mae West's *Diamond Lil* at the Shaw Festival in Niagara-on-the-Lake, Ontario, fell apart. He was devastated. He just couldn't catch a break.

It seemed the only person he had in his corner was Lori Jenkins, his No. 1 fan turned dresser. She'd been following his career for five years. She'd seen his movie, she saw him perform at Massey Hall and twice at the Imperial Room, she knew his touring schedule, and she had introduced herself to his mother. Now, after their reacquaintance in June, she'd been by his side through *Hogtown* and then the summer stay in Provincetown that ended in more frayed relationships. She was his shadow, an unfailingly loyal supporter and ego booster.

Craig wanted Lori there through it all, but he couldn't help but find Lori overwhelming. He thought it would subside after their summer in Provincetown but it hadn't. She never turned her admiration off. She had been so complimentary, so excitable, so loving. It was like she wasn't her own person and she just meshed into his shadow. He needed her support, but he also needed space. He wanted her to stand on her own two feet and love herself. Yet as expressive as he was, he didn't know how to get through to her.

"I have finally found the person of my dreams and love him very much," Lori said to Craig, after he instructed her to ask him questions so he could practise his Tallulah Bankhead impression before a show. "How can I be more assertive, without being a shadow?"

"Know when to say 'Bye-bye!'" Tallulah replied to Lori. "You have to become more assertive with your disappearance. The greatest thing in the world is anticipation … Do not confuse your love's attention or lack of admiration. Remember, you get what you deserve! The person you are really going to fall in love with is L.W."

L.W. was, of course, Lori Westman, the professional name Craig had given Lori for working in the theatre. She excitedly hung on to every word of his reply to her question, but didn't clue in to anything Craig really meant. Her next question for him was how she could pick up more responsibility. She wanted to be his road manager.

Lori in a top hat and tails to work for Craig.

Getting through to Lori would have to be put aside for now. Craig needed to focus on his act. He desperately needed a win and put feelers out for opportunities. It is telling that even though he was in Toronto all that time, Craig never entertained going back to his roots in gay bars, even just for the money. He still bristled at being aligned with drag and the gay world, and he didn't think the venues he came from were places he could return to.

That was a missed opportunity. Toronto's gay community had grown and mobilized since his early years. In fact, the community marked "Toronto's Stonewall" that year, an uprising that demonstrated the city had hundreds, if not thousands, of LGBTQ2S-identifying people who believed they counted and weren't going anywhere, no matter what ignorance and homophobia they encountered.

It started when police executed Operation Soap, major bathhouse raids that resulted in 286 men charged (the largest mass arrest in Canada since the War Measures Act was imposed in 1970) and damage to four venues. More than three thousand angry demonstrators marched on a Toronto police division and Queen's Park the next day, followed by gay freedom and International Women's Day marches that included thousands.

In June, the infamous "Battle of Church Street" began when more than one thousand gay, lesbian, bisexual, and queer people holding a protest near Church and Charles Streets were attacked by a group of thugs. Police defended the gay-bashers, not their targets. Six people were injured and six were arrested. Eight days later, more than two thousand came out for Lesbian and Gay Pride Day activities at Grange Park.

There were positive community-building events, too. Two organizations amalgamated to become the national nonprofit organization Parents and Friends of Lesbians and Gays (PFLAG). More bars were now licensed and had larger capacities, and with that came increased press, access to advertising, and available information on what was happening on the scene. The gay community even had an information phone line (923-GAYS).

Yet Craig maintained his antipathy. He wasn't part of any of the community activity and barely went there for a drink, let alone to perform. He preferred performing in large theatres anyway.

Craig and his U.S.-based manager came up with another plan. In late October 1981, he and Lori headed to the West Coast for a four-city comeback tour. It would be his return to the stage with shows that were to be of the calibre he was known for in the 1970s. If he couldn't make it as an actor or find a place for himself as a man, he could still bring his ladies to the stage.

The first stop would be at Vancouver's Queen Elizabeth Theatre.

From the outset of the October trip to Vancouver, Craig was in an odd mood. He went out ahead of his entourage to give promotional interviews as he always did, but instead of going with a positive message to catch his show, he was indifferent and defiant.

When he gave an interview to Co-op Radio, a small community radio station, he was uncooperative. He gave flat yes or no answers and challenged the interviewer in his questioning. He called his play *Hogtown* "a snoozefest," didn't seem overly happy or grateful to be in Vancouver despite the tour's intentions, and said he had few plans after the tour was over.

"The public will be there, one way or another," he said.

When Lori and his makeup artist, Paul Raymond, flew in the next day, Craig met them at the airport and told them he was planning to break from convention with a new show where he would only mouth some parts of a song, or perform without stage lights in darkness. He said it would be a tribute to the deaf and blind.

Uh-oh. Paul saw the mess that became the Carnegie Hall disaster. This sounded like trouble. There was little he could have done to stop Craig, but after a technical rehearsal and a full run-through went all right, he thought the threat of trouble had blown over. Maybe Craig's ideas were just callous, offhand remarks.

Paul shouldn't have been so optimistic. Before showtime Craig called the theatre and summoned him to his hotel suite to do his makeup. It was not part of the plan and the clock to showtime was ticking down, so Paul jumped into action and rushed over to meet him, only to find Craig naked in the bathtub.

"Hi there, I'm Esther Williams!" Craig joyously said, jumping out of the water with coarse, shaved hair stuck to his chest, looking nothing like the swimmer-turned-actress. His body was totally bald.

This was ominous, but there was no time to think about it. It took Paul almost two hours to get Craig cleaned up, into a limo, and over to the theatre to get on with the show that was already too progressed to cancel. Shunning any more help to prepare once he was there, Craig strode onstage to greet the audience wearing Japanese kabuki makeup and a kimono with a parasol in his hand.

"Good evening Radies and Gentlemen," he said with a slurred accent. "Tonight, we are not doing the regular show. Instead, we'll do Okrahome, My Fair Rady and Harro Dawry."

He then wheeled his costumes onstage and started to dress himself.

What was going on? What was he trying to do? The audience stirred more. Some were mad; others were perplexed. This was the performing arts, after all. Maybe Craig was trying to break through another level of the outrageousness that he was known for, but it certainly wasn't clear where he was going with this kind of introduction.

Lori and Paul looked on from side stage, horrified. They were powerless to stop him.

As the audience started to stir and boo, Craig responded by throwing his gowns and accessories into the crowd. When the crowd persisted and the band gave up even trying to follow him and play, he picked up sheet music and threw that, too.

The show never got off the ground, no matter what his intentions were. The audience left. More than two hundred people asked for their money back. Legendary promoter Hugh Pickett — known as the "Mr. Impresario" who brought the likes of Marlene Dietrich, Jack Benny, and Bob Hope to Vancouver — called the incident "the most disgusting, disgraceful, horrifying night I've spent in the theatre in thirty-five years."

The incident made headlines across the country and the rest of Craig's western Canada shows were cancelled. Still defiant, he told some people he was upset because he had missed out on a movie part. He told others he was getting the runaround ahead of some planned shows in Quebec. In a story that ran on the front page of the *Globe and Mail*, he said he thought the audience was the problem.

"They looked like a pretty poor crowd and I figured I'd cheer them up," he said. "The ones that wanted their money back were the ones who wanted the same old Craig Russell, and didn't want to be reminded that it's an act. Nothing in my contract says I have to be nice to my audience or not use profanity."

He told *T.O.* magazine he "ended a career with a headline…. [The audience] didn't realize I was giving them a fabulous new angle on Craig Russell."

The fans certainly had their expectations of who Craig was as an entertainer.

"Part of the crowd seemed to have the expectation that he would fulfill their every fantasy," one fan told the Canadian Press. "He reacted to the audience in their negative reaction to him."

Another fan said he felt "awkward for Russell because he had an audience that didn't appreciate him."

The feedback was true to the review he got after his last performances at the Imperial Room. Craig believed audiences were bored and no longer thought of him as sensational, and he really was just trying to reach the next outrageous level. Where were the limits? Or perhaps that wasn't it at all. Maybe his actions were just the behaviour of a drug-addicted, spoiled misfit.

Gene Mascardelli feels Craig was trying to "do something deliberately outrageous that would in fact inoculate him from the failure of Carnegie Hall and put him back on that path … Part of the feedback was, it quite possibly might be the most amazing avant-garde experience. But other people thought it was so disgusting and stupid."

Even Craig's mother, Norma, chimed in at the time with some defence.

"It's not easy for him to be all these different people," she said. "Everybody has their up-and-down days."

His aunt Cathryn came to his defence too.

"I think [pressure] just gradually built up, unfortunately," she said. "And it exploded."

Regardless of what it was, the most lasting theory was that Craig totally sabotaged the Queen Elizabeth Theatre show and at the time he wasn't apologizing. He stormed back to the hotel after the show, ranted to everyone that he would never do another show ever again, and had a physically abusive altercation with Lori. She called it "a Joan Crawford and daughter Christina routine." Craig later had a shouting match by phone with Bud

Haas who said he was "frankly disgusted" by his client's behaviour. Their relationship was over.

It took years before Craig reflected on the whole episode and took accountability for what happened. He told a documentary film crew "demons were starting to come out in me. I did terrible, terrible things."

It was more lost fans, bad press, and damage to his reputation. It was also more burned bridges. No one in Canada wanted to book him now.

He said he "understood perhaps what Marilyn Monroe must have felt like when you think you're on top and then you're fired, and nobody wants you at all."

A bizarre few days followed what became known as "the Vancouver incident."

Craig and Lori fled the hotel, flew back to Toronto, and made a trip to Craighurst, his family cottage outside the city, in the middle of the night. He insisted to their driver that they be dropped off more than a kilometre from their destination "to keep his whereabouts secret." They walked through an early winter snow to get to the cottage, and dove into roadside ditches whenever a car approached so they would not be seen.

Craig was nearly psychotic. Lori thought it was an adventure. They stopped only to make a wish under the stars. Lori said she wished that "all of Craig Russell's expectations of me will be fulfilled."

They spent the next day lying low at the cottage as Craig came down off the high that had taken him over the past week. What Lori didn't know was that he had been formulating a plan. On the morning of their second day, as they lay together in bed, Craig proposed marriage.

"Would you marry me if I asked you to?" he asked.

Lori said she would say yes. She would marry him if she were asked.

"It's all settled, then," he told her. "We'll be courting until we get married!"

The proposal didn't get further than that. Craig ran from the room and returned with a red ruby ring he said he'd been given as a child. Lori accepted it, and put it on her finger, delighted. He didn't have to say or ask anything else. She had agreed as far as he was concerned.

Having never been a couple, Craig and Lori were now engaged.

Craig was not in love with Lori. He was grateful to have her. So many of his relationships were damaged. If relations with people like the Hofferts, Bud Haas, and Michael Oscars were not totally severed, friends like Lenore Zann, Margaret Gibson, Shirley Flavell, and Phil Buckley were alienated. They were unsure of who their friend had become or how to be in his life. Lori was the most loyal person he knew. A marriage would be a thank you.

It was also an opportunity. Craig wanted to continue making headlines. A wedding to a woman would distract attention from what had happened in Vancouver, and it would be true to the outrageous reputation he was trying to build as his act seemed so tired.

He had talked about his plans with Gene, now his Canadian manager. The two met in 1979 when Gene approached Craig for a show at Casa Loma in Toronto. Gene became a close confidante and held the reins of Craig's career, something he likened to "trying to manage air."

"Craig was an opportunist," Gene says. "A wedding would take the outrageous reputation to another level."

Craig thought about the idea for weeks. He had shown interest in marrying Lenore, brought up the topic with Margaret, and then asked his old friend Helen Phillips, saying how good they were together and that he thought it would be good for their daughter Allison, who was then just about to turn nine years old.

"He said we needed to make [Allison's] life more normal," Helen says with a laugh, remembering her skepticism of his intentions. "You really think so? He thought it'd be good for her ... I just remember thinking, 'This can't be happening.' That wasn't the nature of our relationship."

The spotlight then landed on Lori. She had unconditional love and loyalty, and no idea she was not his first choice.

Proposal complete, Craig was on the phone to his publicist and reporters in Toronto before he and Lori even left the cottage. Manic and excited, he called many before office hours, leaving messages on answering machines along the lines of: "Hello, Gino. It's Craig Russell. Guess what? I'm getting married!" He'd hang up without leaving details and be on to the next call.

"A fine romance?" Gary Dunford reported in the *Toronto Sun* on November 1, 1981. "Page Six — so easily confused ..."

Lori did not realize the proposal was even really official. She thought he was just being his usual silly self, delighting in the world of make-believe. She didn't give it another thought until she got home and her father said he read Dunford's article. News story? Engagement? Her father asked her who the lucky lady was.

"Holy shit, it must be me," Lori replied, as surprised as she was pleased. "He did ask me but I didn't think it was serious."

Lori bought ten copies of the *Sun* for that article. She was in disbelief, but it became even more real when columnist Sylvia Train picked up the story and named her as the bride-to-be. That confirmed everything. Lori really was the fiancée of her No. 1 movie star. She was getting married. She kept a cut-out of the article on her desk at work and showed it to all of her colleagues.

Craig took Lori out on the town over the next months as news spread of their plans. They made a splash wherever they went. They partied with drag friends at the Toronto Press Club, were interviewed by CBC broadcaster Barbara McLeod, went to the Elliott Research Christmas party with Lori dressed as Tallulah Bankhead wearing makeup courtesy of samples from a department store makeup counter, and went to Gino Empry's garden party, where Craig introduced Lori to actress Barbara Hamilton, broadcaster Lynn Gordon, figure skater Toller Cranston, and ballet dancer Alexander Grant. Someone told Lori they "could see magic happening" between the happy couple. The bride-to-be said she could feel it.

They lived separately, with Lori renting a furnished room for Craig on Sherbourne Street. On his invitation, she moved in with him that December and they decorated the walls with pictures of Mae. Lori found a Christmas tree, and for their first holiday together as a couple Craig gave her an oil painting of Marilyn Monroe.

Craig made several gestures of thanks to Lori in their short time living together. He was growing fond of her. He bought them bottles of Mumm champagne to share and gifted her with another ring, this time silver and set with small diamonds. One day he gave her a makeover and placed a blonde wig with a towel as a turban over the mane of hair, just as Mae had taught him.

"I know you can't see it, [but] you're beautiful," he told her, tearful and more creatively inspired than he had been for a long time. "Look at yourself! I know what I can create!"

He often cooked for the two of them and would greet Lori at the door dressed as one of his characters. One day he'd be Barbra Streisand, the next Bette Davis. Lori's favourite dinner was when he dressed as Tallulah Bankhead.

"Welcome home, dahling," Craig said at the door, before presenting her with a candlelit dinner of pasta dyed pink with food colouring. He called it gay spaghetti.

Another day he greeted her at the door with a favourite cocktail.

"Welcome home, most honourable lady," he said with a kiss to her hair, forehead, eyes, and shoulders, just as Mae's father, Jack West, kissed her beloved mother, Tillie.

Lori was simply in awe. She wrote in her journal that Craig "made my whole life worth living again! I cannot believe how much I love this man, Russell Craig Eadie!" Could it be any better? Maybe so. A psychic told her "a big wish is coming to pass and will come true.... You are wishing for the moon and you are going to get it."

Six months after Prince Charles married Lady Diana Spencer and made headlines everywhere, Craig told Lori that Canada needed its own royal wedding. Since he was a queen, they'd be it. The two of them watched reruns of the official royal affair to assure that when they did it, they would do it right.

That was the only planning they did. There were no traditional pre-wedding events, no engagement party, no bridal shower. Lori said they didn't even realize they would need a marriage licence.

The wedding date changed multiple times. As Craig thought Lori was setting up a date and his manager would take care of preparations, Lori thought he was taking care of things. They told the *Toronto Star* on December 24, 1981, that they were aiming for a wedding the following Monday. Craig didn't sell the story as a total spectacle. He implied that he was ready to settle down.

"It took me a long time to grow up," Craig said. "I finally developed an identity realization that Craig Russell is a star but he doesn't have to go around acting like one ... Now I feel secure; I now have someone to share the joke with."

Lori told the reporter they were planning children.

"I have the feeling we'll have three boys," she said, matter-of-factly.

The December wedding didn't happen. Neither did the New Year's Eve wedding, but they did go to city hall to get their licence. After the holiday Craig was back on the phone to reporters.

"Mark your calendars," he said. "January 11 is the day Princess Charles will marry Boy Di."

CHAPTER TEN

YOU MADE ME LOVE YOU

On the day of her wedding, Lori assumed her husband-to-be would be wearing the dress. She didn't mind at all. Lori was more comfortable in gender-neutral clothes and she already had a tuxedo anyway. She'd bought it earlier that year to wear in her job as Craig's dresser.

The wedding itself, on January 11, 1982, wasn't going to be a big affair. Only a small handful of Craig's friends and Lori's family were invited. But recognizing the occasion with publicity was another story. More than fifty reporters, photographers, and camera operators were on hand. They came from television, radio, magazines, and newspapers; most were invited by Craig. He called them in advance, encouraging everyone to come out and cover Canada's royal wedding.

Royal wedding? Few grabbed onto that hook. The fact that a sensational, outrageous personality like Craig was getting married was enough. Wasn't he gay? Who was the mystery woman? What would he do? There were plenty of questions for Craig and Lori that Monday, but perhaps surprising no one, the media had a wait on their hands. The bride and groom were running late.

Craig and Lori got ready at their apartment on Sherbourne Street. They still had not done any planning, but with Craig's ample wardrobe, their attire was more than taken care of. Craig wore a suit with an open collar, a starched white shirt and a thin red scarf that matched his red high-heeled shoes, the same pair he wore when impersonating Judy Garland. When he saw his bride planned to wear her tux, Craig nixed the idea and took over. He helped her out of the suit, pulled out his gold Marlene Dietrich outfit, and made alterations so she could wear it as a top with veil. Lori then chose black-and-gold leggings to match and slipped on a pair of suede black flats.

Gene Mascardelli and his wife, Gloria Martin, were on hand to help. They knew the whole affair was an outrageous stunt on Craig's part. Gene admitted there was "something so tragically insincere" about the marriage, but he felt Craig and Lori might as well go ahead because it was like they were married already. There was no mistaking that the couple seemed to be a match.

"They both revelled in being unique and not being that boring, normal person," says Gloria. "They liked being their own unique selves."

Gloria could see how Lori brought a sense of normalcy to Craig's life. She made arrangements to see family and took on responsibilities to buy birthday cards and Christmas gifts, and she made consistent money to cover their bills, including the small apartment they now called their own. Gloria observed that Lori was "trying to create this normal, sweet little life."

Both Craig and Lori were grateful for the support and understanding from friends, but particularly Craig. He was growing sentimental despite his intentions with the marriage. His family would not be at the nuptials and that disappointed him. His mother, Norma, and stepfather, Eric, were snow-birding in Florida. He was not in contact with his father, and the rest of the Hall family simply chose not to go. There was no ill will. They just assumed it was a publicity play; any sentimentality he had wasn't apparent to them.

That was a miss. As the date got closer Craig was, in fact, looking for support and ways to make the event meaningful in his own way. It was an opportunity for people to share in a joyous occasion and for him to demonstrate that maybe he could be just like everyone else. That included recognizing at least one tradition. Craig reached out to his old pal Phil Buckley to ask if he would be his best man.

He was in for disappointment. Phil said no. Just like the Halls, Phil didn't know what to make of Craig's plans and what outrageous headlines would come of it. He was still a very shy man and preferred a low-key life.

"I kind of knew it was going to be flashy and [not really] something I would want to be a part of," says Phil. "He didn't take that very well."

Craig felt rejected. He turned his back on Phil, as well as their mutual friends Shirley and Margaret, and kept looking for someone to stand for him. He thought to ask Paul Hoffert — a peace offering, he thought — and entertained the idea of having Gene. The person he finally settled on was Gino Empry, the PR man from the Royal York.

Gino had done so much for Craig by then. He acted as his de facto publicist and scheduled most of Craig's time when he was in Toronto. It wasn't all business. Gino was very fond and protective of Craig. He wanted him to be well. He wanted him to be happy. Gino accepted the offer to be best man and seemed genuinely excited to get in on the fun when the day of the wedding came around.

His advice for the groom? "Remember that you aren't the bride," he said.

Toronto Sun gossip columnist and friend Sylvia Train was asked to stand in as maid of honour for Lori. She had written quite a bit about Craig over the years. She was hot on the wedding scoop and wouldn't have missed the event for anything. Now she was part of the story. She even paid the $15 marriage fee. The couple said they couldn't afford it.

Gino picked up the group in a limo and together they headed to Old City Hall, a building once a symbol of power and the heart of municipal politics that was now used for court, office space, and the department that provided civil, non-denominational wedding ceremonies. Such occasions were usually quick and low key, but today there was a spotlight on the happy couple, and a gaggle of media creating a fuss as soon as they walked in the door. They clamoured after Craig and Lori and peppered them with questions.

"Are you really getting married?" a reporter asked.

"There's nothing like love between a man and a woman," Craig said. "I finally found the right woman."

"Aren't you gay?" another queried.

"I'm a 'try-sexual,'" Craig replied. "I'll try anything once."

Craig and Lori pose for the news scrum on their wedding day.

Craig was in his element. He was an interviewer's dream. He had quick, clear, zippy responses for all of the reporters' questions. He looked right into the video cameras, and he stopped and posed perfectly for the photographers. He even kissed an unexpecting male reporter in view of everyone and hugged another. That made for great colour, the perfect little quirky detail to an already outrageous story.

Lori stayed by his side through it all, clearly shy and nearly silent except for the occasional smile and giggle. With the gold veil from the Marlene dress placed perfectly over her small head, and a fur coat that matched Craig's, she looked both demure and new-wave hip. Sylvia would later write in her follow-up column that Lori "looked lovely, although a little frightened." When a reporter asked them if they were happy, the soon-to-be wife smiled and nodded that they were.

Everything was going just as planned, except for one kink. Craig intended for the press to join them in the wedding chamber to photograph and film the ceremony, but an official intervened to say cameramen would not be allowed. It was against the rules. Craig spoke out, as did at least one broadcast news crew member, and things got heated. But after a security guard appeared and told them any breach could result in a $10,000 fine, everyone agreed to forget about the idea. The show would go on without the press.

Craig and Lori headed into the wedding chamber for the ceremony. Gino and Sylvia were by their side, as were Gene and Gloria and Paul and Brenda Hoffert. They still didn't want to work with Craig after their rocky interactions in *Hogtown* and at Carnegie Hall, but they wanted to support him. This was a spectacle not to be missed.

Most of Lori's family were there, including Eddie Jenkins and his girl-friend, Sandi Dobrowolski. Lori's brother Paul was there with his first wife, Dawn; her sister, Dena, was there with son Danny; and her brother Marc was also in attendance. Hazel was not there. She had never been a fan of her daughter's groom. She thought he was trash and freely said so.

Paul admits the whole thing seemed unusual, but he was more surprised that Lori was getting married to a man. He assumed his sister was a lesbian. He was happy for her, though, and when it came to the scene at hand, including a groom in a fur coat and heels, he wasn't put off at all.

"That was just Craig," says Paul. "If he showed up like a groom in a tuxedo, that would have been wrong."

Dena, meanwhile, was thrilled for Lori. Her sister, with her "child-like fascination and adoration," was marrying her idol! But when Dena had met Craig just two months earlier, she admittedly felt a little cautious. Craig always seemed so over the top. It was like he was compensating for something.

"I loved him, I thought he was an amazing and talented human being, but I felt also a little sorry for him," she says. "I think he got caught up in the [idea] that if you're not on, you're not a person…. He was losing Craig Eadie. You didn't see a lot of Craig Eadie."

And now here they were, engaged, mere months after Lori went to work for him. Dena couldn't ignore that they were marrying for factors other than love. But she kept her thoughts to herself and put the practical observations aside. This was Lori's day. She didn't want to consider the event to be anything other than a special occasion that meant the world to her sister.

Norma, meanwhile, had been more outspoken. She cautioned Lori when she found out about the marriage. Craig would not be a traditional husband. Did Lori realize that? What kind of union was she expecting? She asked her future daughter-in-law if she knew "what she was getting into." Lori said she did.

Norma nodded her understanding but concluded with one point: "It's not going to be an easy life."

The wedding itself, just after 2:00 p.m. in Room 203, was quick and by the book. Any silliness was put aside. Craig took off his heels but kept his fur coat on. Lori held a small bouquet of red, white, and pink flowers. They listened to the officiant carefully, answered the questions exactly right, and exchanged simple vows.

When they were pronounced man and wife, Craig lifted the gold veil and gave Lori a lasting, passionate kiss. Excited, he then kissed the officiant. The man was shocked. Everyone laughed. It was the perfect Craig moment.

Wedding over, the "royal" couple was ready for the world. It was time to ramp up the fun. With family and friends tailing around and behind them, and his new wife on his arm, Craig headed down the staircase of Old City Hall toward the awaiting media scrum and proclaimed: "Introducing Princess Charles and Boy Di! It's straight for the '80s because the gay '90s ain't coming for eight years."

Lights were on them, flashes fired, microphones were pushed in their faces, and tape recorders clicked on. And then excited questions came, as both man and wife held each other and complied with genuine answers. One reporter asked Lori if she would enjoy being married to a celebrity.

"I'm going to love it," she said, after thinking for a second. "I'm his biggest fan."

Then in a scene that could be in a movie, she let out a loud giggle and Craig took the response over.

"I needed a big fan to cool off," he said. "I've been fooling around with boys long enough. It's time to get married to a woman."

He then pulled Lori into another lasting, not-quite-made-for-TV kiss. They continued to pose for photos and answer questions. Lori said she hoped

First kiss as husband and wife before Craig kissed the officiant.

in her marriage she would be loved, happy, and they would stay together forever. She also reiterated that she hoped they would have children.

Still, this was Craig's show. Sylvia reported it was like he was the "bride and the groom rolled into one."

Things got serious for another minute when Craig acknowledged everyone who was there for them. He seemed genuinely thankful. He said he hoped he and his wife would be like Paul and Brenda, who he called "the Alan and Marilyn Bergman of the '80s." He was grateful they were there for this and that they recognized he was more than his behaviour.

"It's nice to have friends around, you know," he said. "It's a serious day."

With news deadlines looming, it wasn't long before the media gaggle disbanded and everyone from the wedding headed to a Rosedale mansion for a roaring celebration. Judy Welch, a Canadian model who participated in the Miss World competition and was now an agent representing supermodels Linda Evangelista and Naomi Campbell, hosted. She pulled out all the stops for the best party she could have.

All of the Jenkins family went along, as did Gene and Gloria, Paul and Brenda, Gino and Sylvia. Other notable guests included actress Barbara Hamilton, entertainment broadcasters Bob McAdorey and Jeanne Beker, and a gaggle of models from Judy's agency.

The owners of Toronto bakery Patisserie Kever, and fans of Craig's, donated the wedding cake. The impressive creation included a topper that was a replica of Mae West sculpted out of marzipan. It was unusual but perfect. Craig was excited, perhaps too excited, and dug his hand into Mae's face to grab a handful and smear Lori with it. He would have done it, if not for Gloria.

"I saw Craig wanted to throw the wedding cake in her face and I told him, 'Don't do this. Do not do this to her,'" Gloria says. "It's like that little demon on his shoulder telling him, and I was like, 'No, no, no, no, no.'"

Craig listened. He was manically excited but, at least this time, he was able to pull it back. Instead, Craig took off his high-heeled shoe, had it filled with champagne, and poured the bubbly into his and his wife's mouths. Lori happily obliged, as did a *Toronto Sun* photographer when he was asked to capture a shot of the moment. It later ran in print with their story.

Gino Empry toasts Craig and Lori at the home of agent Judy Welch in Rosedale.

Craig and Lori pose with Danny, son of Dena Jenkins (partially obscured).

There were a few traditional elements, including toasts and gifts. Craig and Lori drank champagne in hand-carved silver goblets, posed for photos with their guests, and read cards and telegrams that had been sent along. Their gifts included candle holders, a Chinese vase, a brass elephant bowl, and two poems. One, called "A Man and A Woman," was written by Craig's friend Ian Craig McKinnon. The other was written by Paul's wife, Dawn, and perfectly titled "Six O'Clock News."

Lori cherished not only her gifts, but every detail of the day. She documented everything. This was her day.

"MARRIAGE DAY," she wrote in her journal. "Absolutely flawless!!! … Happiest day of my life! … Divinely Wonderful Wonderful Wonderful Day!"

It was all a fantastic success. Craig got the positive promotion he wanted; Lori married the man of her dreams. Both were happier than they'd been in years. Everything seemed to be on the up. The next day major Canadian newspapers ran the story.

The *Toronto Star* piece by reporter Bruce Blackadar, written in Craig's voice, carried the headline "Look Ma! I got married after all."

But it was the *Toronto Sun* headline with Sylvia Train's column that said it all: "Goodbye Mae Hello Lori … this wedding takes the cake!"

Through the rest of January and into February, Craig and Lori lived the movie star life.

They went to a studio and posed for photos by music photographer Peter Noble, filmed a segment for the TV show *Backstage*, attended a charity telethon where Craig performed as Judy Garland, and went out dancing at the Hotel Isabella jazz bar. In between they were feted with dinner and drinks all around town. Everyone wanted to meet the happy couple. Craig's status as a man happily married to a woman certainly was cause for intrigue. Maybe the outrageous performer really was settling down — at least in his personal life.

Craig was used to such attention, but for Lori each day brought something new and exciting. Her activities were totally different from what had previously filled her quiet days usually spent alone. She changed her wardrobe and had her makeup done by professionals, met musicians Bill King and Jodie Drake, modelled with Craig at a celebration auction connected to the posh King Edward Hotel, and got an advance read of scripts that had parts for her husband. She also had multiple meetings with a high-powered celebrity lawyer to potentially seek a financial settlement for the 1980 accident that left her injured.

Ironically, despite all of their celebrity-life activities, they had no money. Craig did not have a movie star's bank account. His lack of wealth would be a point of conjecture to others for his entire life. Most people assumed that someone who had been in a movie as big as *Outrageous!* would be filthy rich. Craig definitely was not, and as a result people concluded that some movie or music executive somewhere had ripped him off and got rich off his hard work.

That wasn't the case. With the slim budget *Outrageous!* had when it was made and a rocky U.S. distribution deal, Craig never made much money from it. He profited more from his act, but with that income, he chose the finer things that came with big price tags. There were elaborate gowns and accessories to buy, hotel suites to lease, and rocking parties to bankroll. He had chauffeurs and bodyguards, limos for family visits in Port Perry, and the best champagne and finest meals on a menu. Those choices were often made with indulgence and a desire to be seen as having everything afforded to a movie star. That came from his insecurity. The real Craig would have been just as happy with a bar rail cocktail and a sandwich.

Craig was always generous, too. There were $1,000 tips for band members and all the food, booze, and drugs anyone could want at the after-parties. He gave to family, friends, and strangers. Musician and friend Alan Ett says one night, as the band jumped into a cab to head out for a meal after the show, Craig gave the cab driver a $500 tip and then invited the driver to join the band for their meal. It was important to Craig to have people around him, and if that took some money, so be it. He valued the company more than he valued his earnings and savings.

When Craig was not indulgent or generous, he got careless. He was often paid in cash, and it was not unusual for him to leave wads of bills around his apartments and hotel rooms. His mother was forever gathering the money when she was around, stashing it away, and telling him to put it in the bank. But even that seemed to be a convention that Craig avoided. With such a lax approach, greedy hands with sticky fingers were always on his earnings. Any number of strangers, in and out of his circles for parties and events, took what was available. Craig was having too much fun to notice and believed any money lost would simply come back after another show, TV spot, or movie part.

The onus of expenses would fall to his new wife while Craig was not working, but despite her usual maturity with budgeting money, Lori made mistakes when it came to taking care of their finances. She quit her file clerk job at Elliott Research the week before the wedding to focus on supporting Craig's career, but with no work, they had no money, and weeks after the wedding they had to give up their apartment and move in with Lori's dad.

Nobody seemed to mind. Craig got along great with Eddie Jenkins. Craig nicknamed him "Mr. Snacks" and once impersonated Eddie, with Lori dressed as her brother Marc, at a roaring family party. Eddie thought Craig was absolutely hilarious.

Their new living arrangement would be temporary, Craig and Lori said. Many plans were in motion for Craig's career. First up was a series of shows at the Stardust Dinner Theatre just outside Toronto. The pressure was obvious. Things had to go smoothly. Craig took weeks to prepare and drum up interest, including meetings with owner Lloyd Whiteway, a jovial, theatre-loving man who had just opened the promising venue complete with a dining room and bar, ample stage space, and seats he said were straight from the set of *The Jackie Gleason Show*.

Craig did numerous interviews ahead of the shows and brought Lori along for the biggest one: a broadcast interview with journalist Bob McLean, the host of a go-to daytime television show called *McLean at Large* that aired on the CBC. The interview was a good grab for Bob and the show's producers. It was the first time the newly married couple had sat down on camera together.

Lori got a makeover for her appearance. She was dressed in a black-and-silver sequined jacket with white blouse, full makeup, and flashy earrings with Craig's Barbra wig styled over her short hair. She looked great in a flashy '80s glamour way, yet in her moment to shine, her facial expression said she was less than pleased.

After Craig performed "Evergreen" dressed as Barbra Streisand, introductions with their interviewer did not go well. Bob seemed too shallow and invasive, more interested in sensational headlines from the wedding and the Vancouver incident than he was in celebrating their marriage and the next steps in Craig's career. Lori concluded he was a jerk, and when cameras started rolling for broadcast, the awkwardness among the three of them only grew.

"The headline says 'Outrageous wedding: We're fighting over who gets the dress,'" Bob began. "Did you really? Come on, you've been sitting here for half an hour. Say something."

Lori smiled politely and kept silent. Craig smiled, too. Just as annoyed as his wife, he mouthed his answers but spoke no words, all while the cameras were rolling. Bob laughed, tried to push an answer, and didn't seem to know what to do. Craig only continued.

Bob then got on the topic of what happened in Vancouver. Craig danced around a direct answer, made a sexual hand gesture, told a racist joke, and said he thought the show had been a success because he was able to insult people better than the prime minister, Pierre Trudeau.

Trudeau insulted the Liberals, Craig said. "He missed the NDPs and the Conservatives," he countered. "I got everybody."

Dead end established, Bob attempted to change topics. After he mentioned Craig and Lori came from broken homes ("Well, bent," Craig confirmed) and said they were admittedly bisexual ("Sylvia Train doesn't stop here anymore," Craig said), Bob brought up their marriage. He begged them to respond and turned his attention to Lori.

"Lori, did you chase him for four years?" Bob asked.

"Yes, I did," she said proudly, but unamused by her interviewer and increasingly uncomfortable as Craig stroked her hair and face. "Everywhere he went, I went."

"Who proposed?" Bob continued.

"He did," Lori said.

Her answers were short, succinct, and without depth — very uncomfortable for a journalist doing an interview for broadcast. Things only got worse as Craig turned the attention on his interviewer. He told a fat joke and made a crude gesture in reference to beloved CBC broadcaster Barbara Frum.

The interview at last concluded with the original point of their being there. Craig explained that he'd been booked at the Stardust — "a bar, grill and lunatic asylum," he said, in jest — in Whitby, Ontario. He teased about the location ("I'm finally going to where everyone has told me I belong," he said) but it was nonetheless going to be steady work with a full band and the first full shows he'd played since his failed appearance at the Queen Elizabeth Theatre.

"Lori has encouraged me after three months off," he said. "I got sick of being the national joke, so I happily pass on the title to Margaret Trudeau and I'm going back to work."

The Stardust was a beautiful theatre, but it was a far cry from the likes of Carnegie Hall.

It was a small venue housed in what had once been a church, and it was off the radar in the sleepy suburban community not known for its arts scene. There was a time Craig would have bristled at being booked there, but now it seemed he was lucky to get anything at all. Musician Billy Reed, head of the band Billy Reed and the Street People, calls the booking a seminal moment for Craig.

"He was a remarkable talent; he was brilliant," Billy says. "But I can't say he was respected by others anymore."

The Vancouver incident was still top of mind. No one was sure what would come of the shows, but a gig was a gig and there was no denying Craig's talent or his ample repertoire. That made an opportunity to play with him very attractive for a lot of people, no matter what the headlines had been.

A top-notch band was brought in. In addition to Billy on drums were guitarist Dave Gray and saxophonist Margo Davidson, members of the Canadian pop band the Parachute Club. A smattering of other musicians, including pianist Steve Hunter, bassist Russ Boswell, and keyboardist Evelyne Datl, also dove in and out over the month. Some took a pay cut. They were paid as little as $50 a night, half of what was an unofficial industry standard at the time.

Rehearsals had gone well, so everyone was excited by opening night on February 1.

Craig did everything he could to bring his A game to the show. He performed his usual ladies — Mae West, Marlene Dietrich, Peggy Lee, Barbra Streisand, and Judy Garland — with all of his gowns and materials perfectly prepared by Lori. On opening night he introduced her to the audience and dedicated two songs, "Evergreen" and "For Me and My Gal," to her. The next night when the show was over, fans followed Craig to the dining room and bar downstairs, where he signed autographs.

"An absolutely brilliant, flawless performance," Lori wrote in her journal of their second night. "All of Craig's ladies were there physically and spiritually. Magic! Magic! Magic! Craig is Magic!"

She journalled about each show diligently, all with warm, excited praise. She called the shows "wonderful," "flawless," and "divine." In her writing it's clear she liked working consistently in the theatre and was tickled to befriend the likes of musicians like Margo and Evelyne. She spent her time off shopping for the show, maintaining Craig's wigs, and sewing a white dress to wear when she met his aunt Zula and cousin Jennifer. She thought it made her look more like a dutiful wife.

Reviews were positive for the most part. Critic Alex Law reported that audiences should go because of Craig's courage and talent. But he also warned there was one kink: the show's star was drinking too much.

It was a fair point. Craig had been drinking heavily through January, into rehearsals and the first few shows. Everyone saw it, including teenager Bill Whiteway, son of Lloyd, the owner of the theatre. Bill spent a lot of time at the Stardust. He'd hang out in the lighting booth, check things out backstage, and deliver drinks to Craig's dressing room when he demanded them.

"Craig said, 'I want twelve rum and Cokes or I won't go on,'" Bill says of one particular night.

Craig had a few of the drinks and hit the stage. His intoxication was apparent as the show began. It ended, as Bill remembers, with Craig singing his final number sitting on the edge of the stage wearing an outfit that, in his drunken haze, was pulled up just enough so his genitals were visible to all.

When his uncle Howard Hall caught one of the early shows, he sat his nephew down to talk man to man about "getting off the hooch." Embarrassed, Craig listened. Howard was the only father figure he had.

That was good advice. By the second week, tickets sales were dropping and a few shows were cancelled. Craig needed a clear mind as he went out to do more interviews to ramp up publicity. He also had work to do in the kitchen. When the chef at the theatre was fired after a conflict with Lloyd, the show couldn't continue without food, so it was Craig who stepped in to keep things going. He cooked and managed the kitchen for many nights over the rest of the month's booking.

Soon after that Craig also took on the role of ticket agent working the door. Suspecting that someone might be stealing cash from the ticket sales, Craig set up his makeup table by the front door so he could oversee how the money was handled while simultaneously doing his makeup and wig preparation right there in front of his guests as they came in. It was a lot of hard work before he stepped foot onstage.

Lori was with him every step of the way. She worked as the dresser, managed the curtains, helped in the kitchen, and kept a financial record of their income and expenses. Everyone knew she was the wife of the show's star. That was curious to some. Many assumed both of them identified as gay. Still, it was apparent that Lori was an entrenched part of the show.

"It did seem like she was his caretaker," says Evelyne, a keyboard player who came into the fold through Margo. The three women partied together and shared a few rides on the commute to and from Toronto. "She made things happen, but I don't know how much he listened to her."

Howard's advice forgotten, booze came back into the picture as stress mounted, and with that the band seemed to come apart. Billy Reed quit in a huff one day. Another day, right in the middle of a show, Craig fired a piano player. Everyone had to react quickly to keep the set going. Margo stepped in on piano between her saxophone parts until a replacement was found.

With each obstacle and the persistent stress, Craig became more unpredictable onstage. He would go off the set list and the band would have to scramble to catch up. The musicians didn't feel respected, and the opportunity to play with him lost its lustre. His commentary with the audience got edgier and everyone seemed uncomfortable.

Craig's behaviour became more agitated and manic offstage, too. He was up and down. One moment he'd be an angry diva; the next minute he'd be an excited hummingbird, flittering around the wings of the venue. His tendency to stay in character before and after the show was obvious to everyone, and they came to notice that whatever character he was would be indicative of his mood and if he was approachable.

"Craig would be in total character; it creeped me out," says Bill. "It's like Craig wasn't there.... I was a little nervous, but never afraid."

Not everyone could say that.

"He would be going around backstage, massaging people's heads, offering to give them chiropractic adjustments," says Evelyne. "That would never fly now."

Everyone kept quiet. No one defended themselves if they were uncomfortable. They didn't want any public embarrassment or to put their pay in jeopardy. Speaking up could cost them their job.

No one knew the career pressure he was under. These bookings had to go well. No one knew how hard it was for Craig to cope, and no one thought to ask how he was doing or if he needed help. No one knew of his depressive history, or that he thought his alcohol use was a struggle he couldn't handle, not an indulgence. They could only see him as unpredictable Craig.

The show closed on February 27, 1982. Most of the musicians say they were glad it was over. The show didn't do anything to advance Craig's career or get him back on track in Canada.

If Craig was disappointed, he didn't say so. Neither did Lori. The block of shows was simply over and now they had their eyes set on a European tour. Germany would be their first stop.

CHAPTER ELEVEN

DON'T RAIN ON MY PARADE

Gene Mascardelli says the Germany move was not only his idea, it was his insistence.

So much press surrounded Craig after the disastrous New York and Vancouver performances. His behaviour was so erratic that he couldn't be trusted. The wedding generated the publicity he wanted, but it didn't garner any new respect, and after the shows at the Stardust Dinner Theatre, there were few job offers. He was called disgusting, indecent, and unprofessional.

"It was so blown out of proportion," Craig bemoaned.

While the political situation in Germany going into the 1980s was not exactly progressive, it was at least gay friendly. Same-sex sexual activity had been legal in East Germany since 1968 and in West Germany since 1969. In 1980 West Germany was one of the first countries in the world to pass a piece of pro-trans legislation. LGBTQ2S people and gay culture were more tolerated than in many European countries and were an expected part of the entertainment world.

Female impersonation also held a place there. Performers included Bob Lockwood, a female impersonator who parodied the likes of Tina Turner and Marilyn Monroe; and Mary & Gordy, a rare drag duo with active careers on stage and screen. All of them were appreciated performers and well regarded. It seemed they had no shortage of work.

But for Craig Germany was more than a place for drag. The outrageous things he was doing onstage fit there, too. The arts scene was seen as more expressive and progressive than in countries with dated morality, attitudes, and expectations. His antics weren't likely to raise eyebrows as they had in Canada and the U.S. Gene reasoned that if he was outrageous or bizarre in Germany — if he did anything outlandish or offensive onstage — it would more likely be seen as edgy or avant-garde and part of the act. It would also be far away from North American media still hungry for another story on the star who crossed the line all the time.

"You go to Germany," Gene urged. "Come back when the mess is cleaned up and we have a film for you."

It might not have been all that long. Plans were already in motion. Gene was in talks with Dick Benner to strategize an *Outrageous!* sequel, and together they started to feel out possible producers. To keep a tie back home, Dick's boyfriend, Bruce Calnan, went along to act as Craig's European tour manager.

Craig and Lori headed to Berlin on March 21, 1982, and celebrated their arrival with a bottle of champagne that cost 380 German marks — about $300 Canadian. Lori wrote all of the details in her journals, including an account about waking up in their Hotel Arosa penthouse suite to the sound of birds chirping and church bells ringing. Every day was special.

Craig played two shows in Berlin before they were off to Hamburg, Cologne, and Bremen. His shows were sold out, just as they had been the last time he was there. Interest in his act had not dampened. Bouquets of flowers were thrown to him onstage. Fans clamoured to get into his dressing room.

"The audience was so appreciative," Lori wrote in her journal. "They applauded his every sentence. After the show, they kept up the applause for fifteen minutes. Magic in the air. I've never seen Craig perform better."

Craig worked with notable musicians, including Dave Gray and Alan Ett, and his entourage grew to include a publicist, a promoter, a booker, and bodyguards. Dick joined them for a visit in Cologne. He was in town to see Bruce and to soak up more ideas for the *Outrageous!* sequel. He took

Outrageous! had a following in Germany for years, a guaranteed audience for Craig.

time to get to know Lori, and noting her tendency to write backwards, he incorporated the trait into the script for the character Liza.

Craig was excited and revelled in all the positive attention. Everywhere they went, he was treated like a star. But that didn't stop his overconsumption. He drank daily. He was on cocaine and hash, sending Lori out to acquire the substances even though she knew little German to ask around and find it. His odd, erratic behaviour surfaced along with the drugs. Lori wrote about a train trip to a new city during which he smeared windows of their boxcar with shaving cream to "assure their privacy."

There also seemed to be problems with money. Three weeks into the tour, everything they had seemed to have dried up. Their bank balance was never replenished even after Craig's sold-out bookings. He argued with Bruce about the problem and they parted ways just a few short weeks after they got there. He and Lori soldiered on, often relying on complimentary meals in restaurants and hotels.

Lori loved Germany. She developed a taste for schnitzel, marvelled at the sights, shopped frequently in markets, and found an appreciation for leather and the bizarre punk fashion that German women favoured. She saw them as more like her — feminine but in touch with their masculinity.

She particularly liked Berlin because David Bowie recorded part of his album *Low* there. Bowie reportedly stayed in the same posh suite they had in the Hotel Continental. Craig and Lori celebrated their stay with champagne, caviar, and smoked salmon. She compared their new life to Robin Leach's television show *Lifestyles of the Rich and Famous*, which was known for its "Champagne wishes and caviar dreams" tagline.

As she absorbed these new experiences and feelings, Lori said she was reminded of the song "Courage, Madame" by Peggy Lee. The song is about not having an easy life but nonetheless living with dignity, allowing time to heal. That was exactly where Lori was in her mind. This was her time after so much pain in her early life, and her reward for living life on her own terms. It was the perfect way to start her marriage.

Lori and Craig flew to Munich — "Munchkinland" as Craig called it — on April 15. He sang "You Made Me Love You" two nights later at the Brienner Theater and dedicated it to Lori.

"I love you very much you know," he sweetly told her one night over dinner.

They continued like they had in Provincetown. Lori shopped during the day to buy props for Craig's characters, including glasses for Ella Fitzgerald and purple freesias for Mae West. When he needed shoes, she bought him eight pairs. Another day she bought purple grapes for him as a treat. He danced on them like comedian Lucille Ball's character Lucy Ricardo did in an episode of *I Love Lucy*.

Craig would do rehearsals and interviews during the day before showtime in the evening. They partied all night together with whomever happened to be around, but at Craig's insistence they had separate sleeping quarters, something Lori did not question.

"The Queen does this with her husband," Craig told her. "This way we know that when we share a bed, it will be for romance."

One night while Lori slept, Craig went into her suite and left her a love letter, quoting "The Right to Love," a song Peggy Lee sang about having each other in a judgmental and unfriendly world.

She responded with a poem she wrote herself. In part, it read:

> This is my first poem ever
> I hope it does you justice
> 'Cause I will leave you never.
> I've loved you from afar
> For so many years
> 'Cause you've turned sad to joy
> My tears.
> You've made my every dream come true,
> And being with you for the rest of my life
> Is what I've planned to do.
> I don't think I can thank you enough
> For the many opportunities
> You've given me.
> And I know my life
> Will never again be as rough
> As I've experienced it to be.

I'm deeply in love
With you and your magic world of fantasy.
'Cause working with you and being with you
Leaves me in pure ecstasy.

True to form, and their habit to not talk about all of their feelings directly, Craig responded with another poem. In part, it read:

You're learning secrets
Never told.
Nothing's new
But nothing's old.
…
I'm jealous that you've
Managed to
Learn a lesson
Maybe two
'Cause I bore myself
And ain't that a shame?
And I bored you
Fame is a game.

Two weeks into May Lori found out their money problems had continued and their hotel bills weren't being paid. She had not been responsible for finances as she had been in Toronto and asked no questions when her payments as his dresser stopped coming. She wasn't reimbursed for her shopping, either. She assumed this was because they were married. Wives aren't paid to support their husbands. They relied even more on friends and fans for their meals but went forward with plans to take Craig's act to Switzerland.

On May 16 they made the ten-hour trip to Zurich by car. They arrived at another posh hotel, both of them drunk from the rum and triple sec they had been drinking on the drive. Lori was excited by this next stage of the tour despite the money problems, and as she wrote in her journal, she was "feeling no pain." When Craig drew a bubble bath in their bathroom, his excited wife thought it was for them to enjoy together. But she was wrong. Craig had drawn the bath to enjoy with their chauffeur.

That deeply hurt Lori. She was enraged and, in a rare move, tried to stand up for herself and express her emotions more openly. She had a total temper tantrum right there in the hotel room in front of Craig and his would-be lover. She barricaded herself in her small room, angrily flailed around, and kicked a French door until a pane of glass broke and cut her leg.

Craig jumped on top of her and tried to restrain her.

"Do you want some attention?" he asked, angered and still drunk. "What's wrong with you?"

He was confused by her response. Craig had never been exclusive with her, and while they had been sexually intimate, they had never discussed ever being monogamous. They were each free to be involved with others, at least he thought so. He didn't know how to help her.

Lori was jealous and embarrassed. She spent the next day alone, drinking from the mini-bar and eating complimentary peanuts. The day after that she went shopping for props with the 20 marks Craig slipped into her coat to buy food. She thought hard about what happened and how she could pull her dignity back together.

After a few days of cooling off, Lori was back to work as Craig's dresser for three days of shows at the Bernhard-Theater Zurich. It was better for her to focus on her work and the show. It must have been a little healing. In her journal she described Craig's efforts as spectacular, flawless, and fabulous. A review with compliments on her work made her feel pretty good, too.

When they did take some time to talk alone, Lori cried, trying to explain how she had felt and what she had done. It was her fault, she said. She was jealous for nothing. Marriage is forever. Craig was indifferent and distant. He was not receptive to her feelings at all. The door that had been open to his world was now closed.

Craig told Lori that she reminded him of his failures in Canada and he wanted her to be invisible. Lori was stunned and she watched helplessly as he went to a TV appearance the next day without her. When she got to the theatre for work that night, she found that he had a new dresser, and her services would not be needed there either. He said she could still watch from the audience.

Alone, Lori sat through his performance that night and cried, contemplating suicide. She was devastated. One misstep and she had been shifted from part of the crew to a member of the audience. She was serious about taking her life but held back because, as she wrote, "that would only give him more publicity." In her mind, not taking her life was a negative, a way to get back at the man who had hurt her.

She was in the audience again the next night after spending the day wandering around Zurich's sloping cobblestone streets. She put on a brave face, went to the show, and went backstage between acts to congratulate Craig on another great performance, saying nothing about her feelings. He thanked her for her class, asked no questions, did not offer any consolation, and did not offer for her to return to her work as his dresser.

But he did conclude that he no longer wanted Lori on this tour whatsoever. Craig went to Lori's hotel room and told her to go home to Canada alone. He told her to find a lover and to reconnect with a lawyer so she could continue to pursue a financial settlement for the 1980 accident that had left her badly hurt. He promised to meet her again in Canada in a couple of months.

To Lori this was déjà vu. He was sending her away just like he had done in Provincetown.

She did not fight to stay this time. If this was what her husband wanted, she would do it. She fought back tears all the way home to Toronto, clutching a stuffed toy monkey Craig had given her as a gesture of comfort for her pain.

It was the last time she heard from Craig for four and a half years.

Back in her home city without her husband, Lori tried to hold her head high. She stayed at her grandmother's apartment and spent her time watching old movies, napping in the sun at Ward's Island Beach, and writing in her journal, trying to sort out her feelings.

"Craig is making $3,000/night and he can't afford to keep me on tour," she wrote. "What a fucking insult! The more I think about it, the madder I get at myself for not standing up for my own beliefs."

A few weeks later she wrote, "I love him and respect his wishes ... I did have some wonderful moments when I was alone with him. Oh my man, I love him so, he'll never know."

She faced the anticipated questions from family and friends with grace. She told people Craig was away touring. She was just another wife with a musician husband on the road. Very few came to know the truth, and those who did kept conclusions to themselves out of respect for their friend, a new wife who was all but abandoned.

She was still so sensitive. Inside, her emotions were volatile. She was sad and bereaved, and even suicidal at times. She wrote in her journal about how she missed Craig and did not understand why he didn't want her with him. She could not see his side of things at all. To her, this was simple rejection. It took all of her strength to go forward.

Priority one was taking steps to build a case and sue the driver who had hit her in the 1980 accident. To build a medical history, she amassed the thorough documentation of her pain and discomfort, collected her medical records, and saw a psychiatrist.

"Relived my childhood," she wrote in her journal after that meeting. "Yuck!"

She later saw a doctor and had several meetings with her lawyer. She eventually did get a settlement but felt insecure, under duress, and in need of third-party advice when she signed it. She said it awarded her $14,000, with 50 percent going to her legal fees.

Around this time, Lori changed her last name to Russell Eadie, tying together Craig's stage and legal last names. She met up with some of their mutual friends and attended Lady Iris Mountbatten's funeral at St. Paul's Basilica on Craig's behalf. She wore a black dress and a black hat with matching veil to the church, wanting to play the part of grieving British royalty. She cried throughout the service but was thinking of her marriage.

By the summer Lori moved out of her grandmother's apartment and back to her old neighbourhood in Rosedale. She took a night-shift job with Brink's and later a day job in data entry at the Dominion of Canada General Insurance Company. She made a little time for old loves. She saw Stevie Wonder at Maple Leaf Gardens and Peter Allen at the O'Keefe Centre. She spent hours watching movies with actress Greta Garbo, went to see *E.T.* in the theatre with her brother Marc, and worked for two days as an extra on the set of a TV movie about Canadian athlete Terry Fox.

She met Gena Rowlands at the Festival of Festivals and Peggy Lee at the Imperial Room, introducing herself as Mrs. Craig Russell.

Lori said she never heard from Craig. She tried to keep face as the happy wife but remained upset by the separation. She wrote less in her journal as time went by, but when she did, her thoughts would shift from being smitten in love to being anguished with grief for what she thought she was missing. She sometimes would write notes to herself to stay strong and keep going. Other times she would write love notes, including writing the lyrics to Joe Cocker's song "You Are So Beautiful."

"I've never felt lonelier in my life before," she wrote one New Year's Day. "Half of me is missing."

A week after that entry, her last documented journal entry for several years, she wrote, "The most important thing is keeping yourself together."

Craig kept working in Europe without Lori, performing in theatres, cabarets, and nightclubs. His show wasn't making headlines but he had steady gigs.

His prospects shot up in September 1982 when he met talent manager David Lieberberg. A talent manager, agent, and booker all rolled into one, David was well-connected in Europe and worked with some of the greats, including Pink Floyd, James Brown, Barry White, and Diana Ross. Now his eyes were set on Craig.

David not only had all the contacts needed to keep Craig's career moving forward, he had one of the best venues available. David says he primarily worked as director of the music department at the Alte Oper, an opera house in Frankfurt. It is an impressive venue that was inaugurated in 1880, destroyed in the Second World War, and slowly rebuilt for a grand reopening just before Craig returned to Germany. It was the perfect place for him.

David came up with a plan and went all the way to Paris to find Craig and work out details. He found his target performing at a small club, went backstage, introduced himself, and laid out a deal right there in the dressing room on their first meeting. Bolstered by the offer, Craig leapt onto David's lap, covered David's face in white face powder, and licked it off of him. They had a deal.

Robin Turner and Liza Connors, played by actors Craig Russell and Hollis McLaren, as seen in an Outrageous! *publicity still used in Europe.*

They returned to Germany where David and Craig, with help from Craig's German manager, Volker Steppat, polished his act and built it up to what it had been in his best days in Canada and the U.S. A band of great musicians was brought in. They worked on his set list and Craig worked on his gowns, wigs, and materials. They hadn't been taken care of well since Lori left.

Craig was energized. He gave no indication anything was bothering him, or that any of his past actions troubled him, including his marriage or reputation in Canada. He told one interviewer that going onstage and listening to applause was like coming home.

"The light gives you a kick, and everything else is forgotten, everything," he said. "I'm totally at home here. I can be completely me, do what I want, even if I'm very dirty."

According to David, things went well for a while. The show at the Alte Oper — called *Craig Russell: A Man and His Women* — was a hit. The reviews were great. The venue was selling out. When the first block of shows ended, the act was renewed for another run. Craig was getting attention from fans everywhere he went. It was like he had regained his status as a superstar.

He could sometimes misbehave — he had diva-like demands and fits of temper — but the management and musicians around him seemed to be able to handle it. David became a mentor, and David introduced Craig to his wife and children. As with Paul and Brenda Hoffert, Craig became part of the family.

By 1983, with demand for performances in other venues, a tour was organized and Craig hit the road. David couldn't join but would pop into town every now and then to check on how things were going. Craig resented that. He was jealous that David had other obligations. As well, while the shows and audience response were good, they were not as great as when he had a consistent venue. Craig drank more and became more aggressive. Things went sideways. Shows were cancelled.

Craig was also increasingly needy on the road. He had no romantic relationship or companionship. He had no one around who knew him intimately and cared for him. David said Craig was spending any available money on male prostitutes, looking for comfort in the arms of temporary anonymous lovers. David says he tried to talk him out of it.

"You earn so much money, start putting it away," he told Craig. "You spend it on those motherfuckers who just take advantage of you and don't love you."

But Craig longed to be loved. He only stopped paying for companionship when the money ran out. David believed that not only was Craig spending thousands per day on hustlers and prostitutes, but that also many robbed him of what was left. After a night with a stranger, "Craig would wake up the next morning and all the money was gone," he says.

Drug use did not help. David admitted that cocaine was always around. Craig was not the only one partaking.

"If you can remember the '80s, you never lived the '80s," he says, noting that unlike others, Craig didn't know his limits and would often cross the line with people around him.

Craig could be belligerent and insulting — one time he called David's wife and children "dirt" — or he would be totally destructive to dressing rooms and hotel suites where he was staying. Eventually David had to step away.

"It was just unbearable," he says now. "No normal or regular person had the strength to be around or with him anymore.... He was going down the drain."

David, like everyone else, did not try to get Craig medical help. Mental health was not discussed and drugs were seen as a choice — you did drugs or you didn't. Detox or rehabs were not seen as options. Craig would just have to rely on someone else who could tolerate the insanity.

Enter Manuela Mock. Born and raised in Germany, Manuela is an artist with a love for drag. She once lived and breathed the nightclub life and respects drag as much as other arts, just as Lori had. Manuela had heard of Craig — "We didn't have anything like him," she says — loved *Outrageous!*, and jumped at the chance to see him when he was in town.

Craig and Manuela were first introduced after a show at the Alte Oper. Manuela was immediately drawn to him. She found him fascinating because he eschewed convention and the typical idea of "good behaviour." They were fast friends as Craig wrapped up the stay and started touring.

Manuela had yet to see how Craig was slipping, but she knew he needed a place to live. As at so many of his hotels and temporary lodgings before that, Craig destroyed a suite given to him as the artist in residence at the opera house. When he was kicked out, Manuela's small flat became his home base.

At first she was caught up in the fun. There were sold-out shows and glamorous parties. There was fashion, music, and plenty of booze. There were always people around. Everyone wanted to meet the big star. Manuela shared what little she had with Craig.

But very quickly, as his relationship with David was broken and he was overconsuming drugs and running out of money, his behaviour turned erratic, angry, and dangerous. He acted out. He urinated from her balcony onto people below. He toppled over cocktails at a party and threw his prosthetic breasts in a pot in the kitchen. He cut up dresses and burned not only his, but also her, possessions.

"He messed up all my things," she says. "He ruined everything. He smashed everything. One day in my apartment there was nothing left."

Manuela said very little to him about his behaviour, but she stood up for herself better than Lori did, including some physical altercations where she says they "beat each other up like mad." Still, Manuela accepted him

Manuela and Craig with his dog Nancy, named for Nancy Reagan.

as he was. She knew he was suffering emotionally and asked no questions, forgiving everything. She saw he was trying, appreciated when he could be loving and caring, and accepted his generosity when he had money.

"I cannot say we had one bad day," she says, looking back some thirty years later. "I was the right person to share [this time] with. I would not miss one second of this craziness."

It helped that Craig recognized his behaviour and regretted things that happened. He would snap out of his destructive mood eventually, realize what he'd done, and cry to Manuela for forgiveness.

"Sometimes I'd throw out a demon and later open the door to a baby," she says.

It was a roller coaster, with good times and bad. Craig and Manuela went everywhere together, attended countless parties, saw dozens of shows, and travelled. He cooked her elaborate meals and bathed her feet in champagne. He shared his personal emotions, intimate details, and told outlandish tales, including a horrific story about waking up in the middle of some plastic surgery he had had. At one point they thought the government was watching them and had bugged their phones. It was worrisome but exciting.

They had heart-to-hearts that lasted for hours. Craig confided to Manuela about his childhood, being rejected by his father, being an outcast, and living with Mae West. He told Manuela the falling-out with Mae happened after he was caught trying on her dresses. He said nothing of a sexual assault. He showed her a copy of Mae's death certificate that he kept in his diary. He also told Manuela about Lori and his confusion over her sudden expectations of him.

Despite his marriage in Canada, Craig suggested marrying Manuela. She certainly had the same loyalty Lori did, and as in his relationship with Lori, sexual involvement was not a priority. They each had the freedom to associate with whomever they chose. Manuela believed Craig was bisexual and says he was free to carry on with whomever he wanted.

"It was not so important that he stay with me," she says. "There were several guys. There was one guy from the army. He was around the house often. He was taking Craig to a men's leather club every night."

Craig was still getting some work doing shows and TV spots. He got a lot of work in Berlin, Stuttgart, and Hamburg, and had an almost three-week stay at Frankfurt's Café Theatre in December 1984. Singer Eartha Kitt watched one of his shows and teased him about his weight gain after they met. They laughed. He was pleased to be known by another one of the ladies he revered.

Once Volker was out of the picture, German actress Doris Egbring-Kahn stepped up to the plate to help manage Craig for a while. They were both eccentrics and got along great, even living together for a time, but Manuela says they had a falling-out after a fight over money, a common point of contention in his working relationships. Craig believed he was getting ripped off of his pay.

It wouldn't have really mattered if he was paid. If he had money, he would spend it as fast as he earned it. He had no savings, no investments, and no independence. Overconsumption abounded.

"He was just playing to feed the dogs and afford another bottle of booze," friend Leszak Liz told a documentary crew ten years later. "He didn't care…. He just wanted desperately some physical and tender attention and affection and love."

A 1984 ad from a German newspaper advertising The Craig Russell Show: A Man and His Women *in Frankfurt.*

As time went on, the quality of his performance ebbed, the venues got smaller, and the audiences got sparser. Craig would say later, "[I] worked my way to the bottom ... after three years the places get smaller and smaller until you're in the *ratskeller.*"

The misbehaviour continued, onstage and off. He disrobed in interviews, imitated Nazi leader Adolf Hitler, tore into borrowed dresses with scissors, and, according to Manuela, narrowly escaped bigger trouble when a home where he was staying burned to the ground in a fire. He had a destructive weekend in Amsterdam, including a disastrous performance at a large theatre, much like what had happened in Vancouver and New York. The incident hit the papers and job offers tapered off.

"Craig misbehaved like hell," Manuela says. "News travels so you don't get engagements anymore. You are box office poison."

After three years in Germany, he spent most of his time alone in the apartment he shared with Manuela, watching Mae West movies, listening to music, and drawing. He'd cook for the two of them or show up in a club where she tended bar. Sometimes he'd make a little money combing wigs for performers who worked in a cabaret; other times he'd nurse a drink, look at an empty stage, and think about the aspirations he had had.

"Do you know what the word 'star' really means," he asked Manuela one day, depressed and disillusioned. "It's 'rats' spelled backwards."

One thing Craig did a lot of was writing. He wrote poetry and planned multiple biographies. They would be like his impressions, tributes to the women he loved. One of the projects he worked on was a film manuscript that would feature fictionalized lives of Judy Garland and Marilyn Monroe. The storyline would imply that not all people are as they seem.

He also wrote letters to a few people back at home. He was in touch intermittently with Gene Mascardelli and Gino Empry with short letters or postcards. One note was written on toilet paper. He wrote thoughtfully and tenderly and made no mention of his persisting struggles. In April 1985 he sent Gene a book called *Idole* that included a chapter about him, alongside chapters about Pete Townshend and the Who, Frank Zappa, and David Bowie.

Craig was very reflective in his interview for the book, honest and direct at times, vulnerable and nostalgic at others. He talked about the state of his career, his shows, and his projects. Translated, he said his dreams had

Craig looking well with friends in Germany.

come true, and now it was about making the dreams of others come true by performing for them. He was happy as a stage performer versus a career as a movie star, and he was not inclined to share more of his personal self in any art form because it would be too painful if he were rejected.

"Ambition only leads to disappointment," he said. "I have enough of that."

If he could have something for himself, it would be a place to call home. He felt misunderstood at times and believed his tendency to stay in character was a defence mechanism. Still, he was hopeful for the future.

"My soul is so deeply hidden, but now and then something glitters," he said. "I feel a pretty strong hope that even if you don't get what you want, someday … you are going to be recognized.… I'm just trying to own myself, as good as I can."

He also talked candidly about Lori and their marriage; although, he was at times misleading. He said he married her because he had fallen in love with her and thought it was the right thing to do. It didn't work out in part because she wanted the celebrity life and didn't want to work anymore. They also disagreed about the topic of children.

"I expected to go into the marriage on common ground, sharing problems, but our problems annoyed me," he said. "Then I ran away. The marriage was a flop. It was my only real flop in life. It should have been a hit."

Despite that admission, he didn't ever reach out to Lori, nor did he reach out to his mother or his aunt Cathryn. He did phone Yanka Van der Kolk and Brenda Hoffert on Mother's Day holidays, and he spoke to his uncle Howard Hall, who sent him some money to get by.

Manuela says she never saw any drug use — he likely couldn't have afforded it then — but there was no doubt Craig was a heavy drinker. He drank everything he could get his hands on. Craig said nothing to Manuela about being diagnosed as a manic-depressive, but his emotional struggles were prevalent, and only getting more intense. At times he was suicidal and told Manuela he was ready to die.

"He'd cut himself and want me to cut his wrists," she says. "You have to really love somebody — I mean love, really love somebody — to keep up with all this behaviour.... I would never consider him a bad person, never ever. He was a lost soul. He did terrible things. But most of the things were awful against himself."

Into 1986 Craig got involved with a man named Jurgen, who came into the picture as his boyfriend and a de facto manager. Manuela distrusted him right away. "This guy was criminal; I can smell evil," she says, but she asked no questions when Craig would be off with him for long stays in Hamburg and Munich.

Manuela grew increasingly worried as the months went on. After one weekend when he had been away with Jurgen, Manuela found Craig in rough shape. He was beaten and bruised, and he had a cut lip. He had lost a lot of weight and looked very sick. Craig told Manuela that Jurgen was the culprit. He said Jurgen angrily beat him and locked him in a room for two days to ensure Craig would be available for a show booking.

It took a lot to clean Craig up, find him medical attention, and get him back on his feet. It was just in time. Craig had a plane to catch.

Gene had been in touch with good news. A feature film script was ready for a follow-up to *Outrageous!* with Craig reprising his role as Robin

Turner. A production schedule was in place, with Dick Benner still at the wheel to direct it and Hollis McLaren back to play Liza Connors. It had the potential to be as big a hit as its predecessor, and to put Craig back on track and in the spotlight.

Craig boarded a plane to go home to Canada four and a half years after he had left. Manuela wished him well, and to this day feels only positive about their tumultuous four years.

"He was unhappy with himself; he couldn't find out where he belonged," she says. "We were two lost souls, but we were glamorous lost souls."

CHAPTER TWELVE

TOO OUTRAGEOUS

Craig arrived back in Toronto on October 19, 1986. Lori had been waiting for this day for years, and as it turned out, she could have missed it. She only knew he was coming home because she read a news story reporting it. He didn't tell her in advance.

Craig did, however, think of her when he landed and invited her to the Brownstone Hotel, where he was staying, as soon as he got in. Still dutiful and doting, Lori dropped everything to go. She couldn't have been happier when they at last reunited. His spirits were good and he looked well. He'd had plastic surgery in Germany and had dropped weight. She thought he looked wonderful.

Lori didn't address the abrupt separation or his silence. She didn't want to nag, and Craig wasn't offering explanations. He didn't ask how she'd coped or what she'd been doing with her time alone. But he knew enough to know that their separation would have been hard for her. She needed him. She needed his attention.

Craig and Lori made love that night, and the next morning he gave her a poem that he had written for her. In part, it read:

I always thought her cool.
She must think I'm a fool.
Not to pay the price she demands.
I still think she's real cool.
But I'm not enough of a fool
To put my whole life in her cool, cold hands …
Getting married,
I threw up
'Till I grew up.
Now I know
No longer scared,
All things shared,
Getting married.

Lori accepted the poem like a renewed wedding vow. She was in heaven. They spent that morning together walking hand in hand from the Brownstone to her Rosedale apartment, where she gave Craig the few belongings he had left behind, including his Mae West memorabilia. He was pleased she had kept everything and humble enough to know that she didn't owe him anything.

They saw each other regularly after that and went to numerous events like any other married couple. Craig introduced Lori to his fellow cast members, brought her to a dinner at the home of film critic Jay Scott, and joined her for visits with the Jenkins family. Curious about her intentions and motivations after all that had gone on, Craig asked her if she'd rather be a wife or a woman. Lori said wife, without a doubt. Her loyalty had not wavered.

Craig was still moody but Lori was just as able to go with the flow as she had been before. She took him at his word that they had to stick together. With Craig more outwardly emotional and wanting affection, and because Lori craved to be with him in any state, they continued a sexual relationship over the next weeks. Craig would often be in drag when they went to bed, dressed as one of his characters.

"When was your last lesbian experience?" he asked her one morning, after they had spent the night making love with him dressed as Tallulah Bankhead.

Craig and Lori, reunited.

"Last night!" she quipped, pleased and satisfied.

With them were Craig's dogs, a pair of mixed-breed pups he adopted in Germany and had brought over. Nancy was a dachshund-corgi mix named after Nancy Reagan, then married to U.S. president Ronald Reagan. The puppy Baby Mae was, of course, named after Mae. The dogs were primarily Craig's, but Lori was always available to help out, and she bought gifts for them on holidays.

With his relationship with his wife re-established, Craig was focused on getting back on track. He told a few people, "If I get only one film in ten years, it's gotta be a hit." Because *Outrageous!* was a cult classic, a sequel seemed like a sure bet.

Too Outrageous! was set to begin filming in late November. It was years in the making. Dick Benner was at work on the script almost as soon as Craig had gone to Germany, with Gene Mascardelli weighing in with ideas for how it should be produced and financed. Dick was prepared to direct again, but Bill Marshall and Henk Van der Kolk were not as prepared to resume their roles as producers. They had moved on. Bill wasn't interested in working with Dick, and Henk wondered about the value of a sequel. The climate didn't seem right.

"The first *Outrageous!* had quite a lot of impact on the world," Henk says now. "*Outrageous!* was a perfectly good idea of what the [gay] world was all about, including the hardship, the joys and including the fun. I think it did a lot to make that world more understood. We didn't think we needed that again."

Gene suggested Dick send the script to Roy Krost to produce in their place. Roy had worked in film for more than thirty years. He had his own film company and his credits included a TV movie with actress Dorothy Hamill and a feature film with actor Richard Harris. This new project was attractive to him. *Outrageous!* had been a hit almost by fluke. Roy felt he had more experience than Bill and Henk, and with his resumé he could take the franchise to the next level.

Still, Roy had reservations. He liked Dick's script but thought it needed some work. For one thing, it had no mention of AIDS in the storyline. It seemed silly to make a film about gay culture and have no mention of the growing global pandemic. Roy also had never met Craig, so he took the time to fly out and meet him in Munich to chat about the project. Craig seemed sober, drug-free, and past the nonsense he was known for. None of that was true, but in their meeting, Craig proved himself a good actor. He was willing to do what it took to get the film going.

Roy still had reservations when he returned and wondered if maybe someone else should play the Robin Turner character. Four years was also a long time away from the U.S. and Canadian film market, and the entertainment world in general. Would moviegoers even remember him? Was his name still marketable? Could they rely on him? Had he grown up since New York and Vancouver?

Gene not only insisted Craig was ready, but also that there would be no movie without him. His character arguably made the original, and it was Craig's performing career that helped market it. He had broken ground as a gay icon. His reputation could take a sequel global, especially considering the following they believed he had nurtured in Europe for the last four years. Dick and Roy were apprehensive but they proceeded.

Craig had a month to prepare before principal photography began. He got some publicity in early November when he appeared in a small film called *A Virus Knows No Morals,* which screened at the Harbourfront International Festival of Gay Cinema. The film was a satire about the AIDS crisis directed by German producer Rosa von Praunheim, a man who called himself "the queer of the nation." It was a forgettable piece of work with an offensive concept, but one of Craig's interviews about it offered a bit of an apology for all that had happened before he left.

"I got self-involved," he told the *Globe and Mail.* "I lost my sense of humour. I took this brilliant joke of a career seriously and started feeling 'victimized' and starting crying the blues about being lonely at the top."

He said he was hopeful that he had turned a corner and his time was now.

"Now, I've been given another chance," he said about his part in *Too Outrageous!.* "They say life begins at forty, but it begins anytime you want it to.... I have a producer and director who believe in me; this is a sequel, but it will be something new. It feels good."

Craig also gave a shout-out to Lori, totally changing his stance from what he had told the German interviewer on the state of his marriage. "She's been totally supportive. You know, when you choose a life partner, it ain't all easy, not all laughs.... With her, I can be myself totally."

Still, he insisted theirs was a "legal friendship." He did maintain his support for her though, at least so far. Craig encouraged Lori to get a small part in *Too Outrageous!* and helped her with preparations for an audition with Dick. He arranged for her to get her hair dyed at the Robert Gage Salon in Yorkville and made plans for her to rehearse lines with Craig's friend Lenore Zann, who was now living in Toronto and pursuing her own acting career.

Lori was excited but never got that chance to go further. When Dick arrived at Craig's apartment for her audition, he found Craig in a manic state and doing somersaults after throwing pieces of chicken at the walls, telling his company that he delivered on his promise to "throw lunch." Dick was incensed and fired Craig from the film on the spot, no questions asked and no opportunity given to explain.

It took a lot of coaching to turn Dick's head on the issue, but when Craig arrived on set for the first day of filming bruised and bleeding, he fired the lead all over again. Dick figured he'd been on a bender, but Craig quietly told Lori his German lover had come to town and roughed him up. Jurgen was a dominant man, and Craig's strong personality was beaten down to a diminished submissive in his company.

Regardless of the cause, Dick said that was it. He was done and made it known that he intended to hire Kenny Sacha, a talented comedian and female impressionist, to take over Craig's role and get back to filming. Time was money. Gene ran defence, pushing to get Craig back in. Hollis McLaren did too, as did financial backers. They said Kenny wasn't a big enough name to sell tickets and make money as Craig could. Even Roy thought it was best to keep him. They won out. Craig was back in.

The story of *Too Outrageous!* picks up nine years after the original ended. The character Robin is still chummy with mentally unwell Liza and still works at a gay club. As Liza makes progress in her dream of becoming a famous writer, Robin has a chance at a cable TV show but worries fame and fortune may not be good for him.

"[It is about] the nasty choices of becoming an adult," Dick told entertainment reporter George Anthony of the *Toronto Sun*. "But it's also about what the world does to talent that doesn't know how to protect itself. Because it will re-do you completely, and neither of them are prepared for that."

Once again, the script was mirroring real life. Craig could relate to all of that.

Shooting began in late November and continued over five weeks. Craig was still bruised and healing from Jurgen's beating when they started, so some of their first scenes were shot from only his right side to hide his mangled face. It fell to Gene to keep Craig focused on the task at hand. That became a group affair. Because there was still concern about Craig's drinking and drug use, handlers were hired to keep him sober. They were with him on set and in his off hours. It was a kick to his ego but he seemed to accept it.

"With me, drinking and career are so closely related," he told Toronto gossip reporter Rita Zekas, noting he had given up his vices and was now totally sober. "A calmness came over me and I thought, I don't need it. I might as well stop ruining my looks."

He was self-deprecating yet confident and determined in another interview, this time with *T.O. Magazine*. Referring to his old persona and reputation, he said: "That Craig Russell is dead. He's my monster and I killed him. I'm just going to drag him out of the bag when I need to pay the rent."

Filming proceeded efficiently. They filmed across Toronto, including at the Spectrum, the Big Bop, Showbiz, and the Adelaide Court Theatre — popular venues of the day — as well as the Winchester Hotel in the Cabbagetown neighbourhood and CFTO television studios in Scarborough. Craig particularly enjoyed filming at Theatre in the Dell.

While they filmed with gusto under Dick's and Roy's hands, energy was missing among the cast and crew that existed on the original film. They weren't breaking ground this time and with everyone more experienced, they weren't operating with the same passion and guts that come from taking risks with something new. The making of the film was about business, not the magic of moviemaking. That was a bummer.

It also couldn't be ignored that the lead star was faded and set a tone over everything, despite their intentions for this to be his comeback.

"There was an edge to Craig that had gone ... you'd see this self-destructive guy self-emulating," says Helga Stephenson, who was by then director of Toronto's Festival of Festivals. "Nobody was ever mean. They wanted his life to work."

No producer, director, or cast could ignite what was missing in Craig's eyes and spirit. He looked depressed, tired, disengaged. The spark that gave him so much life in his performance seemed to be gone and Craig couldn't hide it. Helga says he was simply "more disintegrated as a person."

Craig was still manically depressed, but he also admitted he was frustrated through the process. He didn't like working for Dick and Roy. He was doing his best but said he felt like he was being raked over the coals and was a scapegoat when things went wrong because he had the reputation of an out-of-control star.

When he wasn't defeated by that dynamic, he acted out. Dick told Richert Easley, the actor who played Perry in the original *Outrageous!*, that Craig was giving him trouble when he had to repeat takes. Craig nicknamed Roy "Double Crost" and relied on Gene more and more to look out for him.

"Craig was very much a handful," remembers Gene. "It was exacerbated by the fact that he felt that what was happening was seriously flawed."

Gene points to Dick's perceived approach. After the release of *Outrageous!* in 1977, Dick was recognized but didn't get the accolades Craig did. He had made one other film, *Happy Birthday, Gemini,* with actress Madeline Kahn in 1980, but he still wasn't a big name in the movie business. Gene thought Dick was jealous of Craig's success and the spotlight *Outrageous!* brought him. On the set now, Dick said the filming of *Outrageous!* was weighted too much on the actors, and while it may have been successful for the original picture, the sequel would be "a director's film."

"To me, it meant abbreviated performances, and the whole idea of this film was that you want those performances to be as prominent as you can possibly make them," he says. "I voiced that concern both with Dick and somewhat with Roy."

Roy doesn't remember Dick's comments or Gene's feedback but does say this was a bigger film. They had more experience than Bill and Henk did, multiple production companies were involved, and, at $2 million, the budget was much larger. That meant they had higher production values than the original. Following the same formula to make a film "on a prayer and a song" was not so simple.

"Dick Benner was aware of the circumstances shooting the first film and wanted certainly to upgrade it in terms of quality and photography," he says. "We had to capitalize on the success of the original but at the same time we tried to differentiate it to make it more palatable to a later audience."

Too Outrageous! wrapped on time after five weeks. Gene says Roy deserved a medal for what he had to go through with Craig. There were no big incidents or disasters, but he had not been easy to work with. Despite reservations about Craig's spirit and whether or not the film captured the original magic, plans were put in place to play it up big in the entertainment world. Interviews were booked, parties were planned, and a publicity machine ramped up to share their work.

Craig poses with hired entertainers at the Too Outrageous! *premiere party.*

Everything started with a premiere at Toronto's annual Festival of Festivals in September 1987. They had a packed house for the screening at the Ryerson Theatre followed by a roaring premiere party at the Royal York Hotel where, as *Toronto Star* columnist Rita Zekas reported, "there wasn't a dress code as much as an undress code."

Kenny Sacha worked the stage while drag queens worked the crowd. Male strippers danced down to their underwear; others served food and drinks. Legendary names in entertainment like actresses Beverly D'Angelo and Megan Follows, writer Norman Mailer, and producer Peter O'Brian partied among them, yet somehow with such outrageous cast members and party elements, they paled in comparison.

Craig wore a white tux, fake eyelashes, and Day-Glo nails. He celebrated his success with Lori, Norma and Eric, Helen Phillips, and other family and friends he invited. It was the party to be at that year.

"I thought it played really well; everybody laughed in the right places," says Gene. "The event itself and the party was the best party at the festival. The actual gala premiere and the party was the toast of the festival in 1987. Everything was great."

Craig, Dick, Roy, Gene, and company took the film on the road with premieres across the U.S. When Craig got out of the limo to walk the small red carpet, Gloria Martin said, "The energy would blow the top right off your head.... You could imagine how it would be hard to have that attention day after day."

But Craig took right to it, just like old times. It felt good.

"When we saw the other drag queens who were fabulous, they adored Craig," she says. "He was their king."

At his premieres, Craig took time to talk to all his fans, particularly the women. He took so much time that things often ran behind. He didn't care. This was the moment he had been waiting for. He had done his time in Germany and had now proven that he still had potential. He wasn't a lost cause after all.

"I know now from personal experience that you can survive without money or friends if you believe in yourself," he said. "I haven't changed so much, but the people here in the business maybe took a scorecard and put the pros and cons together and realized I had not been so errant as they thought."

At least one reporter shared the notion that Craig and his character Robin Turner were imperfect humans who had trouble, and the film was genuine in capturing that.

"*Too Outrageous!* ultimately wins you with its relentless sincerity, its glorification of outcasts, and humanization of types most contemporary filmgoers would rather not deal with," writer Michael Musto wrote in the *Village Voice.*

Too Outrageous! eventually played in a few dozen theatres in the U.S. and Canada. It was a promising start, but it struggled and plateaued as its distribution company went bankrupt. That hampered getting the film in more theatres. According to Roy, a deal to get it on home video also fell through. It was a mess. It is not clear what the film earned at the box office.

But it wasn't just distribution problems. *Too Outrageous!* didn't play well with many reviewers. The *Montreal Gazette* said the film lacked outrageousness and gave it one and a half stars. The *Vancouver Sun* called it "something of a drag," while the *Ottawa Citizen* said it was "more of the same."

"*Too Outrageous!* suffers from the usual symptoms of sequelitis," critic Noel Taylor wrote. "It's got a lot more of the same, but that's all. It's so busy looking at itself in the mirror it doesn't notice that showbiz is passing it by."

Ouch. Yet Taylor was not alone in the sentiment.

"The *Outrageous!* formula, translated to the jaded, big-budget '80s, no longer seems to click for either critics or movie goers," reviewer Thomas Waugh wrote in *Cinema Canada* magazine. "The basics are there, to be sure, but writers, directors and actors all get rusty without a chance to practice and polish their craft."

Critic Bruce Kirkland also was less than flattering. "Benner has stretched the story out to thinly deal with a clutch of other assorted friends, leaving the new film muddled and misguided," he wrote.

It was like something was off. Something was missing.

"Though the film seems intent on embroiling Robin Turner in a story, Mr. Russell works best when left to his own devices," critic Janet Maslin wrote in the *New York Times*. "Dick Benner, who wrote and directed the film in a very low-keyed and often clumsy style, too often forces Mr. Russell into more dramatic situations than readily suit him."

Reviews like Maslin's seemed to point to what Gene had been worried about. The film didn't capitalize on the charmed relationship between a gay drag performer and a mentally unwell woman, nor did it put enough weight on Craig's talents and ability to hold an audience. It was well made, on time, and on budget, but it tempered him down with formulaic moviemaking elements instead of bringing up its stars and didn't capture anything special.

Roy points the magic wand at Craig.

"The real problem was that Craig had really not updated his choice of material, although he said he had, he actually hadn't," he says. "He was fine doing Sophie Tucker or Mae West or these older ladies that he'd grown up with but by that time, there was a whole slew of people who'd never heard of them."

It is true that Craig still had not diversified his impressions, either in his show or in advance of the *Too Outrageous!* filming. That was something even he identified as necessary, even before he went to Germany. Did anyone even know the likes of Mae West, Bette Davis, and Carol Channing? If they did, did they care about them? At Dick and Roy's urging, Craig worked on impressions of more contemporary artists, and they tried to work them into the film. He did a passable impression of Tina Turner singing "Proud Mary." He wasn't very good as Janis Joplin. An attempt at Madonna flopped. All of that probably was because Craig didn't love those performers as he did his original ladies. How do you put your heart and soul into an impression of someone you don't care about?

Waugh pointed out that Craig's Mae, Judy Garland, and Peggy Lee impressions were "inspired," but his other impressions were weak, stale, and seemed to just "involve Russell impersonating Russell." In the end, Waugh wrote, Craig's persona may not have been strong enough to carry the film.

Maybe it was more than the characters. Was Craig Russell the entertainer a thing of the past? He had been away for over four years, and now another entertainer named Harris Milstead was on the scene, building on his own path to stardom.

Going by the stage name Divine, Harris's career was built on the Craig Russell formula over the same time period. He had an outrageous persona, a large presence with a forty-pound blonde wig on top of his 320-pound frame, and he could hold an audience.

Harris had more than a dozen film appearances, most of which were made in close association with filmmaker John Waters, and an established position in drag clubs, theatres, and on television as a recording artist. He was very successful. Harris even conquered Toronto's Massey Hall before Craig, doing a show in December 1977 called *Restless Underwear* while clad in a tiger-skin bikini and blonde beehive alongside hypersexed, provocative Toronto singer Carole Pope, lead singer of the new-wave rock band Rough Trade.

Craig and Harris were both outrageous, but were far from carbon copies of each other. While Craig thrived on tributes to his ladies, his talents as an entertainer, and his impeccable transformation, Divine thrived on sensationalism. His trademark was trashy. He donned skin-tight clothes and abrasively applied makeup. He thrived on a brand of filth, and his antics were at times revolting. In the 1972 film *Pink Flamingos*, playing a character described as "the filthiest person alive," he ate dog feces.

People magazine would eventually name him "Drag Queen of the Century." By 1987 when Craig was out promoting *Too Outrageous!*, Harris was gearing up to release his fourth studio album and star in the musical film *Hairspray*, a project written, produced, and directed by Waters, which also starred Sonny Bono, Ricki Lake, Debbie Harry, and Jerry Stiller. It became a cult classic.

MuchMusic VJ Kim Clarke Champniss remembers running into Craig at the Queen Street studios in Toronto around the time he was out promoting *Too Outrageous!* While Craig was still the same "mischievous rascal," Kim was also slightly surprised to see him there at all.

"He was largely forgotten," Kim says. "[Craig] had such a low profile.... Divine was a hit."

Was Harris's style what it took to be a successful drag artist in film and television? The answer isn't clear, but regardless, Craig's talent and reputation weren't enough to lift *Too Outrageous!* to the level its predecessor reached. Still Roy doesn't consider the film to be a failure. He sees it as a success "in relative terms."

"It was pretty good value for what it was," he says. "The film itself played, it had its amusing moments, and it had its musical moments that I think were very good."

Craig thought the film was boring — "Two laughs is not enough for a feature film," he bemoaned — and said he was less than pleased with Dick as a director.

"He edited it like a rabbit on speed," he said. "He kept cutting out the funny parts. I had no input ... Without me, the man has nothing to write about."

Craig walked away from the whole experience defeated.

It wasn't a disaster shattering his reputation like what happened in New York, Vancouver, and Amsterdam, but any hope Craig had coming back from Germany for a major career resurgence was gone. He felt like he had failed.

Through the filming, promotion, and first screenings, Lori was on the sidelines. She never did get her part in the film, and other than getting to be in one scene as an extra, she wasn't invited on set or to promotional

January 1987
Dear Craig: 11 Years Later
and we're still here!
Love, respect and
Good Cheer,
Brian
Your City Light

Craig, feeling playful, and swooning friend Brian Linehan, a Canadian entertainment reporter.

events. It didn't matter anyway. She was happy simply to have Craig in Toronto and in her life.

But Craig's interest in her was again starting to waiver. He was feeling pressure and again felt her admiration was smothering. He still invited her out for social events with cast mates, but with more reluctance. He spoke poorly about her and according to one friend, he went as far as to suggest that she was a drug addict only coming around to score through his shady followers who always seemed to be around. That wasn't true, and lucky for Lori, she never heard him say that.

Reality hit her hard eventually though. One night, as the night wound down after a party at the home of actor Ron White and Lori found herself the only female left, Craig pulled her away from the group, walked her to the door, and asked her to leave.

"Now it's an all-male party," he told her. "And by the way, I want a divorce for Christmas!"

Craig slammed the door in her face and went back to his friends. Stunned, Lori walked home from Cabbagetown to Rosedale alone. She was rejected. Again. She didn't understand why he wanted a divorce. He had just got home from Germany after they had four years apart. What had changed? Everything seemed fine. She didn't ask anything of him. She couldn't say she did anything wrong.

She stayed alone and cried for three days straight, trying to think of the answers. Of course, her husband didn't offer any. There was no explanation. But again, as when she left Germany, there was no doubting what she'd do. She'd give her husband the divorce he wanted.

Lori went to a lawyer to get proceedings going. When asked why she wanted to end her marriage, Lori pathetically replied that she promised her husband a divorce as a Christmas present. She still couldn't say what prompted his request or what had gone wrong, nor could she say it was what she wanted herself. She couldn't even put into words how it made her feel. The lawyer took pity on her, told her she could "always break a promise," and encouraged her to think more about it before taking steps to file in court.

Lori wondered if maybe Craig would change his mind or forget what he said so she put the request on the back burner for a few days. But he brought the topic up again and this time coolly added that he only married her to pay her back for loving him when everyone else had rejected him. That was the first time Lori heard the words out of his mouth that marrying her was for anything other than love. She hadn't considered his intentions before. Now he said he didn't need anybody. He only wanted his dogs.

Lori was upset but compliant. She reached out to an uncle going through a divorce to get some advice. When he shared his own divorce papers with her, Lori had an idea. She borrowed the paperwork, got photocopies, used Wite-Out to mark out the completed fields, and hammered away at a type-writer to write in their names instead. Craig would get his divorce after all.

Now staying in the Waldorf Astoria building downtown, Craig invited Lori over that Christmas morning. She arrived early with an armful of presents for Nancy and Baby Mae, and a card for Craig with the doctored divorce documents tucked inside. Craig ignored her sentimental card but jumped up and gave her a heartfelt hug after reading the paperwork.

"Now we can be friends," Craig told her, genuinely pleased.

The whole divorce request was symbolic. Craig wanted Lori in his life — both in his personal life and career — but he was steadfast in his desire for clearer boundaries between them. This was what he'd been trying for since they first spent time together in 1981. He didn't want to feel he had obligations or pressure, and he wanted her to understand they would never be a monogamous couple with a traditional family life. He also wanted her to stand on her own two feet and turn the love she had for him onto herself. He knew the documents weren't real, but as far as he was concerned, they were proof that Lori understood his position, would adjust her expectations, and would relax in her admiration.

Craig and Lori could still be close pals. He still needed her. They had Christmas dinner together later that day with Lori's dad; Eddie Jenkins; his new wife; Lori's sister, Dena; and her brother Marc. They spent New Year's Eve day together, too, walking Nancy and Baby Mae. But when it came time for evening plans, Craig made clear that he planned to spend the holiday without her. He didn't have time for her the next day either, so Lori went to Greenwood Raceway with her dad.

On the surface Lori made it seem she was okay with what Craig wanted, but emotionally she wasn't separated in her heart. She told no one they were "divorced" and identified as his wife when he wasn't around. She also continued to wear her wedding band.

January 11, 1987, marked their fifth wedding anniversary. Craig didn't acknowledge it and never picked up the anniversary card Lori left for him. It was another signal that clearly screamed the message: *We are not a couple.* Lori did not get it. His tough love response made her sad. Still apt to find comfort in theatre, she took herself out to a cabaret to hear singer Bonnie Meyer, accompanied by saxophonist Carrie Chesnutt, in an attempt to find solace in her loneliness. The lyrics to Bonnie's song "Just Loving You" spoke to Lori deeply:

> And I just don't know how
> I'm going to make it without you,
> I just can't fake it about you
> Because I love you so.
> And I just don't know how
> I'm going to get it together,
> Now that I've lost you forever …

Lori didn't end up having to spend the day totally alone. Later that night she and Craig went to the club Les Cavaliers (later named the Barn) on Church Street. At Craig's insistence, they toasted their friendship with Brandy Alexander cocktails. Lori seemed pleased with that and put her feelings aside for a while. But there was no changing Craig's mind. He still wanted space and better boundaries.

He maybe could have been more sensitive about it, though. The next day Lori found out he had moved out of the hotel where he'd been staying. He didn't want to tell her where he went.

CHAPTER THIRTEEN

LILI MARLENE

Craig had some soul-searching to do in the months after *Too Outrageous!* wrapped. His career and relationships were uncertain and he didn't want to be alone. The person he turned to was Lori.

After deliberately not telling her he had moved from the Waldorf Astoria Hotel to an apartment on Avenue Road, Craig invited her to see his new place and presented her with a card that said "U and I should be together." So much for the symbolic divorce. Now Craig wanted them to live together. It was a perplexing offer after months of trying to establish boundaries in their relationship. Lori didn't care. She moved right in and set up house, decorating their apartment with pictures of Mae West just as she had done in the first apartment they shared five years earlier.

Despite his lack of interest in Lori as a wife and partner, Craig was very needy. He wanted companionship with someone. Anyone. He was again in a manic-depressive emotional roller coaster like when he'd lived with Manuela Mock. In the day he'd be up and lively, cooking Lori delicious meals and giving her foot massages. But at night he'd go low and dark. He would be anxious, fret and cry, or act out in fits of temper. At first, Craig would kick Lori out of their apartment as an angry, violent episode came on so that she'd be out of harm's way. The next morning when it had passed, he'd sing into the telephone and ask her to come back.

They kept up a social life, with Craig seeing her family and Lori joining him for trips to Port Perry to see the Halls or for visits to the family cottage. Many people, including their friends and associates, thought of Craig and Lori as they thought of any other married couple.

One night Gino Empry had them out to meet comedian Joan Rivers and see her perform at Toronto's O'Keefe Centre. Lori was thrilled by the invitation, but the night ended with disappointment when Craig left the show early, envious that Joan had top billing on a stage in a grand venue and he did not. He went home in a huff and took his anger out on Lori's bike.

"How many nails did you break?" Lori asked when she got home and found her bike crumpled in the street, destroyed. She didn't have to ask what happened, who did it, or why.

"Only two," Craig admitted, coyly. He never apologized.

Norma and Eric Hurst knew he wasn't doing well but did little to help. Norma had strict boundaries and wasn't going to get involved in drama. Craig could live his life as he chose. If he really needed her, he would call. Norma's thoughts were more with Lori. In March 1987 she sent her son a card that read: "Love to Lori. We hope she sticks around to keep you company."

The underlying message was clear. Norma knew the state her son was in. She didn't want him to mess up one of the few loyal relationships he had left.

Craig wasn't doing as much cocaine at that point, but he was drinking more and more. The booze eventually clouded any consideration he had for Lori. He stopped kicking her out of the apartment as his moods went dark and took his anger out on her directly. He'd rave into the night, leave all the lights on, and refuse to let her sleep. He nipped at her with put-downs and biting remarks. One night he pulled the mattress out from under her and made her sleep on the floor. Lori said a few episodes became physically abusive. She took to wearing long sleeves to hide bruises.

Their landlord evicted them that June, and for the first time Lori was relieved to be away from her husband. She found herself a new apartment in Rosedale, her favourite neighbourhood, and in addition to her work as a file clerk for Dominion of Canada General Insurance Company by day, she got evening work as a personal support worker to a patient with amyotrophic lateral sclerosis, better known as Lou Gehrig's disease.

Craig lived for a few months at the Essex Park Hotel before Gene Mascardelli helped him find an apartment on Queen Street in the Beach neighbourhood east of downtown. It was close to where Gene lived with his wife, Gloria Martin, and close to the lake and boardwalk for walks with Nancy and Baby Mae. It was also right around the corner from Craig's daughter, Allison. They were just getting to know each other that spring.

Allison grew up in Toronto just as her mother, Helen Phillips, wanted. She always knew about Craig, who he was, and what he did for a living. Helen told her daughter that her father was wonderful and talented. Allison read reviews her mother had kept, saw stories about his wedding to Lori in the newspaper, and knew about his love of Mae West.

"[My mother] never expressed anything negative about him, his choices or anything," she says. "It was always, 'He's gorgeous. He's talented and he worked so hard at his talent and his craft.' It was modelled for me to respect it rather than to think of it in any kind of odd way."

Allison was thirteen years old when she took the first steps to find her father. Craig was still in Germany at the time, so the first person she found was Craig's father, Russell Eadie. She was less than warmly received, but she persevered and with the timing of Craig's return to film *Too Outrageous!*, she didn't have to wait long. Her mother, Helen, met with him first to ensure it would be okay and he would be in the right frame of mind — no funny business — to get to know their daughter.

There were no antics when the day finally came in the spring of 1987. Allison had no qualms. It was her father who had the hang-ups.

Craig was genuinely pleased that there was someone, his own flesh and blood, who wanted to know him as a person because he was her father, not because he was a star. But his erratic behaviour and emotions were still a roller coaster. He worked hard to be up, share his talents, be funny, stay in performer mode, entertain, and be fabulous. That was the only way he knew how to win someone over.

It was clear to even a young teenager that he didn't know how to be himself.

"Just getting him to be real and to be him was difficult," she says, but she tolerated the unruly behaviour. "How do you hold him back? You're either along for the ride or you lose him."

It was clear to her father, too. Craig's opinion of himself was incredibly low, and he was resigned to the fact that he didn't know how to be anything but outrageous. He didn't know how to relax and nurture himself or others.

"It takes so long to wind down and be me," he said in a candid interview with the *Advocate*. "Because you know what it's like to be me? It's just like you. It's boring.… And I'm so tired and so fucking ugly."

Allison didn't know anything about his manic depression, but she did know about his alcohol use. She saw that Craig was drinking heavily, and as strong as he once was, she told her father more than once that he would have to sober up when she was around or she would walk away. Craig must have cared. He listened and made a point to be sober.

Young but beyond her years, Allison understood Craig when so many people didn't seem to anymore. From the start she was the mature one in the relationship. She set the boundaries and expectations, stepped aside if he was over the top or out of line, and carefully analyzed who he was, what was behind his actions, and what he really meant by some of the things he said. She was the dominant personality to his submissive. In other people Craig would interpret such dynamics as threatening, but in Allison he was able to see that her actions came from a place of nurturing and love.

"He wanted people to love him," she says. "He just wanted to be OK."

Craig wanted to make it work. Allison brought hope to his life and, like any father, he was proud. He first introduced her to Lori, who commented that Allison "looked so much like Craig! I couldn't stop looking at her! She's beautiful!"

Father and daughter spent a good deal of time together. They were different people with different interests, but they had a connection. One time, digging into his roots of transformation, Craig played hairstylist with Allison as his subject, teasing at his daughter's pretty hair and fitting her for a wig. It was his way of showing sweet, tender affection.

There were a few big events, too. Allison was one of his special guests at the *Too Outrageous!* gala premiere party in September 1987. Not many teenage girls in Toronto got to go to places like that. There she was at a posh

Craig in the studio recording Glamour Monster *with Robert Armes (left) and Tim Tickner.*

party in the Royal York Hotel with glitz and glamour, drag and dancers, and so much attention on the father she was just beginning to know. She was dazzled by it all — her father, the movie, the party, seeing actor Brian Dennehy, and the present of a movie poster that Lori had ripped off the wall for her.

Craig's career edged forward after it was clear *Too Outrageous!* wasn't going anywhere. Dance music was on the way up in the 1980s, so Craig recorded "Glamour Monster," an original track that was later remixed to make a high-energy, pop, and electronic track.

He worked hard with producers Syd Kessler and Marc Giaronelli, and later in the studio with Robert Armes and Tim Tickner when it was recorded. Craig's potential as a recording artist was apparent. He was a natural in the creative environment and had the musical chops, particularly for lyrics, while also being the quintessential artist for the era. He was bold, dramatic, and colourful, and he had the edge of new-wave and punk rock glamour.

"He was a harbinger of all sorts of movements, being accepted, valued as an entertainer," Robert remembers. "It wasn't hard for him to feel comfortable. He had very good energy."

The track didn't get much airplay in the end, but Craig was proud enough of the result that he sent it on to some friends, including Manuela in Germany.

In a television interview with the CBC, conducted around the time *Glamour Monster* was recorded, Craig's temperament was calm, but he looked tired and unwell. His dyed hair was unkempt, his skin blotchy. He was fatigued, and in his answers to the reporter, he sounded like he was even trying to convince himself that all was well.

"Sometimes I haven't loved it," he said, speaking about his career. "But then I sort of took a look at myself and said 'Well, you should because you do it well, so love it, enjoy it.'"

Still, his blue eyes were open wide with a look of innocence and hope. He kept going.

Craig turned his attention to projects in front of the camera.

The first was a promising opportunity to star in a movie as a character accused of murder and on the run. He talked less about the script than he did about how the role was a chance to be seen as an actor, not as a man who dressed up as a woman. It was a familiar sentiment, something he had suggested for years yet never seemed to achieve. The other was a comedy series pilot called *Prime Rib*, produced in part by Gloria Martin with Gene as a consulting producer.

Unfortunately for Craig, neither project got off the ground. Two other opportunities proved more successful. Craig appeared on *The Originals*, a Citytv series featuring "portraits in the first person," and at the 1988 Genie Awards with Hollis McLaren. For a bit of fun on the latter, he grew out a beard and began the evening wearing a suit only to reappear later in the broadcast dressed in a gown as one of his ladies. Both got him a bit of positive press.

He didn't have many opportunities to perform his original complete act, but he did perform a few times with musician Dave Gray, the guitar player from the Parachute Club. Craig suggested in a few interviews that he may take the act to the United Kingdom, the Soviet Union, or the Caribbean, but in reality, he didn't get farther than London, Ontario. He didn't seem to care. He still had fun.

There were days Craig was actually feeling pretty good, and he reached out in ways that would make him feel like the star he aspired to be. He would go downtown to Yorkville and visit the posh Robert Gage Salon or make a stop at Vintage Furs where friend and owner Marianne Heller would let him borrow a fur to go out on the town for a few hours. She knew he couldn't afford them. It just mattered that it made him feel good about himself.

Sometimes he "was beyond hilarious," Marianne remembers. He was once so physically affectionate, pouncing on her with hugs and kisses so intensely that his makeup rubbed all over her. But other times it was sad. It was obvious Craig had "a lot of feelings in him." She calls him "a sad sweetheart."

Other days Craig felt outrageously funny, like his old self. After hearing that Gene and Gloria's neighbours, a gay couple, had been rude to them, Craig decided to make a splash. He summoned a limousine and asked to be driven to their house. As the limo pulled up in front, Craig stood through the sunroof and hollered through a megaphone.

"Where is my manager?" he cried. "I need to find Gene Mascardelli."

Catching the attention of the offending neighbours, Craig got out of the limo, sauntered up, and sat on the lap of one of the two of them. He was fully made up in outfit, wig, and makeup.

"I hear you haven't been very nice," he purred. "Are you straight-o-phobic? If you can't handle the heat, get out of the kitchen."

The couple was mortified and moved soon after. Gene and Gloria laugh at the memory. It was their old Craig, being outrageous. Maybe things would be okay for him despite his struggles.

For a while it seemed like Craig wanted to put down roots in the Beach neighbourhood and have more balance in his career and personal life. He grew a beard, wore a tweed coat, and took up exercise and pipe smoking. He'd sometimes meet Gene at a local bar to have a few drinks, talk business, or watch the ball game on TV like one of the guys. He visited friends at their homes, making a few dinners where he would hilariously use leftovers that were a bit too old or sprinkle in multivitamin pills to ensure a balanced meal. Some days he'd walk to the local Shoppers Drug Mart to chat up the cosmetician and help customers with makeup; other days he'd dress up as one of his ladies and walk the Queen Street strip and try to get local bars to hire him to perform. It never resulted in anything, and he quit his efforts after he was beaten by a gang of thugs.

He also again tried to assert some independence from Lori. He wouldn't always answer her calls, and he avoided her if he saw her on the street. It was less about boundaries now and more that he tied Lori to his life as Craig Russell. If he were going to separate from that life, she would have to be kept at a distance. His efforts were futile. Lori was easily able to penetrate the wall if she showed up with a bottle of rum under her arm. Rum was his favourite. He couldn't say no.

One person he did align with was Rita Zekas, an entertainment columnist at the *Toronto Star* who lived close by. They first met years earlier after the release of *Outrageous!* and he was no stranger in her circles over the years. Now he was reaching out to her as a friend. Rita was quite taken by him.

"When he was straight, he was the greatest guy you wanted to be around," says Rita. "Amongst all the bravado, he was a very sweet person."

But when he wasn't sober or was in a manic mood, he caused the same trouble with her as he did with everyone else.

Craig would sometimes show up at Rita's house uninvited, unannounced, and drunk or high on cheap drugs, usually poppers. He wouldn't respect any boundaries. One day when Rita hosted a yard sale, he hung out and insulted anyone who tried to buy something. Rita had a great affection for him and forgave the nonsense. She knew there was more to the person than the behaviour.

Another friend who came to that conclusion was Russell Alldread, the drag queen better known as Michelle DuBarry, whom Craig knew from his Manatee days and the Great Imposters. One night Craig showed up unannounced and drunk at Michelle's apartment, with an entourage of questionable characters in tow. Michelle was annoyed by the interruption, but her heart yearned for the Craig she once knew, the Craig with so much talent who now seemed so lost.

Craig saw the same things as his friends. He was well aware of his emotional struggles and his unpredictable behaviour. He was also reflective about his failings. There were more than anybody knew. That included the Carnegie Hall disaster, the Vancouver incident, the Amsterdam implosion, the people he upset who didn't understand him or his motivations, and the fans he alienated with his shocking behaviour and antics. He admitted he had not a few, but thousands of regrets.

"I would have done almost everything differently," he said in one interview. "Things I thought very amusing at the time turned out to alienate a lot of people."

But still he thought it wasn't overly fair when the star who had to keep being outrageous for his audience all of a sudden became too much for people. He was only trying to give them what they wanted.

"My original idea was to get high, dress up wild and go out and have a ball and shake everybody up and get a lot of attention," he said. "What's a star, performer or entertainer supposed to do? Then they decided you must arrive sober, stay that way, sit quietly in the corner and behave like a proper young man. Somebody got lost in the rules."

That soul-searching often made him sad, and he'd slide back into the grips of depression. Who was he? Why didn't people understand his behaviour? Why couldn't he control it himself sometimes? What life did he have? He thought about what life he could have had if he hadn't pursued the path of being Craig Russell the star. Would he be a happier, more fulfilled person if his career never happened?

The answer was no. Craig couldn't have escaped his mental health struggles no matter what he did with his life and career. He understood little about his diagnosis of manic depression, and though support was better in the 1980s than it was in the 1970s when he saw a doctor, he sought no medical attention for it now. There would be no real peace.

Craig never again talked to his father, Russell, and he had grown to have a great antipathy for his mother, Norma. That was surprising to some. She had been the only mother in the gay bars of his early career, she had welcomed gay men into her home when they had nowhere to go, and she had travelled across Canada and the U.S. to see him perform. She even had an "Outrageous" necklace, just like character Carrie Bradshaw's infamous "Carrie" necklace in the hit HBO TV show *Sex and the City*.

Yet as far as others were concerned, Craig hated her. He spoke bitterly of her and wasn't very nice to her in person either. When questioned about his feelings, he told some untruths seemingly to justify why he felt so strongly. He spoke so poorly of Norma, yet lovingly of his aunt Cathryn, some wondered if his aunt was his actual mother. It wasn't natural to be so hateful.

His devaluation of Norma and their relationship grew from misperceptions. While Norma had been supportive, she was always practical. Over the years she was openly cautious of his outrageous career and sometimes responded to his decisions with concern. She straightforwardly said that maybe it would be better for him to do something else, like a proper job or a trade, and keep his performing career as something he did on the side. She even paid to maintain his hairdressing licence, just in case he needed it.

Norma could also be to the point. Her advice could be very matter of fact and direct. She meant well, but at times her words were cold. Craig said she once told him that he "was nothing without his characters." She meant that he had not nurtured more of a life for himself offstage, which was true, but that is not how Craig took it. He was hurt. He did not see her pragmatism as a mother's love, and her actions tasted like the rejection he got from his father.

Norma knew the intensity of her son's feelings and was unfailingly patient when he was unkind to her over the years.

"It was good to be with you and I hope everything is going OK," she wrote to him in a card after he married Lori. "We think about you a lot and certainly welcome Lori to the family if you can both accept us. We love you and want you to be happy."

She signed the card "Love Mother." It was about as outwardly expressive of her love as she ever was.

"She loved him without reason," Allison says. "But she could say things that were thoughtless, and you'd think, 'Did you just say that?' She was not an emotional woman at all."

But her son *was* emotional. It was all so confusing for Craig. He couldn't emotionally filter her words and actions. He didn't see her intentions and didn't feel good enough, no matter what she'd ever done to support his career. Did she even love him? Maybe she was right. He was nothing.

His low feelings of himself and of Norma were compounded by another secret, something that had happened in childhood. Craig said he had been molested by someone in his extended family. It happened on numerous occasions, and only when he started his fan club and grew more confident did he feel strong enough to refuse advances.

At the time, Craig told his friends about the assaults but kept it from his parents, Norma in particular. He didn't want to upset her when already, as a preteen rejected by his father, he felt unwanted. That made him feel alone and, thirty years later, he resented Norma for it. For her he felt like he had sacrificed some sense of peace and justice that would have come from speaking out and naming the offender. Still, he kept silent.

No one in the Hall or Eadie families knew what had happened. Even Lori didn't know. His high school friends held on to his secret, and when Craig opened up to a writer in the late 1980s, he was so mired with alcohol and known for sensational remarks, it's not likely he would have been believed if the story went public.

Nights were never kind to Craig in those months and years after *Too Outrageous!* His emotions always spiralled downward once the sun set. He felt depressed and alone. He didn't have much contact with his old pals Shirley Flavell and Phil Buckley. They'd gone on and built quieter lives for themselves, while he was off being outrageous.

Margaret Gibson was one person he did turn to. The two were still closely matched even though they had not maintained regular contact over the past few years. Margaret was still actively struggling with mental illness, having been on the slow rebound of a breakdown she said she'd had in 1979. But when Craig started reaching out to her, she was lucid enough to feel like he wasn't the same person.

Margaret told Shirley of one encounter when he showed up drunk, made a pass at her, and wanted to have sex. They had been intimate before when they were roommates, but she felt uncomfortable with him in his present state. Something was wrong. Something wasn't right.

Aaron Gilboord, Margaret's son, remembers another day when Craig showed up unannounced in a manic state. It was clear he was drunk or worse, and when he made suggestive comments in an attempt to be funny, Margaret kicked him out. She quit answering the door and hesitated to take his calls.

With Margaret out of the picture, Craig turned to Lenore Zann. It was not unusual for her to get calls from Craig in the middle of the night, desperate for company. The result would always be the same: Lenore would jump into a cab and find him outside wherever he was staying, drunk, pacing, and crying, sometimes wearing his pink nightgown with fluffy pink slippers.

Lenore would ply him with love, try to calm him, and help him to sleep. She told him he was a person worth saving. He couldn't be made to feel better. One night he showed her his empty bottles of booze and, exasperated, told her: "This is what they have done to me! This is what the industry has done to me!" Another night he turned his sorrow into verbal abuse directed at her. He resented that she was a woman, that she was successful, that things seemed easy for her. It was an exhausting dynamic.

"He was more and more abusive and hysterical," she said. "I had to let him go."

She told Craig she was stepping back from their friendship and that he needed help. The situation with Lenore was much the same as it was with Paul and Brenda Hoffert, David Lieberberg, Michelle, Margaret, and Rita. Lenore was someone stable who loved him and looked out for his best interests, but now she had been pushed to her limit. Craig was almost too intoxicated to acknowledge the loss.

It was lucky he still had some work to bring him distraction. Craig had some big gigs on the docket in the latter half of 1988. After years hosting

Craig as Bette Midler in his last appearance at the Imperial Room.

top talent from across the world, the Imperial Room in the Royal York Hotel was set to close. A lineup of stars was pulled in for final shows and Craig's old friend Gino Empry booked him for a week of performances. It was a significant booking, and his first time at that venue in seven years. The opportunity was great on paper, but in reality, it came with little excitement in his circle.

"I was kind of worried about it," says Gene. "When somebody has been at the top of their game, but their game is low and their ego is high, it is complicated. That's what I worked on with Craig. You've got to rebuild back up. I was nervous about him doing that."

Even Craig scoffed at the plans. He said he was bored of the venue and that he didn't think his performance was up to it. He wasn't prepared to potentially fail. It was only out of loyalty to Gino that he proceeded.

The show was good but not great, and as with *Too Outrageous!*, the audience seemed to change. He wasn't as well-known and not everyone bought into what he was selling. Some bristled at his show altogether. The impressions were passable, but his singing was unmistakably hoarse. His rapport and jokes were inappropriate and on the whole poorly received.

"The people were hoping for a hometown triumph," reviewer Bruce Blackadar wrote in the *Toronto Star*. "But, sadly, they didn't get one … The man's voice was just about shot — a true tragedy for an impressionist … The words to describe the act up to then are … a little dull. Craig? Dull?"

There were plenty of empty seats in the audience through that run, but a silver lining was his ability to perform for family and friends. One of the people in his audience was Allison. She was bursting with pride and found it fascinating that not only did he have the talent but the courage to turn himself into "his ladies" like Peggy, Carol, Barbra, and Judy.

"I was just really, really proud of him," she says. "Maybe because I knew his story a little bit, I knew how hard he worked and how outside the box he was."

Half of the Hall family came out to see him one night, including his mom and Eric; uncle Howard; aunts Zula, Cathryn, and Melba; cousins Jennifer and Cathryn with their spouses; and long-time family friends Kent and Doug Farndale. Lori was there, too. They cheered him on, celebrated in his hotel suite afterward and excitedly posed for a group shot.

Craig almost blending in with the Hall family after his last show at the Imperial Room. Lori is on the far right.

In the photo Craig stands in the back, blending in with the group instead of standing out. He had the biggest smile he had in a long time.

Another event that brought him pride was a "hometown" concert in Port Perry. Craig's uncle Howard was the mayor of the town and invited him to come and perform at a fundraiser for the local theatre and event space, dubbed Town Hall 1873. The opportunity came with rules: no drugs, no drinking, no shenanigans. There was a time Craig would not have responded well to such instruction and done the exact opposite, but he was humbled now, and he always respected Howard.

Craig approached that show with the same focus and drive he brought to his first Carnegie Hall show in 1978. He went to Craighurst, his mother's cottage, weeks before the event so he could dry out and rehearse his impressions. He wanted to put on a good show for all the people who knew his family so well, and he wanted to do well by Howard. It paid off.

"He did a hell of a good show," Howard says. "Exceptionally good."

Kent, part of the group who organized the fundraiser, agrees.

"It was a fabulous concert," she says. "We had a wonderful crowd."

Craig was buoyed by how it turned out. He was also more at peace in his relationship with Norma. The time he took to prepare was also the first time they were alone together in decades. They had a lot of talks. Craig talked. Norma listened. Norma mothered. Craig listened. He was able to understand her more, see what she intended by her practical approach to things, and appreciate her intentions.

He let his guard down in their rediscovered closeness. He told her more than he ever had. That included one detail about his health, something he hadn't told anyone else yet.

Craig told Norma he was HIV positive.

Craig tried to make jokes about AIDS for a while. That was probably not surprising. Of course he would want to find humour in a dark time. But he had also been hiding his own diagnosis, and humour masked his own pain, fear, and uncertainty for his future.

"When I left for Germany, I told all the drag queens in Canada to drop dead," he quipped. "When I came back, they had."

It wasn't a laughing matter. HIV and AIDS were running rampant across the world through the 1980s. Thousands were dying. Little could be done medically once it was diagnosed, and little was understood about symptoms, management, and treatment. It seemed as soon as someone was diagnosed, they'd be gone within months, if not weeks or even days.

Canada had its first reported case of AIDS in March 1982. As the number of those diagnosed rapidly expanded, a national task force was formed in 1983, the first AIDS awareness week followed, and the first gathering of doctors and researchers came together in 1985. In 1988 a community-based activist group for people living with HIV and AIDS called AIDS ACTION NOW! was founded in Toronto. The next year, the group worked with a similar New York–based organization called ACT UP to jointly issue Le Manifeste de Montreal, a declaration of the universal rights and needs of people living with HIV.

Craig knew he was HIV positive when he came back to Canada from Germany in 1986. It was unclear to him exactly when he was infected and by whom, but when he was later asked about the details, he sometimes made up stories. It was as if he wanted to appear more in control of himself and the situation than he was.

"I thought something was wrong in 1980," he told a documentary crew. "I told my friends, 'I've got some kind of cancer. They don't know what it is.'"

That wasn't true. The truth was he had been infected when he was in Germany and had been diagnosed when he was there. He contracted the virus from unprotected sex with someone who was HIV positive. He was not a needle user, nor did he have any blood transfusions. It's not clear if Craig knew the risks of having unprotected sex and nondisclosure of status, or if he cast aside the growing realities and risks in favour of some temporary intimate comfort.

Publicly, Craig admitted that he had, in fact, "lived dangerously, adding excess to success," and said he would have to "make the best of the consequences." But privately, Craig was terrified and ashamed by his diagnosis. To him it was something else he had done to sabotage his life and it was a blow he would not recover from. He just couldn't get a win anymore.

He did not tell Manuela when he was diagnosed (or that he'd even seen a doctor) and said nothing of his status for the first three years after he was back at home. Like many who are living with HIV, he believed the stigma would cost him relationships, respect, and love. When he finally revealed his status, his infection had already progressed to AIDS.

It was 1989 when Craig told Allison that he was ill. Her first response was that he had to be kidding. He was not usually serious and, of course, he had joked about AIDS before. But no, he wasn't kidding. In fact, Allison noticed in their conversation how his defeated voice already sounded gravelly and sick.

The disease was progressing rapidly. Craig had been admitted to hospital with an infection when he told Gene. Gene said he was surprised by the news, too. Craig was so strong and his personality was so big, it was as if he were invincible.

Craig may have believed that as well. He had unprotected sex after he knew he was infected with HIV. Lori was not only devastated to find out about his infection, but also concerned and alarmed. She was at risk.

She didn't get upset that he hadn't disclosed sooner, and after a blood test revealed she was negative and safe, she didn't bring up the topic again.

Margaret didn't have the same response when she heard Craig had AIDS. She was furious. He had tried to have sex with her, and if they had gone through with it, she would have been at risk. How could he do that to her?

Margaret not only told all of their mutual friends (and later a documentary crew) about what happened, but she would also write about their alleged encounter and her feelings in a short story that was published in her book *Desert Thirst*. Like "Making It" and so many other pieces of her writing, it is seemingly an autobiographical piece masked as fiction.

The story is called "Golden Boy." In it, a writer named Dolly has tender feelings for her old friend Phineas, a drag queen who has just come back to town. She cherishes their memories and has flashbacks to younger years that reveal his sensitivity and her fondness for him. But, thinking of the "pile of broken dreams and promises" between them, now she sees him as troubled. He has changed.

Not everyone believes Margaret's claim that Craig tried to have sex regardless of his HIV status. Some were outright angry. They point out that it was not uncommon for her to exaggerate to get a sensational reaction, or, in the grip of schizophrenia, to have delusions and believe them to be fact. It could be another story where she spoke for the two of them.

Margaret didn't see Craig's state of mind or intention. He wouldn't have intended to hurt anybody. He didn't have a malicious bone in his body. It is possible he didn't clearly know the risks and how to protect others. He pushed aside the realities of HIV and AIDS for a long time because he couldn't handle it. It was easier not to acknowledge it.

It was a cruel irony that someone who longed for affection and love from others was now alienated from physical intimacy.

CHAPTER FOURTEEN
THE MUSIC
OF THE NIGHT

Gripped with AIDS, Craig couldn't have been lower.

His dark periods, once relegated to late hours of night after riding the incredible highs that came with performing shows, extended and got longer. He drank more, wrote confused letters to old acquaintances, and called up others, crying and ranting into their answering machines for as long as they could record him. He wasn't totally disconnected psychologically. He had lucidity, but on the best of days, it was clear hope was leaving him.

"I found him a remarkable and deeply engaging man," friend and one-time roommate Garth Douglas, a musician and filmmaker, says. "He was also deeply unhappy. There's no question about that."

After years turning his back on the gay and drag community of his early career, Craig began to toe his way back into that scene. Why not? He had few other options. Much had changed since the late 1960s. Most, if not all, of the venues he knew had closed and newer establishments opened in the area of Church and Wellesley Streets, away from the Yonge and Charles area he had known. The neighbourhood would become known as the Gay Village.

A 1988 promotional shot of Craig, stricken with AIDS and struggling to make it.

Some of the performers he knew from his stage days were still there, including drag queens Michelle DuBarry, Rusty Ryan, Murray Cooper, and Jackie Loren. They remembered him, and with the legacy of *Outrageous!*, their fans knew of him, too. Craig picked up some shows and appearances at a few bars including Chaps, Trax, and Komrads, but inside them he was just another drag queen, not a respected female impressionist, the status he felt he had worked for. That upset him. Craig didn't like it if he wasn't received as a *star*.

Makeup artist Dino Dilio remembers seeing him around the neighbourhood.

"Craig was an outsider, but he made himself an outsider," Dino says, noting that in addition to his absence from the Gay Village in recent years, his show and impressions were outside the norm of what the drag audience was looking for at that time. No one seemed to care about the lives of Mae West, Tallulah Bankhead, or Bette Davis. "They had all moved on to Madonna, Cher, and Diana Ross."

Dino says it was obvious Craig was struggling with alcohol and, likely, drugs. Some days he could be found just sitting alone. Interactions with him could be disconnected, as he talked in and out of character, unable to keep meaningful conversation going. He was like a faded painting that, while once vibrant, was now aged and depressed by the elements it couldn't avoid.

With little money coming in, Craig started collecting welfare and eventually moved into a rundown house in the Parkdale neighbourhood with several roommates. Lori thought two of them were shady characters and believed they were smoking crack cocaine and sniffing glue. She was worried for Craig and suggested they live together again. Craig declined. He was trying to hold on to some pride. He did, however, accept her offer of groceries.

While Craig was down, things were looking up in Lori's life. She had a new career. After she was fired from her job as a file clerk — Lori said the final straw was when Craig showed up at her office and made inappropriate jokes about her co-workers — she thought of her original love of theatre. She put together a modest resumé that included her high school efforts, experience as an extra on movie sets, and time working for Craig, and she got a contract job as a dresser for a travelling stage production at the O'Keefe Centre that August.

It was the right move. She still had the passion and work ethic she brought to the backstage productions at Riverdale, and she remembered every detail Craig taught her about preparing and managing wardrobe. Her first gig lasted only a few weeks but it motivated her to keep going. Her big break followed when she was hired to work for playwright Andrew Lloyd Webber's new Toronto production.

The Phantom of the Opera was the opportunity of a lifetime before it even opened. Not only were theatre greats Colm Wilkinson and Rebecca Caine brought in for the lead roles of the Phantom and his protege, Christine Daaé, but the musical debuted in the glorious and restored 2,200-seat Pantages Theatre on Yonge Street. The show, called "the most complicated show technically ever to be produced in Canada," included an elaborate stage design with cutting-edge special effects. It had a full stage crew, including designers, technicians, wardrobe staff, and hairdressers, for the large cast.

The curtain went up for the first performance on September 20, 1989. Lori was assigned to work with opera singer Lyse Guérin, who played the part of Carlotta, the opera's prima donna. Lori dove into the opportunity with all her heart and soul. She loved the production and her co-workers so much she started to take courses in mask making with artist Karen Rodd between shows. She was full of purpose to be something other than her idol's wife.

In a rare opportunity to look out for herself, Lori chose not to tell her husband any of it at first. She was worried he would show up at the theatre, cause some hijinks, and get her fired again. She valued the opportunity too much to lose it. When she finally admitted what she was up to a few months later and explained her reticence, Craig understood. He stayed away except for the rare night when he'd meet her at the stage door after a show to go for a drink or when he got the occasional invite to a cast party.

While working on *Phantom*, Lori also worked four nights a week as a personal care assistant to a woman named Myra Rosenfeld. Myra suffered from Lou Gehrig's disease and went to great lengths to contribute to the Toronto chapter of the ALS Society of Canada despite the limitations of her physical health. Lori admired her for that, called her a mentor, and got on board to support the cause. She volunteered to help with Myra's society meetings, canvassed in malls to collect donations, and sold cornflowers on the annual Flower Day charity event.

Through her volunteer work, she met several friends, including Dave Jorgensen, a man who was living with multiple sclerosis at Queen Elizabeth Hospital. Feeling relatively prepared to be a caregiver after her work with Myra, Lori took him out for dinner and to the movies several times, even as she suffered from yet another broken arm. She did the same thing with another ALS patient named Carol Nevers and spent hours brushing Carol's hair and sharing Craig's stories about the stars. Caregiving was another role where Lori thrived.

Keeping so busy, it was easy for her to give Craig as much space as he wanted. But she remained repulsed by his living conditions in Parkdale and couldn't shake the feeling that she had to do something to change the situation. Since she had no room to offer him at her Rosedale place, Lori set out to find a bigger apartment so Craig would have the option of somewhere else to stay if he needed.

She looked around for a few weeks, found something promising in the Cabbagetown neighbourhood and asked her mother, Hazel, for a loan to finance her plans. Hazel declined because the funds were meant to help Craig. Unswayed, Lori kept looking and eventually settled on an apartment in a coach house on Ossington Avenue. It was well out of her way from her jobs, but it didn't matter. She had a place to comfortably live with her husband.

Home established, she again approached Craig with an offer to live together. His answer was still no, but the decision had little to do with boundaries or his desire to separate himself from his "Craig Russell" life. He couldn't afford to pay half the rent. He didn't explain, but Lori saw right through his reasoning. She accepted his refusal and gently said the place was hers but he could visit as often as he wanted. Craig took her up on that. He showed up with his dogs the day she moved in and never left.

Craig showed his gratitude for their new home life in his own way, just as he did before when they were engaged and when he returned from Germany. He painted their walls brown and gold. He prepared elaborate meals. On Lori's thirty-third birthday in September 1990, he surprised her at the door dressed as Peggy Lee and presented her with fresh flowers, a Black Forest cake, and glasses of Baileys Irish Cream.

Their relationship had a new-found balance by then. While Lori still loved Craig deeply and thought of him as her husband, not her "legal friend" as he had said of the marriage, she cooled the intensity of her adoration. She had grown confident with a feeling of permanency in their association. Now she was the one with the strength; the one the other was leaning on for support.

Craig, meanwhile, was kinder and more sensitive to her feelings. They shared good days as Lori told tales from the theatre and her time with Myra, and they cried together on bad days, when Craig was feeling unwell after a run to the emergency room or when the older of his two dogs, Nancy, ran away. Craig hauled bags of groceries home that Thanksgiving and prepared a full meal for the two of them to enjoy. But by dinnertime, he collapsed in bed exhausted. He was too weak to eat.

Craig's health was failing fast, and with that, his personality was tamer. His emotions were on a more even keel and he didn't break into characters as much anymore. He didn't try to put on airs or be the biggest person in the room. His moods were less manic. He and Allison got particularly close and had many visits. They would be some of her favourite times with him.

"He was real with me," she says. "He was just at peace … He wasn't on. He wasn't trying to entertain me. He wasn't trying to make anyone laugh. He was just being him. It was really nice to see that."

Craig also tended to his rectified relationship with Norma. Bringing Allison to see her became very important. Norma knew of Allison all of her life, but they had no real relationship before. Now, Craig wanted to change that. He wanted to make a family connection, give Allison a new grandmother, and show his mother that he had done something — parenthood — she would have wanted for his life.

Their meeting was a memorable day. Craig had Lori's father, Eddie Jenkins, drive them out to Port Perry via limousine for the visit. It was less that Craig wanted to look like the successful movie star he once aspired to be and more that he wanted the visit to be memorable and special for Allison. He wanted star treatment for his daughter.

"It was striking that it was important to him," Allison says. "It was grounding for him a little bit and realizing that his time was coming close to an end really soon … He had all this unfinished stuff."

With those relationships tended to, Craig also had a new boyfriend. Few remember Robert. Craig didn't say much about him but he did introduce him to a few people, including Lori and Gene Mascardelli. The best they could say about him was that he was young, good-looking, and a positive distraction. Robert seemed to care for Craig, too.

But at the heart of it, Gene thought Robert was a fuck-up and wondered if Robert was another leech of Craig's celebrity. Lori, too, didn't feel comfortable and wouldn't acknowledge Robert as more than a friend. But she didn't say anything or scoff when he was at their apartment. Why try to take something else away from Craig? Did it really matter anymore? They might as well let him have some companionship.

Few other friends were around; most didn't know Craig had AIDS. They were either out of touch or couldn't get to him if they tried. That was because Gene took it upon himself to limit contact with some of the people from Craig's past. He wanted to keep Craig's old hangers-on at bay and only allow access to the people he knew had Craig's best interests at heart. He didn't want anyone else to use him or upset him.

The few who did get through to Craig uplifted him greatly. One was a man named John Henry Broad, an old friend from his Mae West Fan Club days. Another was Ian Craig McKinnon, a Toronto musician and drag queen who performed on the Gay Village scene under the name Miss Goodwill. Craig's eyes would well with happy tears when someone wanted to talk about better days and the good times. He genuinely appreciated anyone who still wanted to know him at all.

Holding on to hope that Craig's career would swing back into action and all would be well, Gene also continued working on two projects for him. One was an "existential biopic" — a deconstruction of his characters meant to examine "how much of Craig is an act and how much is his personal psyche" — called *Craig Russell: The Portrait of an Artist in the Extreme*. The other was a variety special that Craig would headline with music from musician Jackie Rae.

It was all starting to come together, and in preparation, Craig and Gene got in the habit of getting together once or twice a week. Gene would pick Craig up and they'd share long, thoughtful talks on the drive to a studio where they would meet a designer and Craig could see the wardrobe being prepared for him. He'd try on all of the materials — gowns, wigs, boas, makeup, shoes, jewellery — once staples of his daily life. It was all a reminder of his past and a new-found opportunity for transformation he didn't think he'd get to have again. Each fitting was like magic.

"The moment he put these costumes on, he came alive," Gene says. "There was always something for him to look forward to."

Gene came to see Craig differently. He was no longer the star, the outrageous misfit who Gene once said was so impossible it was like "trying to manage air." He now saw Craig as "a very brave, practical, down-to-earth guy."

Craig Russell was at last being Craig Eadie, a separation that had been such a struggle for him over the last twenty years. It was bittersweet. His time was running out.

Just after Thanksgiving, he was hospitalized with a double pneumonia. He almost died but, with his strength buoyed by support from Lori and a few sips of contraband rum she snuck in to his hospital room, Craig ripped out his IV, defied doctor's orders, and went home. Their attitude seemed to be "to hell with the sick-and-dying nonsense" — Craig had living to do. A holiday was coming up. It wasn't possible to properly celebrate Halloween from a hospital bed.

Craig called Gene to ask if he could borrow an outfit from his wife, Gloria Martin, so he could go out for the holiday in style. Gene was getting ready for a business trip when he called and had a flight to catch, so the conversation ended quickly and was almost forgettable. They agreed to talk in a few weeks.

It was the last time they spoke.

Craig never saw Halloween 1990.

Late in the morning on October 30, Craig was in his bathroom shaving and trying to pull himself together to prepare for the day when he collapsed. He had wasted away to a thin frame and weighed all of one hundred pounds. He was weak and exhausted, void of energy, and gravely ill. Now his body had failed him; he could not get back up.

Craig's fall was loud enough to get Lori's attention in the next room. Alarmed, she ran to him and found him naked, desperately trying to get up from the cold floor.

"Go away," he yelled at her. "I don't want you to see me like this!"

Lori watched in horror as Craig collapsed again and briefly lost consciousness. Recalling her years working with Myra, she knew she had to wake him, get him upright, count his heart rate, and check his breathing. She sprang into action, but despite all the strength and energy she had for her last patient, she found herself unable to move her husband an inch.

She was losing him. That depleted all her energy. She was as defeated as he was.

Lori rocked Craig in her arms and cried until he came to. Carefully and painstakingly, he then got himself into a crawling position, moved across the floor, and pulled himself up into his bed. His face and limbs were numb, his vision blurred, and his breathing laboured. He tried to speak but couldn't and looked to Lori for help. His eyes lit up in horror and fear.

Lori told him to blink twice if he wanted to go to hospital. It was a trick she learned from her time with Myra. Craig blinked twice.

Robert arrived at the apartment at the same time as the ambulance, and together they went to Toronto Western Hospital. As doctors and nurses went to work on Craig, Robert and Lori tried to figure out what to do. Robert notified Norma, who was away in Florida with her husband, Eric, and Lori cancelled Craig's plans for the afternoon.

They didn't think to call anyone else. Craig had made so many hospital visits in recent months that the gravity of the situation didn't seem clear. He was always able to rebound. No one considered that it might be time to say goodbye.

Lori was still due at work, so thinking that Craig was in good hands at the hospital, she told herself the show must go on and headed to the Pantages. Hours later she was backstage on a break when a doctor from Toronto Western reached her by phone to give her an update on Craig's condition.

It was crushing news.

Craig had had a devastating stroke. He had irreversible brain damage, and if they tried to fix one thing, something else might give out. He was not going to recover.

Questions followed. Should Craig go on life support? Should they resuscitate him if his heart stopped? End-of-life care decisions had to be made.

As his legal wife, it fell to Lori to decide the next steps. The choice was clear. Craig had told her he didn't want life support when his time came. The lifelong entertainer didn't want to make a scene of it. There was no need for vigils, no need to call in the masses. Craig wanted to be let go, quietly.

As much as she didn't want to lose him, she didn't fight him on that decision. So right there in the middle of a theatre, a place where she always found comfort, Lori granted permission to allow her husband to die.

"You do realize, of course, that with just oxygen he may not make it through the night," the doctor said.

Lori quietly acknowledged that she understood, in her usual faint voice that sounded more like a scared whisper.

"Just make him as comfortable as possible," she said.

Then she went back to the show, shutting off the emotions that came with the phone call she just had. She didn't get to Toronto Western until just before midnight. She arrived a little later than she might have, but she stopped at home to walk Baby Mae. Craig would have wanted that.

As she approached his room, a nurse told Lori she was just in time. Craig was slipping away. He only had a few moments left to live.

With fifteen years of love and adoration for Russell Craig Eadie behind her, Lori walked into his room to be with him as he died. So much had happened since they met. She was just an adoring and loving groupie then, moved to tears by a casual invitation to share a drink and a record. It was remarkable where that led. They put on heralded performances in some of the grandest venues across the world, met entertainers and artists, went to countless parties, and made a splash everywhere they went.

They also navigated a murky relationship. Craig did not love Lori as she loved him, and he was never totally able to find a dynamic with healthy boundaries that he wanted. He made honest attempts to get through to her, and when that didn't work, he was mean and cruel both to her and when he talked about her. But even those tactics were in vain. Lori wasn't going anywhere. He appreciated her, though, was grateful for her generosity, and acknowledged how much she had done for him. He found it comforting that Lori never wavered while so many of his relationships became alienated by his outrageous ways.

Craig and Lori's dynamic provided mutual strength. She was forever his No. 1 fan, an unfailing supporter no matter what ambivalence he threw at her, and an apologist who cleaned up complicated situations of his doing. That propped him up and kept him going. For Lori, being his wife guided most, if not all, of her life choices. He was her sense of purpose, a place where she fit when she otherwise felt misplaced, and her mentor in her life's work that she had only recently embraced. Standing up to him and for him made her strong when the traumas of her early life gave her every reason to be weak.

Craig and Lori shared a unique bond even though they had been apart for the majority of their married years. But now in these final moments, they were together. That was some justification for Lori. She wouldn't be backstage for this final bow. She wouldn't be cast aside. Fate gave her this moment. She wanted to say so much to Craig, but as she wrote years later, the lump in her throat wouldn't allow it. They stayed in silence.

Lori placed Craig's hands across his body and held them well into the night, long after he took his last breath and slipped away forever.

Craig was forty-two years old.

The day after Craig died, Lori went back to work.

What else could she do? She was never one for self-pity, and the theatre was always a place where she sought refuge. It was a place where imagination stirred, where dreams were found, where magic happened. It was a place she went to for joy and entertainment when her spirits were high, and a place for distraction and escape when she was caught in turmoil. Now the theatre was the place Lori went to grieve.

On her first day as a widow she worked through two performances of *Phantom of the Opera.* She wrote later that she felt lost, but she was determined to go for her love of Craig and her love of theatre. She told only a handful of people what had happened the night before. A few co-workers extended their condolences and hugs, but Lori did her best to rebuff the attention. She wanted her news to be private for now.

But outside of the theatre doors, Craig's death was making headlines across the world. It was in newspapers and magazines, on television and the radio; "a worthy news item" that MuchMusic VJ Kim Clarke Champniss said was about someone who was "a pioneer not just of gay culture, but of popular culture."

It was estimated that more than five thousand Canadians had AIDS in the early 1990s, and while Craig never made a public statement like actor Rock Hudson in the U.S. or rocker Freddie Mercury in the U.K., Craig was one of the first Canadian entertainers who had been open about his AIDS diagnosis. Now he was the biggest name in Canada to be lost to the horrible, raging epidemic.

The media didn't really pick up on that fact, though. His death so close to Halloween was a softer news hook.

"It's somehow appropriate that Craig Russell should die on Halloween eve," friend and columnist Rita Zekas wrote in the *Toronto Star* obituary.

"Every night was Halloween for Canada's best-known female impersonator. It was his favourite holiday."

Allison agrees that the date of his death seemed incredibly fitting, but she was too devastated to romanticize the timing when she got the news. She wasn't ready for the loss of the father she had only recently started getting to know. Another part of her grief was that she didn't get to say goodbye. No one told her or her mother, Helen Phillips, about his hospitalization that last day. Helen had only heard he died when she was out shopping and the news came on the radio.

Old pal Shirley Flavell was also surprised by the news. Craig reached out to her in the last year, but he didn't say how ill he was or how little time he had left. While their relationship wasn't as damaged as his had been with Margaret, his life as a star did fray their closeness. While bereaved, she thought his death at an early age was almost something he would have wanted for himself.

"I always felt that he fell in love with the idea that you die for your art, like Garland, Monroe, that sort of thing," she says. "You weren't supposed to live to a ripe old age … With great talent comes great pain."

Shirley sees Craig as equally legendary to such historical figures. He lived life on his own terms and got further than anyone could have anticipated. He did it by being himself and doing what he wanted to do, no matter what the gender, sexual, or entertainment norms were.

"He was someone who opened a door that hadn't been open before.… It wasn't going to be easy but he wasn't going to deny who he was."

Trying to write the endnote about who the real Craig was certainly is complicated. To those in the land of entertainment, he was an outrageous star who went from being a groundbreaking artist — a talented singer, actor, comedian, host, and impressionist — to an offensive character who went too far and didn't belong in the limelight. To those closest to him, Craig was immensely talented and hard-working, but he was also deeply sensitive, vulnerable, and troubled, rejected by key figures he needed to love him in a world that could be cruel to anyone different. There were other factors not discussed. He was a man caught in the grip of a mental health issue, alcohol abuse, and drug dependency. No one freely talked about those topics.

How do you summarize such a life? Journalist Michael Valpy perhaps put it best.

"The story of Craig Russell — as he was known professionally — was a fable for the lost, the fragile, and the misfits of an unkind world, a black legend of the impersonal metropolis," Valpy wrote in the *Globe and Mail* a week after Craig died. "He was one of Canada's more gifted entertainers, all but unhonoured for his talent…. Mr. Russell was a female impersonator known for his brilliant portraits of Judy Garland, Carol Channing, Tina Turner and, above all, his heroine, Mae West. He also was known for his self-destructiveness, his abuse of alcohol and drugs, his moods that swung from black and savage depths — more often than not with himself the target — to kindness, warmth and generosity."

It's not clear how Craig looked back on it all. As he once told a German magazine, he achieved his dreams. He became an impressionist as he wanted and performed tributes to artists he loved. He was a respected entertainer, at least for a time, and sold out venues to adoring crowds. He strived to be seen as an artist. He was a bona fide star as he always wanted. Deeper in his heart and soul, Craig had come to realize that stardom does not nurture or fulfill. He wanted and needed love, acceptance, understanding, and respect. He did have those things, but a mental illness he could not explain or understand robbed him of feeling them.

A letter written by a friend and sent to Norma in the days after Craig's death is a telling document.

"I am glad that [Craig] gave me the opportunity to know him for a few weeks," it reads. "I admired his tremendous talent … but recognized his vulnerability when he was at home. It took so much out of him to perform — to prepare to perform — to 'get up' to being outrageous — but it certainly took its toll for getting down to ordinary living."

The words of the letter would have been a fitting eulogy for Craig. They certainly were more fitting than the tribute at his actual funeral.

Craig was cremated and his funeral was held at Harold J. Wagg Funeral Home in Port Perry. Norma made all of the arrangements. It was her turn to take care of him her way after years surrendering him to the world. She accepted some help from her brother, Howard, Craig's uncle. It fell to Howard to manage a tight guest list and turn people away at the door. They wanted to be sure there was, in Howard's words, "no nonsense."

More than a hundred relatives and friends came to pay their respects. Allison, then just seventeen, was there with her mother, Helen. Craig's aunts, uncles, and cousins on the Hall side were there, as were Lori's siblings, Paul, Dena, and Marc. Margaret put aside her anger and came from Toronto. She signed the guest book "Dolly," the name she used in her short story "Golden Boy." Shirley and Phil were with her. The "Four Musketeers" were now three.

There was a little colour in the crowd, including drag queens Rusty Ryan and Jackie Loren, female impersonator Murray Cooper, director Dick Benner, actress Dinah Christie, model agent Judy Welch, and performer Ian Craig McKinnon. Derek Stenhouse and Rene Fortier, the couple who ran the now defunct Club Manatee where Craig got his start performing in Canada, were there, as was Kim Clarke Champniss with a MuchMusic news crew.

There couldn't have been much to report. It was a short service with a minister. His cousin sang a song. The whole affair was simple and understated. Not everyone was comforted or pleased by that.

"The funeral was a sham," says Gloria Martin. "It was bizarre because here was this outrageous, bigger-than-life character and they are having like a normal funeral, with a little picture of Craig, his ashes and a priest who knew nothing about Craig saying a few words that were totally irrelevant."

The funeral was simple and traditional, something Norma wanted, but nothing like Craig at all. There was little comfort for many people there.

"Craig would have hated it," Gloria laments almost thirty years later. "It was just so bizarre."

Allison, too, thought the funeral was on the traditional side for someone who was anything but. Still, she accepted that the service was according to Norma's wishes, and Norma was, after all, footing the $2,500 bill. Craig had no money left.

"It wasn't a splashy Hollywood affair," she says. "It was the funeral his family wanted."

Allison had bigger questions than the funeral program that day. Part of her was angry. She was in a room full of people who loved Craig and were bereaved by his death, but she couldn't help but wonder what any of them did to help him quit drugs, stop drinking, or find mental health support when he was alive. There were no answers.

Craig's burial and resting place were equally understated. He was buried on a rainy day just outside Port Perry in a small cemetery. It is off the beaten path and hard to find for someone not from the area, a world away from the stages where he lived and thrived.

Eight years before he died, a *Toronto Star* comedy writer asked Craig what he'd want his gravestone to say. Surmising he'd die in 2001, Craig wrote that his epitaph should read: "Here lies Craig Russell, Who finally got laid with the rest of them."

The idea was of course in jest. Instead, Craig has a simple marker set in grey granite. It would later be shared with Lori, Norma, and her husband, Eric.

Craig's grave is fitting though. It is in a plot shared with his beloved grandmother, Bessie Hall, who had died in 1984. It went unspoken, but one could say that Bessie's gifts of earrings when he was five and music lessons when he was nine, his grandmother had set him on his path to the stars. Now it was as if he returned to her.

"He was an incredible spirit and one of the bravest people I ever met," Gene told Rita Zekas for the *Toronto Star* obituary. "I got the sense that he wasn't sad to die, it was the living he had trouble with."

With Craig laid to rest, Lori headed back to Toronto and geared up for the evening performance of *Phantom of the Opera*.

Word had gotten out about Craig's death, but, for the most part, people left her alone. Not everyone was clear on their relationship or understood that Lori saw herself as Craig's widow. That was fine by her. She was so private, after all.

Still, she could not escape some attention. Before the show began, she was summoned to singer Colm Wilkinson's dressing room. He wanted to share his condolences. He didn't really know Lori and he didn't know Craig, but Colm thought it important to tell her he had recently lost a close friend and former dresser to AIDS. He could understand the pain of losing someone so close.

It was a thoughtful gesture. Lori took his words to heart and thanked him. They even shed a few tears together, something Lori did not like to do in the company of others. But it wasn't until later in the show when Colm's words truly spoke to her.

Colm played the Phantom in the production at that time. In the classic tale, the Phantom is a social outcast totally infatuated with Christine, the emerging star of the opera. Phantom rebuffs social convention and pursues her. He not only loves her, he is driven to help her and others to see her gifts. He wants the world to hear her.

In one of the more dramatic moments of the elaborate production, the Phantom sings "The Music of the Night," a powerful ballad of seduction and desire. He sings it to Christine after coaxing her to be with him. While they at last have time together, there is a tinge of pain in his singing. He knows being with her will not last.

Later, in the final moments of the performance, the Phantom realizes he cannot force Christine to love him in return and releases her to the arms of her true love. He is alone again. The Phantom then sings abridged lyrics from "The Music of the Night," and instead of delivering the ballad with passion and love, he sings with powerful heart-wrenching defeat, slowly and carefully, as he is cast aside, alone forever.

"It's over now, the music of the night," the Phantom sings, bellowing out the final note for more than a minute in an intense emotional expression of grief and pain.

It is a poignant moment as the show ends.

Listening from backstage, Lori wept.

CHAPTER FIFTEEN

COURAGE, MADAME

After Craig died, Lori carried on as privately as she could and threw herself into work. It was her way of hiding her incredible pain.

She continued as a dresser for *The Phantom of the Opera* at the Pantages Theatre for the next two years. The show was very well received and continuously extended so her job was secure. She joined the International Alliance of Theatrical Stage Employees (IATSE) Local 822, a union for stage workers, and continued taking classes in mask making. She implied she was interested in picking it up as a trade, but when those plans fell through, she internalized her disappointment just as she had done with the other feelings in her mind and heart.

No one knew, but Lori was in great turmoil through the first few years with Craig gone. Her devotion to him had guided her life, and without him she was adrift. Her position was much like Craig's with his ladies — she had been so consumed by a character she loved that she did not nurture herself as a person. Without him she was lost.

"I've never seen someone so doggedly devoted in every way shape and form," says Miriam Goldberger, the wife of Lori's brother Paul. "It was her entire identity."

Few thought to consider how Lori was coping after Craig died. Not everyone understood that Lori saw herself as a devoted wife who'd just lost the love of her life. She always seemed to be solo when Craig was alive, and he had said so casually that they were just legal friends. They didn't even live together for most of their marriage. Lori didn't fit the standard picture of a grieving widow.

Losing Craig was traumatic and, while she might have needed it, Lori took no time off and sought neither professional help nor the support of friends. She didn't think to, know how to, or even identify that she needed to. That's not the way she was. Years earlier, she had turned off the switch in her mind for pain. That shutdown had lasted all this time.

All Lori knew was to compartmentalize her feelings and keep working. On workdays, she'd get to the theatre in late afternoon, work the show, head to a bar when it was over, and sleep all day before starting again. In her off time she was devoted to Baby Mae, and she took herself out to lunch downtown. She told people she loved to go to the beach to soak up the rays — she said she was a "sun worshipper" — but, curiously, she never seemed to have a tan.

While usually alone and on her own, there were some good times with her dad, Eddie Jenkins, and siblings. Her brother Paul and sister, Dena, had children by then, and she had a soft spot for her nieces and nephews. Rather than being a daily figure in their lives, though, she was more of a gifts-on-the-holidays kind of aunt, the last to arrive at and first to leave the party. When she was around, her behaviour was sometimes a little odd, in a humorous way.

Dena remembers an afternoon when she pulled everyone together for a casual family picnic near their dad's apartment. Instead of the usual sandwiches-and-chips fare for such an occasion, Lori brought crackers and caviar. Paul and Miriam remember how she'd call up their family with an out-of-the-blue offer for free tickets to the latest show she was working on. She spoke in her usual whisper so quietly you'd have to strain to hear her.

Lori also called Craig's mom, the Hall family, and their friends with offers of tickets. She even gave some of them backstage tours. She went to the family cottage several times and often made appearances at the annual family party around the holidays. She sometimes would bring a friend with her, only vaguely introducing them and explaining their role in her life.

Occasionally, Lori met up with her mother, Hazel. She took her mother at face value and paid no mind to how Hazel was usually terse and indifferent to her. She did not seem to harbour resentment about how Hazel treated her either now or when she was a child. In fact, Lori recorded in her financial records that she sometimes paid the $500 rent on her mother's apartment.

She didn't tell anyone about that, or about much else. Lori kept most of her family and friend relationships private. Everyone was fragmented; few of her friends knew of any other relationships she had. The people in her life did not cross paths. Just as family members believed she was a loner when she actually had many friends, most of her friends assumed she didn't have a close family. Some thought she was an orphan. It was an impression she was aware of but did not correct.

"She would focus on other people so much, ask you questions, buy you drinks, support you," says her niece Nora Jenkins. "[It was] almost so you wouldn't ask her about her."

That even included her siblings at times. She spoke to her brother Paul the least, but the two of them made a point to get together about once a year, usually for dinner. Paul knew little about his sister's life. He wasn't invited to her home and knew little about what work she had, and based on how she presented herself, he assumed she was broke. He slipped her money sometimes to help her get by. Years later he found out she was working a lot and making a pretty good wage most of the time.

Lori accepted his monetary offers, anyway. It was true she had a good salary, but she was living paycheque to paycheque because of her choice to spend everything she had on the people around her. Her generosity knew no bounds. She gave elaborate gifts to anyone who was kind to her, bought rounds of drinks for co-workers and strangers, and would slip more than a few quarters to someone begging on the street. Lori lived poorly — in small apartments with no extravagances, no investments or savings — but to others she gave with the hand of someone wealthy.

One person who benefited from Lori's generosity was a woman named Sandy. The details about her are vague. She was older than Lori and quite masculine. Family and friends believed they were girlfriends, but Lori never said so. She still did not label her sexual identity and did not identify Sandy as her significant other. She did not share any details about Sandy, who no doubt meant a lot to her. No one even knew Sandy's last name. She just started coming along one day, and attended several Jenkins and Hall family events.

Lori didn't express it to others, but her actions demonstrated that she loved Sandy. They had a long-distance relationship and took turns travelling between Toronto where Lori lived, and northern Ontario where Sandy was based. Lori was unfailingly generous to her and supported her daily life just as she had with Craig. She gave Sandy an expensive radio and posters from ballets, and she covered everyday expenses like her cigarettes, magazines, and parking.

Dena thought Sandy was almost like a mother figure to Lori. Sandy was nurturing and supportive, more than Hazel ever had been. Lori would come to depend on that when her father, Eddie, died suddenly in 1992. She grieved that loss more outwardly than she had for Craig and turned to Sandy for support.

Part of Sandy would always be kept at a distance, though. Craig still held a large part of Lori's heart, more than Sandy ever could. After Lori's father died, Lori took time off work to live with Sandy up north. Her motivation was to have the time to start writing a memoir about her life with her husband. She was very proud of her manuscript — she called it *What a Drag!* — and made multiple copies of the final product to give to family, friends, and co-workers.

The front page of her manuscript made one point very clear. Lori Russell Eadie was "Mrs. Craig Russell." Lori still identified as his wife and in that role she did everything she could to remember and represent him. She paid for in memoriam ads that ran in the newspaper, had flowers delivered to his grave, and attended several benefits in Craig's name in the Gay Village.

Friend Mark Stenabaugh met Lori through the bar Sneakers, where he worked as a manager. He says Lori frequented there before and after work, and when she met anyone new, she always made a point to mention her marriage. She was quick with an offer of a drink on her, but there was one caveat: the offer was only good if the person accepting it chose her husband's favourite cocktail. She talked about him so much everyone at the bar joked "as long as Lori is around, Craig will never be dead."

Lori was in and out of the theatre scene, too, except her role now was less as a patron and more as a representative of a veteran who'd been through it. She always introduced herself to the talent she saw, and just as she did with strangers, she made a point to mention Craig and their marriage. Impressionist Christopher Peterson remembers her approaching him late one night in an alley behind the gay bar Trax on Yonge Street. They had not met before and out of nowhere there was Lori with a greeting and a purpose.

"I am Lori Russell Eadie, Craig Russell's wife, and I want you to have this," she said quietly, handing him a ring she said had belonged to Craig.

Christopher was stunned. He didn't really know Craig and knew even less about his wife. He thought she was strange, maybe even crazy. Lori slipped away into the night without another word of conversation, never to introduce herself again. She also did that to actor Thom Allison, who was playing Craig's role of Robin in a production of *Outrageous!* at Toronto's Berkeley Street Theatre. She gave him a sequined top Craig had worn when performing as Judy Garland.

The private Lori also granted numerous interviews. While her current personal life was off limits to family and friends, her life with Craig was open for the taking. She gave several interviews for newspapers and magazines and, despite her discomfort with attention, stepped out of the shadows to appear on the CBC program *Life & Times* in an episode called "Russell Craig Eadie: The King of Queens."

"We had a real marriage. I think he saw in me [that] my adoration for him is what he felt towards Mae West," she said in the interview, elaborating about how it wasn't always easy. "A lot of the times the characters did take him over, and so he actually became these people. And sometimes these people were difficult because he became them and lost himself."

Lori was dressed to the nines for her appearance, filmed at Harbourfront with Baby Mae lovingly perched next to her and a picturesque city scene behind them. She wore a white blouse and black slacks, with her hair and makeup done to look very femme and affluent, even glamorous. It was not her style at all, but Lori wanted to make a statement. She was the wife of a successful movie star.

Steven Marks, in character as Madame Outrageous, with Toronto city councillor Pam McConnell at a Toronto Pride parade.

"Everything about Craig was so important to her," Miriam Goldberger says. "She did everything in her power to celebrate everything that he was and ultimately wasn't."

But sometimes Lori did not have power, and she felt it. She spoke about having struggles with an associate of Craig's who claimed, she said, to have legal rights and blocked her from trying to put together a tribute to Craig. She was set on the idea and even visited local TV studios in search of tapes from their archives, but the project went nowhere.

She later sparred with a man named Steven Marks, a drag queen who performed under the name Madame Outrageous. He was active on the scene for a few years and, as the founder and president of the Craig Russell Fan Club, hosted a handful of benefit shows to raise money for charity, including Princess Margaret Hospital.

Steven says it was Craig who gave him the push to go into drag.

"Craig made it possible to be taken serious as an entertainer," he says now, over thirty years later. "[He] wanted me to be his protege, but I insisted I couldn't do what Craig Russell could do. Craig was the best you could get."

Instead, Steven says he chose to honour Craig in drag through name and fan club "to keep his name alive." He built his own Madame Outrageous persona and brand, did impressions of everyone from Barbra Streisand to Barbara Eden, and for a touch of class, was known for arriving to events in the back of posh luxury vehicles. He spoke openly about his position as founder of the Craig Russell Fan Club, attended a handful of Pride parades behind a Craig Russell banner, and gave out community achievement awards in Craig's name at benefit events, recognizing Gay Village community members and allies from every corner of the city.

Steven's intentions were good, and he had a lot of local support and friendships, including powerful Toronto women like city councillor-turned-mayor Barbara Hall, school-trustee-turned-councillor Pam McConnell, and social justice activist June Callwood. He also grew close with the biggest queens of the day, many of which Craig knew, including Michelle DuBarry, Rusty Ryan, Sacha MacKenzie, and Miss Goodwill. He has folders of records and pictures that document all of his efforts, and in between the pages, his adoration of Craig is apparent.

Despite that support and his intentions, Lori was threatened by Steven. His public stature and easy confidence made it seem like he was in the driver's seat of Craig's legacy, not she, and as he motored along with shows and charity work, she felt a complete lack of any kind of control. Making matters worse for her, Steven also shared unflattering stories of alleged run-ins with Craig when he was alive.

"[Craig] was nuts," Steven told writer Paul Bellini for an article published in *Fab* magazine. "We'd find him in the washroom blowing some guy fifteen minutes before a show. Then there were the phone calls at two in the morning, just babbling into an answering machine ... He was always taking aspirins and Ex-Lax to keep his figure."

Saying things like that would be very upsetting to Lori. On one hand, Craig was her husband, and she wanted the narrative of his life to be respectful. On the other hand, Lori was fighting for her place in Craig's life and legacy, and she wanted some control. She had already fought for her place when he was alive. Did she have to fight now?

She may have fought harder for this than she ever did for herself. Steven says she slapped him with a cease-and-desist letter not once, but twice. To calm things down, he invited her to join the fan club board of directors. She accepted and posed proudly for a photo with other members at one of their meetings.

Lori's tension eased with time. Craig faded from public consciousness, public interest waned, and the media mentioned him less frequently. Very few projects about his work ever came to light, and Lori fell out of touch with people who had known him.

Even Steven faded from the local scene. He stepped away from the Gay Village spotlight and built a quiet life with his partner outside of the city, working out of drag in community service. He still maintains a Madame Outrageous website and has performed in character at special events and parties.

"It doesn't matter where you are, people want to see a female impersonator," he says.

In between that conflict in her mind, Lori quietly went about her life backstage as a dresser in some of the grandest theatre productions in Toronto. The theatre scene in Toronto was booming over the decade thanks to productions brought in by entertainment moguls Ed Mirvish and Garth Drabinsky. Lori rode the wave of opportunities that came with it.

Much of her work was in Mirvish theatres, but she also spent time at the Hummingbird Centre (formerly the O'Keefe Centre), the Four Seasons Centre for the Performing Arts, and Ford Centre for the Performing Arts. She worked on *Crazy for You*, *Sunset Boulevard*, *Les Misérables*, *A Chorus Line*, *Beauty and the Beast*, *Jane Eyre*, and *The Nutcracker*, among many others. Along the way, she moved up the ranks and worked with some of Canada's biggest stars. One of her favourite assignments was working with legendary prima ballerina Karen Kain — "elegance personified," Lori said — in a National Ballet of Canada production of *The Taming of the Shrew*.

Lori identified as a dresser, more commonly known as a wardrobe attendant or wardrobe assistant. It was her job to care for, maintain, and restore all elements of a production's costumes. Her work before the curtain went up included washing and steam-cleaning the costumes, as well as mending, sewing, labelling, hanging, organizing, and storing them. During the show she'd work with one or numerous performers at a time, staying ready to dress them and assist with costume changes between scenes, and ensuring every detail of their transformation was in place, from their gowns and suits to their shoes, undergarments, and personal props.

Productions usually have one or more wardrobe attendants per show who work in an intricate choreography backstage with the cast and crew. Successful attendants are resilient, physically fit, and efficient under pressure, and they have a respect for theatre and the etiquette that comes with life behind the curtain.

It isn't all magic and wonderful, as Lori once believed. The schedule is gruelling. Some stage crew members work from 8:00 a.m. to 11:00 p.m. Dressers are prone to repetitive strains, physical injuries, and feelings of isolation as they work long hours in an insulated world away from family and friends. Some struggle psychologically as they deal with stress, pressure, and testy interpersonal dynamics with demanding stars and quirky co-workers.

"Dressers don't work in a bank because they can't," one of Lori's colleagues says. "They are all a little bit crazy."

The Princess of Wales Theatre is one of a handful of theatres in Toronto capable of housing large-scale productions. Inside there is a tingle of excitement in the air, even after a show. It is also overwhelming. Backstage is a maze of suites, dressing rooms, trap rooms, gondolas for supplies, road boxes for performers, props large and small, spools of rope and wires, and countertops covered with makeup and hair paraphernalia. Lists are posted with tape everywhere and tubes of lighting line the floor to guide where to walk.

Of all the rooms backstage, the laundry room is a central hub. It is a gathering space. Most of the production's costumes move through this room, where they are cleaned, tailored, sewn, and repaired. Countless containers of thread, buttons, beads, sequins, and needles line the tables, and multiple sewing machines buzz with activity while the clocks tick down to showtime.

"Open-ended" or "sit-down" productions last for a long time, even years. Others come to town as part of a road tour and stay for as little as a few weeks. Wardrobe attendants like Lori are brought in through the IATSE union, assigned by seniority, and given "track notes" that outline the cast, who they are working with, what their scenes are, their costumes and props, what presets need to be done before scenes, where to be, and what to do when.

Lori's days could start around lunchtime up to thirty minutes before showtime. She was never on time. Colleagues say she was perpetually early or obnoxiously late. She'd take her track sheet and a daily list with updates on what to expect and head to a dressing room, backstage corral, or side stage area to ready everything and ensure she could work quickly and efficiently to keep the show going and the performer happy. She sometimes went the extra mile and did someone else's work, even if she didn't really know exactly what was needed. She was disciplined for that at least once, but it didn't stop her.

Lori was notorious for her fanny pack, a black three-section purse she fashioned with a strap to keep it around her waist. In it she kept sewing supplies, scissors, bobby pins, a notepad, a multi-purpose tool called a Leatherman, medications from Aspirin to lozenges, lip balm, hand cream, tissues, markers, index cards, calling cards, and lighters — anything, in other words, that someone might need. She had needles already threaded in white and black at the ready so she could pull them out and quickly reattach a loose button if needed. She also had Krazy Glue and was known to use it to reapply a broken nail so she could keep on working.

Cast and crew all remember Lori's helpfulness in times of urgent need. She was the go-to girl, whether for supplies or to learn the ropes. Wardrobe assistant Sara Moodie remembers working with Lori on her first production. Sara says when she arrived, she felt totally unprepared for the demands of a production already well underway, and it was Lori who saved her. She showed Sara how to write out the track notes and personal reminders on index cards for each costume change to help her stay organized.

The trade is evolving and some attendants take a different approach to their job description, tailoring it to their skill set or union contracts. Some stick to wardrobe and have less interest in the needs of the performer they work with. Others act more like the performer's personal assistant, making themselves available not just for wardrobe but for private needs that extend from getting a cup of tea to personal shopping.

Lori saw herself more as a personal assistant to the performers. Her approach was natural, given her admiration for and occasional fandom of them. She questioned nothing when she saw the opportunity to go the extra mile, including running errands outside the theatre, or as she did once, sewing up holes in a couch in a cast member's dressing room. She was kind, thoughtful, and hard-working; a "pleaser of the highest order" with a "weird, crazy, strong independent strength." Even Lori recognized her own value. She proudly told Paul that some entertainers coming to town for a production would request her by name.

"She felt she had made it," former teacher and friend Ian Waldron remembers. "And she made you feel like you shared in that glory."

Most also thought Lori was eccentric, from her soft-spoken and quiet demeanour to her "obsessively attentive" nature — she carried a Ziploc bag to pick up and save feathers, sequins, beads, and broken buttons that fell off costumes. She even kept some discarded props, including sheets of paper and grass from a set that had been used in an outdoor scene. It was a habit she continued for years that evolved into compulsive hoarding. Her apartment was so full she couldn't sleep in her own bed much of the time. It was covered with stuff.

More than a few people wondered what she was doing and why. Some describe her as "compelling and fascinating," but others were put off by her behaviour paired with her additional habit of gift giving, and they questioned her motivations. There were gifts for birthdays and anniversaries, to celebrate the beginning and end of a show, to cheer someone up on a bad day, or for no reason at all. Lori gave more than one person a designer handbag or purse. She gave another person a hand-painted tile. She even offered some of her own personal effects, including a pair of cufflinks that belonged to her father.

Some whispered that she was "obsessed," "crazy," or a "stalker." Why else would she offer up these gifts? Everything about her was questioned. They saw her taking notes and writing, often backwards, setting off rumours of what she was planning with her observations. Was she writing love letters? Would she tell secrets? At least two performers from two different shows didn't click with her at all and demanded Lori be assigned elsewhere. That hurt Lori as did some of the rumours about her. Regardless, it never changed her choices.

Conflicts, clashes, and bullying were inevitable in their work environment, and Lori, with her misunderstood behaviour, naive nature, and obvious history of trauma, was an easy target for someone's ire. The gossip at times turned personal and some people were outright mean to her. One performer who didn't like her deliberately ignored her in the company of others.

Sara, who ended up working with Lori on several shows and saw how people treated her, likens it to "a pack mentality."

"It's the odd little quiet ones who get beat up," she says. "A lot of people were mean to her ... She took it more than she ever told someone to fuck off."

Grant Heaps, one of her supervisors at the National Ballet of Canada, observed this dynamic and tried to segregate Lori, assigning her tasks away from poisonous people. But when she couldn't avoid it, Lori took the mistreatment. One colleague astutely said she was "invisible if someone tried to make her so."

But Lori was getting stronger. She was able to be outwardly upset and talk about what bothered her at work with colleagues she trusted. She hadn't done that before. Speaking up was new for her and now, even in her midthirties, she was like a little doe learning to stand on her feet.

Sometimes she fell. On the day the Toronto Blue Jays won the World Series and parties raged downtown, Lori told her boss she couldn't come to work because she didn't feel safe navigating the overwhelming crowds to get there. The attempt to stand up for herself backfired. Colleagues say she was told not to bother coming back. It took some time before she was able to rebound and return to a lesser position at the production.

Lori's work was her life. Some of her most lasting memories were made when working for *The Phantom of the Opera*. She logged more than 1,100 performances on and off between 1989 and 1999. She spent ample time with her co-workers in wardrobe rooms, dressing rooms, and after-parties. Lori built trust with a select few and after years being so private, she shared broad, vague details about her past.

She talked about her marriage to Craig and described him as the love of her life. She said the years with him were sometimes hard and that she felt like she had abused alcohol to cope. She said she'd been in an accident in 1980, bitterly referenced "the Jew who ran me over," and reiterated that she didn't feel fairly compensated when the case was settled. She gave mixed details about her family — hardly anyone knew how many siblings she had, if any, and if she did reference Paul, Dena, or Marc directly, she wasn't always

Lori's essence captured perfectly in a photo taken by photographer and friend Nancy Paiva.

honest — but she was clear in saying she "didn't have a good childhood." She went a step further with one colleague in saying that her mother had "rejected her" because of her premature birth and the death of her brother Eric.

Colleagues observed that Lori reminisced more about her past than her present. She said little of her current life, her home, her side job, her hobbies, her friends, her lovers. She didn't talk about how she spent her days outside the theatre. She didn't introduce friends who came to visit her backstage or who appeared at parties. She did not complain of physical or emotional pain even if, as one colleague says now, "it was apparent she had trauma."

Lori was in control of the narrative of her life. People knew about topics and aspects she was willing to share and respected her boundaries on things she didn't speak about, despite their questions. Sometimes they were personal curiosities. Where did she live? Where was her second job? Was she a lesbian? Other times their questions reflected significant concerns, particularly about her health.

Lori looked increasingly tired, pale, gaunt, and unhealthy into the late 1990s and early 2000s, but given her private nature her colleagues had to arrive at their own conclusions. They thought she was working too hard, spending too much time at the theatre. She wasn't taking breaks. She wasn't stopping to eat. She was doing too much for others and not doing enough to take care of herself.

But Lori had another secret all that time.

She had cancer. She had been diagnosed with advanced melanoma.

Lori's cancer diagnosis seemed inevitable.

She had so many traumas, accidents, and ailments over the years that the writing was on the wall that something else would come up. Of course she would get a terminal illness. Her diagnosis just was what it was, even to Lori.

"I think she thought it was inevitable that bad things would happen to her," muses one family member. "Because [she thought] maybe she was less than others."

Her work had given her distraction — she had physical signs of melanoma for at least a year before she addressed it — but she could hide no longer. Cancer stopped everything. She was in a fight for her life. Melanomas are more commonly treated with minor excision procedures and sometimes reconstructive surgeries, but because Lori had ignored her symptoms, her cancer was aggressive. She was given an intense treatment plan that included rounds of chemotherapy so strong they knocked her off her feet.

Her family came together to support her. Because Lori had no income, no savings, and no benefits to sustain her, Dena covered Lori's shifts at her bartending job and passed along all of the earnings to keep a roof over her sister's head. Lori was grateful but had odd priorities. Dena remembers Lori, still sick and weak from chemo, visiting the bar to collect the pay

Dena had earned, only to turn around and cheer to patrons that the next round of drinks was on her.

Cancer did not stop her generosity. Colleague Bonita Ubell remembers the day she moved and how, despite Lori's delicate health and physical limitations, Lori showed up on Bonita's new doorstep on moving day ready to help. She hadn't asked to be there and didn't tell anyone she was coming. She just caught wind of Bonita's circumstances and took it upon herself to be available. Still the stage manager at heart, Lori grabbed a clipboard to manage the movers and set up Bonita's bedroom. She built a make-shift dresser with empty boxes, folded and organized clothes by colour, and placed a few candles on the bedside table.

After a few months, Lori gathered her strength and went back to work. She wanted things to be as normal as possible, so when more tumours developed and her treatment changed, she chose to deal with it largely by herself. Her doctors gave her daily chemical injections and a different drug mix she could self-administer at home. Along the way she figured out how to make herself comfortable — hot bubble baths with music and candles to relax, ice water in small bottles because they were easier to handle when she was weak, and plenty of Tylenol for the headaches caused by her medications.

She found ways to make it work on the job. She brought a small folding stool so she'd always have somewhere to sit when she got tired. She took hot showers on breaks to change bandages and clean drainage tubes from her treatments. She exited through the front door instead of the stage door at the back — against the rules — partly to limit climbing stairs and partly to demonstrate self-respect. That was something Craig taught her, she said.

Working took immeasurable strength. Her colleagues saw she had obvious physical limitations and challenges that made her function with a diminished capacity. No one really knew exactly why — she didn't give clear details about her accidents, exactly what kind of cancer she had, or what her treatment entailed — but it was clear she had discomfort. She "popped Tylenol like Tic Tacs," used a cane when the pain got too bad, and showed prying eyes her disfigured legs where tumours had been gouged out of her flesh.

Where theatre once gave her emotional salvation, it now kept her functional, putting one foot in front of the other. It made her feel vital and alive, no matter what state her cancer was in. She was particularly proud to

Lori proudly posed with a Lion King *cast member at a party between shows while on a rebound from her cancer.*

be part of the production of *The Lion King*. Pictures she kept from a cast party show her in her black stage garb (with bright red fingernails, true to her style to have a touch of colour), posing with cast members and looking proud as a peacock. She hadn't looked that way since photos were taken of her in the high school drama club at Riverdale. Her involvement in the production at the Princess of Wales Theatre was also a little bit of a family affair. Her brother Marc worked as a security guard at the stage door.

Another production she was proud to be a part of was the Mel Brooks hit *The Producers*. She was personal dresser for actor Michael Therriault, who played the lead character, Leo Bloom. She said he was "absolutely delightful" and was tickled when he won a Dora Mavor Moore Award for the part at the annual ceremony celebrating the best in Toronto theatre.

She was heartbroken when her cancer battle sidelined her work. She didn't want to leave that show.

CHAPTER SIXTEEN

WHAT'LL I DO

Cancer made Lori more reclusive.

After all of her years in theatres and spending all of her time out downtown, she spent more time at home than she ever had. She took to watching cooking shows and wanted to try her hand in the kitchen. She liked comfort foods — stews and casseroles, shepherd's pie, and chicken florentine — and began a journal with recipes from people like Giada De Laurentiis, Bobby Flay, Lynn Crawford, and Michael Smith.

Quite humorously, on the journal's first page she kept a list of Rachael Ray's basics for a productive kitchen: a plastic cutting board for meat; a bowl for scraps; a big pot for chili, soup, and stew; and "a good wooden spoon so [the] pot doesn't scratch." Years later, the pages of her recipe book are clean and new. She didn't get around to doing much cooking despite her thorough preparations.

She still took time to explore her theatre and film interests, but now from the comfort of home. She was a fan of the rock musical film *Hedwig and the Angry Inch*; followed the careers of actors Richard Chamberlain and Marcel Marceau; chipped away finessing her manuscript about her life with Craig; and took time to stitch her initials into her favourite leather jacket.

She was on her computer endlessly and used the internet to keep up with her favourite stars, making notes in her day planner when they were coming to town or appearing on TV.

Lori was a frequent user of email (she had at least two accounts) and instant messaging, and across the digital lines she was reintroduced to her high school pal Tom Veitch. They picked up where they had left off with tales of the old times and exchanges about musical theatre. She shared her deepest secrets with him. Tom knew all about her upbringing, sensitive details of her life with Craig, and some of her sexual tales, including a possible affair with a *Phantom* cast member.

There was room for love and lust in her life, too. Lori had her eye on someone new. That person was Carrie Chesnutt, a saxophonist and singer who plays often in the Gay Village and once had a standing gig at the popular bar Crews & Tangos. Carrie is exactly Lori's type: theatrical, expressive, and funny; and talented at her craft with a sense of sexuality and control in her delivery. She has a way of talking to strangers and making them feel like she values them, like they are the only people in the room.

Lori was first introduced to Carrie's music in the 1980s when she spent her wedding anniversary alone listening to Carrie play with singer Bonnie Meyer. She went to see Carrie regularly through the 1990s and approached her with the same gusto and tactics she had employed with Craig and Dorothy Poste. Lori often sat in the front row, gave Carrie roses, and slipped her "complimentary and a little romantic" notes, written backwards.

Carrie remembers Lori well. She knew Lori was infatuated with her, but intimate involvement was not on the table. They would never be lovers. The rejection never stopped Lori. She kept going anyway. Her attention shifted a bit later when she fell for guitarist Jeff Healey. Lori went to see him at numerous venues, had his albums and posters, and talked about him so much at least one co-worker thought they were dating. Lori told her niece she assertively cornered the blind rocker one night and gave him the most passionate kiss she could. She had no idea Jeff was happily married.

It was apparent to others that she had romantic interests in her life, some temporarily living with her and casually mentioned as "roommates." Yet just as she had done with Sandy, she did not share details and was guarded when questions were asked, even if the inquiries were genuine and supportive. At times Lori was feeling more sexually confident than she ever had. Friends remember her making a very obvious pass at a strikingly attractive woman she met at a party, not knowing the woman was heterosexual. The woman's surprised and uncomfortable reaction made an amusing anecdote but also begged the question: Would Lori ever find nurturing, lasting companionship?

No one could say if Lori was satisfied in love. She at least seemed happy in her friendships. She spent a good deal of time with Kevin Curriston, a friend she had made when he came to town to help a friend promote a book. Lori and Kevin formed a friendship alongside Dena, and Dena and Lori showed Kevin the sights, went out for dinner to numerous restaurants, and hosted him at a holiday dinner. They had such great times Lori said her cheeks ached from smiling. She didn't remember being that happy since she met Craig.

They met at Café DJ's, the bar where Lori bartended on the side. Not a lot of people knew she worked there, but it was nonetheless important to her. The bar was located in a rough neighbourhood between her apartment in Rosedale and the theatres of her career. It was rough around the edges, far from hip or trendy, but Lori paid no mind to such standards, befriended its patrons, and was always welcoming. The bar had a karaoke machine, and Lori treated its users with the same respect and enthusiasm she gave to professional entertainers.

Lori encountered a lot of people at the bar and in that neighbourhood as she commuted between home and work. Many lived in nearby halfway houses, some were homeless, and most were down on their luck. It became Lori's habit to buy things from them when offered, regardless of where the items originated or who was selling them. Her siblings later found numerous purses that were clearly new or lightly used, without sales tags, each typically stuffed with a newspaper or maybe a candy bar wrapper from whatever day it was purchased.

Lori never needed what she bought. She merely wanted to help somebody who was in a rough spot in life. Her purchases gave her things to use as gifts for others who were kind to her.

Lori's contact with family and friends grew to be sporadic. Her work schedule was partly to blame for that, but it was also her wish. It was as if she preferred diving in and out of the lives of many instead of being consistent in the lives of just a few.

Lori rarely saw Allison, even if she was the flesh and blood of the man she still so loved. Lori did, however, make a point every January to drop off gifts for Allison's birthday. She did the same for the birthday of Allison's first-born son, Declan, after he was born in 1994. She also reached out with offers of tickets to the latest show she was working on. She made little time for catching up in their brief contact. Lori had battled her cancer for several years before she told Allison a thing about it.

Many friends recount her tendency to pop up on their doorstep out of nowhere, recall running into her on a street corner while she was en route to a theatre somewhere (again with more offers of tickets), or express surprise at how she would attend a funeral for an old teacher, classmate, or extended friend when no one had heard from her for years.

"She would always pop up on my birthday," remembers her old Riverdale teacher Alex Bostock. "She was a drifter, there was no doubt about that ... She had the life she wanted as a totally unconventional person."

One event where Lori popped up was a public memorial for beloved Toronto businessman Honest Ed Mirvish, who died in July 2007. She had never met Ed, but she wanted to pay her respects after years working in his theatres. She was among thousands of people in the crowd that hot August day, and in typical Lori fashion, the event became an opportunity to make a new friend.

Photographer Nancy Paiva remembers it well. She worked in news and was assigned to cover the event. As the storm clouds gathered, Lori noticed Nancy working and adjusted her umbrella to cover Nancy's expensive camera equipment. The two of them fell into conversation and sensing warmness in each other, they went for coffee after the memorial was over.

In their brief association Lori shared things with uncharacteristic candour. She told Nancy all about her life with Craig, her work, her love of the sun, and her melanoma battle. The cancer started as a mole on her leg, she said. She now had multiple tumours in her legs, arms, torso, and lungs. Her doctor told her she had five years to live. That was a year ago.

It was a sad statement, alarming and horrifying all at once, but Lori said she wasn't worried. A psychic told her she would live until the ripe old age of ninety-four.

Terminally ill with less than a year to live, Lori found time to be carefree. Note her red fingernails, her signature style.

Lori was dying. The prognosis was clear and there was nothing she could do to change that. But it wasn't her nature to dwell on things. She had remained an excellent compartmentalizer when it came to her feelings. Increasingly spiritual, she believed what the psychic had told her. She didn't spend a day grieving the years she was losing. What did it matter? When she told Nancy her prognosis, she was simply enjoying spending time with a new friend, not worrying about what the future held. That was what mattered to Lori.

A few weeks later the two women met up again at BuskerFest, a festival for street performers and vendors in the St. Lawrence Market neighbourhood. They spent some time outside and made their way into the market when the day got too hot. Lori still must not have been worried about her longevity; she bought an old pine box to use as a coffee table that day. When Nancy admired a vintage umbrella with silver-plated handle, Lori bought it and gifted it to her.

Nancy snapped a few shots of Lori on their visits, including a touching colour photo of Lori blowing bubbles, relaxed and delighted in the simplicity of the moment. Another photo taken on a different day is in black and white. Lori is wearing a checkered shirt with popped collar and a sharp-looking Australian hat, her thinning brown hair flowing down her neck.

She looks as handsome as she does pretty. She has a few wrinkles around her slightly pursed lips as she holds back a full smile, but there is no hiding the sparkle in her eyes. This photo's subject has history, a story to tell. It captured her essence perfectly.

Lori turned fifty in September, and while she should have been out celebrating five decades lived on her own terms, much of her time was spent with her medical care. She had tumours everywhere. She was treated at Princess Margaret Hospital in Toronto and Roswell Park Comprehensive Cancer Center in Buffalo, both considered world leaders in cancer treatment. Her care included surgeries to remove tumours on her back and rib cage, chemotherapy and radiation, CT scans to monitor her progress, blood transfusions, and a pain management specialist to ease her incredible discomfort.

She had some scares. Her white blood cell counts were dangerously low, leaving her at serious risk for infection. She was anemic and had a fainting spell that resulted in an emergency run to hospital. One day an accident resulted in her nearly breaking multiple bones in her left hand, and she was left with a nasty contusion. Another day she said she was erroneously given a potentially lethal combination of drugs and her care team had to scramble to save her life.

Lori kept track of every appointment, treatment step, and mishap in a small day planner. She wrote down questions for her doctors and also for herself. Her words are simple, their meaning startlingly powerful.

"What should I be doing now," she wrote on January 10, 2008. "To live as long as I can."

Lori tried to keep working through it all. She was a dresser for the Canadian Opera Company production of *Tosca* at the Four Seasons Centre for the Performing Arts through February, and she worked a long week at the Sony Centre for the Performing Arts (formerly the O'Keefe Centre) leading up to the annual National Aboriginal Achievement Awards gala in March. She was gradually less able to work and attend functions as the weeks went by. After working one day of rehearsals for the opera *Eugene Onegin*, she could not go on.

"Last day of work officially," she wrote on March 15, 2008. "Boo hoo hoo!"

Things were looking rough. At one point she was admitted to hospital in such bad shape that a minister visited and began to administer last rites even though he'd not been asked. The innocent gesture angered Lori. She stood up to the man, insisted she was not ready to die yet, and demanded that he leave. Somehow, after a lifetime of submission, Lori found the strength to stand up for herself, even in the crippling pain of cancer.

She told Tom all about it. They had frequent contact by computer and phone, and made time for a few visits in the city when Tom could come in from his home in Peterborough, Ontario. He sent Lori CDs with music from the productions she'd worked on to lift her spirits. She loved that.

Her siblings did everything they could to help out. They drove her between her apartment, hospitals, and bus stations, and went to some appointments when she couldn't figure out the best questions to ask.

One issue was her home. Lori had been living in a one-bedroom apartment in an impressive-looking Rosedale mansion with multiple units, but as her funds dwindled, she had to downgrade to a one-room unit in the basement. The place was dingy and smelled of cat urine. Sister Dena and Tom did everything they could to clean it up: pulling up carpets, painting the floor, and trying to make Lori comfortable.

Other help was needed for mundane logistics, too. Lori needed to figure out her finances, look into Ontario Works for welfare, and organize her internet service provider in the new place so she could stay in contact with people. Everything got taken care of, with more help than she ever asked for before.

During that period Lori got close to her niece, Nora Jenkins, Paul and Miriam's daughter. Nora was young, vibrant, and the spitting image of Lori, and her mother says Nora and Lori were "very intrigued with one another in a special kind of way."

They became friends. Nora helped Lori get to some of her appointments and stocked her fridge with meals. Other days they'd sit by the pool at Lori's Rosedale place and just talk. Lori, of course, had stories many young women would love — an impulsive marriage to a man she was infatuated with, a whirlwind two months touring through parts of Europe, a career rubbing shoulders with the best stars, and nights spent in the hippest discos, clubs, and theatres.

"She was the person who could grab your hand and take you on an adventure," Nora says. "She loved these delicious, fun situations."

Nora could also see that Lori was generous, and that her generosity was both an outlet to thank anyone who was kind to her as well as a mask for her pain, a way of finding joy and not thinking about the bad stuff. They didn't talk much about Lori's early life — her mother's abuse, her accidents, her rape, the tough parts of her marriage — but Nora was able to see how the trauma of her past impacted her, how it damaged yet also strengthened her. It made her a lone ranger who blended in with the most outrageous people, crowds, and atmospheres; a woman who found and felt love in being selfless and giving.

"She had no confidence or self-interest.... The things that made her happy were seeing other people happy and escaping to a world of fantasy," Nora says. "She found her people in the theatre world, the camp world, the Church Street world. She made her own life there."

Despite all that had happened to her and how she viewed herself, Lori was a happy person. She harboured no resentment toward anyone who had hurt her, and she did not fault herself for her mistakes. If she had regrets, she didn't mention them. And she still didn't seem to grieve that her time was running out. She felt she'd lived a full, meaningful life. Her heart was full.

She wouldn't get to feel that for long. Lori's body continued to betray her. She could not get ahead in her cancer battle or the complications that came with it. Things all came to a head when Tom called her one night and was alarmed to hear his friend totally out of it, confused, nonsensical, exhausted, and dehydrated. She was likely going septic as an infection coursed in her blood and made her delirious, a common problem in the vulnerable and terminally ill.

Tom called 911. Paramedics came and had her admitted to hospital immediately. She would never be discharged again.

* * *

In the final weeks of her life, Lori kept a journal written on white loose-leaf paper. Each entry is carefully dated, with notes mostly in bullet points in black ink, her favourite colour.

Much of the content could be expected. She wrote down questions for her doctors and words of encouragement to herself. She made note of the names of her hospital care team — the doctors, nurses, administrative assistant, and worker who made her bed. She wrote down her roommates' names and the names of their guests.

She wrote down songs she liked from the radio, upcoming TV specials with her favourite entertainers, and her favourite snacks, and she took note of the day actors Brad Pitt and Angelina Jolie became parents to twins. One day she made note of an early wake-up call thanks to an emergency hospital fire alarm; another day she mused about some of life's small joys.

"Here comes the sun, poking through," she wrote on June 24, 2008. "Come on, you can do it! Come on! SUNSHINE! Good morning Sunshine!"

Two days later she wrote how she was pleased to have a room with a view and to feel like she was being cared for with "professional TLC, at a level which every human being on this Earth deserves."

"I held a cancer blanket [today], which is so darned soft," she wrote, noting it reminded her of Craig's dog Baby Mae, who had died a few years before. "It smelled like her. I cried tears of happiness."

In between her notes were statements, reassurances, that maybe she would eventually be well: "I'm healing every day," she wrote. "I'm holding on to hope because hope is hold-able…. Fearful to fearless."

She also wrote about Craig. She thought he was far ahead of his time, wanted him to have a star on Canada's Walk of Fame in Toronto, and believed they had somehow come full circle.

"Nobody's perfect," she wrote. "But we were perfect together."

She did not write much more about him but made note of the album *Exit Strategy of the Soul* by singer-songwriter Ron Sexsmith and the song "Who Knew?" from the album *I'm Not Dead* by rock singer P!nk. They were both in rotation on the radio at the time.

"The answers are in the songs," she wrote.

Now admitted to the care of Princess Margaret Hospital, Lori was able to feel. She spent so much of her life compartmentalizing her feelings and emotions, flicking off the pain switch so she could function despite the traumas she faced. Now with work put aside and help from a psychologist (a first in her life), Lori reflected on her life and how it made her feel.

"Princess Margaret ... had a really fantastic counselling program and Lori dove into it," says sister-in-law Miriam. "That was when she started reaching out to their mom, trying to see clear on everything in her life and make sense of it. She became a lot more communicative."

At last Lori acknowledged that she had been a child of abuse. She hadn't said that before. The most she ever acknowledged before was to say she hadn't been treated well and that her mother rejected her. She also had believed that how her mother treated her was normal. She didn't consider otherwise. Now she was angry. Laying it all out in her journal, she found the person she was most mad at was herself.

"I never ate breakfast as an adult, remembering the horror as a child," she wrote one day. "Who knew? Not me."

"Abused psychologically," she wrote another day. "I suffered unspeakable abuse.... I'm entitled to speak my truth, no matter who I say it too [sic]."

In another startling statement, she wrote: "I was never wanted or loved by the person who was supposed to love me the most; the person who gave me life."

After a few days of this Lori put pen to page to get to the heart of the matter.

"All I ever wanted is to be loved by my mother and for her to be proud of me," she wrote on June 27, 2008.

A positive distraction came in the middle of it all when her bother Marc and his partner Zoe welcomed a new baby daughter. Lori was overjoyed about the news, wrote about it in her day planner, and gushed about the beautiful baby to anyone who would listen. She told Tom all about it, and by happenstance the two of them were visiting one afternoon when Dena and her daughter Keleigh walked in and offered to take Lori to see her new niece.

Tom remembers the day well. He noticed how the mood was light and happy. Everyone was chatty and animated, clearly delighted to share in happier news that didn't include Lori's cancer prognosis. They left the hospital together, Tom headed home and the girls went on their way to meet the rest of the family.

Frail and sick but uplifted, Lori had some of her spunk back. She stopped in the middle of the road, turned to Tom, wrapped her arms around him for a hug with all the strength she had, and gave him the best kiss she'd ever given.

"Call me, honey," she purred, bursting with love and wanting to share it with anyone she cared about.

It was the last time he saw her.

Lori was moved to palliative care at Toronto Grace Health Centre at the end of June 2008. Treatment of her cancer stopped and her doctors focused on keeping her comfortable. Her days were numbered.

Lori was not going to live to age ninety-four as she had counted on. She didn't put much emotional energy into that fact. Instead, she kept busy. She watched shows on TV that she'd been looking forward to, listened to the musicals on CD from Tom, and made notes of books she wanted to read. She made friends with her roommate Francis — calling her a "partner in crime" — and read a complicated scientific paper about hydration in the dying.

One day she learned about the history of the hospital; another day Nora took her to a pub next door so Lori could enjoy a drink on the patio. She even made plans to return home for a few hours to help deal with her things.

"I haven't got time for pain," she wrote on July 17, 2008.

She did, however, have time to carry the banner as Mrs. Craig Russell. The title, and her wish to recognize and celebrate Craig, would define her to her end. While admitted to the Grace, Lori reached out to *Toronto Sun* entertainment journalist George Anthony, admitted her health prognosis, and asked for advice on what she could do to get her *What a Drag!* manuscript published.

"She was looking at the clock, it was just a question of time," George says. "She still wanted to get it out there."

George agreed to help and got her manuscript in front of a major Canadian publisher. They declined to proceed with it. Lori would never know that outcome, but her efforts spoke volumes about her character. Confined to palliative care and facing the end of her life, Lori was more concerned with sharing the impressions and lessons from her husband's days than from her own.

To Lori, Craig's life remained for public; hers was private. She did not recognize that she possessed her own strength, talents, and value — a tale worth telling — yet it is loud and clear in her daily writing, safe in her naïveté and innocent honesty. In her journal Lori wrote out parodied song lyrics ("I'm singing in the pain...."), made quips ("No use crying over spilled champagne"), and acknowledged what it took to live her life ("I have a unique ability to compartmentalize ... I worked so hard through a lifetime of injury"). She wrote that she had determination to keep going despite her prognosis ("I will fight with everything I have").

Her introspection continued, and with it now gratitude.

"I'm just so glad someone cares," she wrote.

A lot of people did. A steady stream of people went in and out of Toronto Grace to visit Lori, including her family; friends; Craig's mother, Norma Hurst, and his aunt Cathryn Hall; colleagues from countless shows and theatres; and members of the IATSE union. On more than one occasion, family and friends would cross paths and an uncomfortable exchange would ensue. No one knew anyone else and they were all protective of their sensitive, vulnerable friend and guarded with new people in the picture.

"So many people popped out of the woodwork and said, 'I'm Lori's only friend.' Then someone else would say, 'No, I'm Lori's only friend,'" notes Nora. "It was very strange to all run into each other. She had these intense relationships with different people and friends that had no connection to each other.... A couple of them were very protective of her."

Paul, Lori's brother, notes how strange it was to get close to his sister at the same time as he was losing her. In addition, he didn't know a lot of the people who were around to help because she'd never mentioned them, but they questioned his presence because they thought Lori was alone and had no family at all. There wasn't time to dwell or make sense of it, though. It was best to make the most of the little time she had left. Lori's siblings loved her just as she was, and she knew it.

"She was really trying hard ... all of us, to get to know each other better," says Miriam. "Her illness accelerated so fast. It was hard. The last few times we were together, it was very real. She couldn't say a lot. It was very poignant."

Lori died on August 15, 2008.

* * *

Lori (Jenkins) Russell Eadie slipped away quietly without a fuss. Unlike Craig, she had no headlines about her death. It wasn't covered in the papers, there was no TV crew, no benefits were held after the fact, nor were documentaries made about her life. Only a short, condensed obituary marked the occasion.

But the loss of Lori was as big as the loss of Craig. Her death represented the loss of someone who struggled; who yearned to feel loved; who worked so hard to make it; who overcame incredible trauma, obstacles, and challenges to her heart, mind, and soul; and who eventually found a way to make a meaningful, impactful life for herself on her own terms.

Craig lived outward. Lori lived inward. The lives of people who live outward make the news, and Lori was okay with that. She wouldn't have wanted attention, anyway; she'd turn that spotlight back to Craig.

Many family and friends took time to memorialize Lori on a web page for condolences managed by the funeral home hired to handle her affairs. The contributions recount her kindness, generosity, love of music and drama dating back to high school, and talents as a dresser working in theatre.

"It was wonderful to hear that you had employment as a 'dresser' in the world of professional theatre after high school," wrote Riverdale friend Philip Cheong. "My world will be poorer with the absence of your soothing voice and infectious smile."

"She was an incredibly generous person, and we were lucky to have spent time with her," wrote Susan Dunstan and Michael Therriault, actors who had crossed paths with Lori between *The Lion King* and *The Producers*. "We both loved her backwards cards, funny stories, and especially her warm smile."

Linda Ash, a fellow dresser who worked with Lori on *Crazy for You*, wrote how Lori was an "incredibly hard worker ... extremely concerned with the comfort of the performers she looked after. Her desire to continue working despite her illness was an example of her dedication and love of theatre."

Linda had visited at Toronto Grace in Lori's last weeks. Lori told them she had been on a journey of self-discovery and made a commitment to herself to be positive, no matter what, "grateful and happy with whatever life had left to give her."

There was more to Lori's life offstage, too. She was an accomplished caregiver. That hadn't stopped with Craig, or even Myra Rosenfeld, Dave Jorgensen, and Carol Nevers. It continued during her own cancer treatment. Eileen Morrison, whose mother roomed with Lori at Toronto Grace in her last days, wrote that Lori had helped ease her feelings of grief and guilt while dying herself.

Others remember her as a "one-of-a-kind original," with "something unforgettable about her," who set a high threshold for "tolerance and humility."

"Lori, I shall remember you always ... in so many supporting roles," wrote her high school teacher and friend Ian Waldron. "You never wanted to be on stage, but you always helped others to shine.... You may have been a supporting player all your life, but I will forever see you as a 'star!'"

Friend Bob Trower concluded simply, "We are all better for the time she was with us."

While news of her death and reflections of her life were more private, Lori did get a more personal and touching funeral than Craig. Her ashes were taken to Port Perry where family and friends gathered for a small wake and graveside service to share stories and memories.

Everyone who spoke saluted her with a rose, just as she had done for the performers she loved. One friend recounted how Lori had been born prematurely, and now she was prematurely gone. Another recited lyrics from the song "For Good," from the Broadway musical *Wicked*. It is a moving testament to thankfulness for knowing someone who made an impact on the people around them. It was the perfect tribute, even more so because it came from a theatre production she so loved.

Friend Kevin Curriston shared his memories in a piece of writing.

"The theatre was really Lori's first passion, because even as a child, everything was always perfectly glamorous and impeccably done," he wrote. "Life can be gritty at times, but when the lights go down, and the actors take their places and know their lines well, the world is magnificent and a beautiful place.... Life was worth living, and live it she did."

Lori was buried next to Craig in the Hall family plot at Pine Grove Cemetery. They would be together for eternity, just as she wanted.

Their shared gravestone misstates her name.

CHAPTER SEVENTEEN

OVER THE RAINBOW

Not far from where Craig got his start performing at Club Manatee, and mere blocks from Toronto Grace Health Centre where Lori died, the Gay Village has lived on.

The lights twinkle a little brighter, music beckons an echoing call to action, and the atmosphere among patrons has an edge of excitement and belonging. It is easy to see why Lori and Craig would feel they had a place in the Village. It's vibrant, brazen, and daring, just as they were.

Many venues have come and gone over the years, but a few mainstays endure. Few who are there now can say they remember Toronto's original gay destinations — places like the St. Charles Tavern, Parkside Tavern, Studio II, Jingles, Chaps, Komrads, and Trax. There are few bathhouses and even fewer cabarets. Crowds ebb and flow, constantly changing.

One would think the political tension, social consternation, or even danger of Craig and Lori's time in the gay community would have subsided in the fifty-year evolution, but recent events prove they have not.

Thirty-five years after the 1981 bathhouse raids, called "one of the largest mass arrests in Canadian history," Toronto police chief Mark Saunders made a public statement to express regret and "acknowledge the lessons learned about the risks of treating any part of Toronto's many communities as not fully a part of society." The intention was good. It was supposed to signal the start of healing. But one word was missing. *Sorry.* Saunders did not apologize.

Days after Saunders's acknowledgement, the Toronto chapter of an international activist movement called Black Lives Matter (BLM) interrupted the annual Toronto Pride parade and staged a sit-in. The demonstration, at a major event drawing more than a million people, was intended to bring attention to the BLM stance against the participation of uniformed Toronto police officers. The organization said the police represent a reminder of brutality and accused the Pride Toronto organization of anti-Blackness and anti-Indigeneity.

"Folks are forgetting that we haven't all made it to the point of queer liberation," Alexandria Williams, a co-founder of BLM Toronto, said ahead of the parade. "Not all communities who participate in Pride are actually able to be free in that celebration."

The group was so visible, and so politically strong, Pride Toronto executive director Mathieu Chantelois was forced to sign a list of demands from the group before the parade could continue. Their demands included an increase of funding for Black youth events; hiring more Black, trans, and Indigenous people; and banning police floats with uniformed police officers from future parades.

The incident stoked at racial tensions, and made many question whether Pride Toronto and the LGBTQ2S community as a whole were as diverse and inclusive as they seemed.

Between those headlines, danger was also lurking. In November 2017 two women disappeared and died under alarming circumstances, highlighting the vulnerability of women, people of colour, and marginalized people on the Church Street blocks. One, Alloura Wells, was a biracial trans woman who vanished over the summer and was found dead in a ravine. Her body went unidentified for months and her cause of death remains unknown. The other was a young woman named Tess Richey, who was murdered after a night out on the strip. She was later found dead by her mother in an outdoor stairwell as a police search for her was underway.

Both incidents led to questions about the Toronto Police Service's handling of missing persons cases. Those questions would only expand when, two months later, an unassuming sixty-six-year-old landscaper named Bruce McArthur was arrested, and eventually charged, with first-degree murder in the deaths of eight men with connections to the Gay Village who had disappeared over the last eight years. His arrest was the culmination of years of work from police, alarms from the LGBTQ2S community, and minimal information or warning that a predator was afoot.

McArthur pleaded guilty to the charges and was sentenced to life imprisonment a year later, but even while he was off the streets and no longer posing a threat, anger at Toronto police remained, with countless accusations and questions. Where had police been when different men were reported missing? How could police have known about McArthur for years and done nothing? Why had this taken so long, with no arrest made earlier to potentially save lives? Where was the public warning that a potential serial killer was among them?

Anger seemed to permeate the community, and not just because of the McArthur case. Cities across the world have seen a rise of anti-gay hate activities at the hands of people connected to political, religious, social, and extremist groups that serve to directly and indirectly stoke divisiveness and hostility. Toronto has not been immune with the Gay Village frequently a target of what one city councillor called "extremely homophobic" and "alt-right" individuals who are "essentially praying for our souls."

The actions of one individual led to large outrage that felt like a déjà vu to decades past. It started in June 2019 when David Lynn, an evangelical pastor and founder of an organization called Christ's Forgiveness Ministries, took to the streets in the Village to preach what he called pro-Christian messages and suggest that the LGBTQ2S community does not tolerate Christians.

"I'm coming out as Christian," Lynn told onlookers. "You don't want to talk to me — you have your backs faced against me, and you won't tolerate me."

In hand with a group called Christian Positive Space, Lynn returned with a September rally and march to promote "civil liberties." Their planned march included the section of Church Street where the Gay Village is located to recognize the meaning of the word "church" and its significance to the Christian faith. Members of the LGTBQ2S community saw Lynn and the group as a threat and planned a counter-rally and protest in response.

Hundreds came out on both sides. Many members of the Christian group wore black and cheered behind an amplified band while others carried signs that said "Diversity includes Bible-believing Christians" and "Civil rights are for Christians too!" One member had a T-shirt that read "Make Canada righteous & Godly again." The LGBTQ2S group, as organized by The 519, an inclusivity and advocacy organization, were more colourful, carried their own signs — "No hate in our village" and "Keep calm and queer on" — and showed up ready for a showdown, chanting "Love, not hate, makes our city great!"

The whole affair closed streets as the groups edged through one downtown intersection after another, stopping for several standoffs cheering and chanting, at times in the pouring rain. It went on for hours and only stopped when the groups were forcibly moved apart and dispersed by countless police officers, some at the ready for a potentially dangerous riot.

The LGBTQ2S community was not without support in their stand against anti-queer protestors of Lynn's group. Ahead of the march, at a rally held in the Village, Toronto mayor John Tory called out anyone promoting "division and polarization and stigmatization against the LGBTQ2S community or anybody else … that's not what we're about in Toronto." Alongside him, faith leaders reminded those gathered that many people of faith believe lesbian, gay, bisexual, transgender, transsexual, queer, Two-spirit, questioning, intersex, pansexual, asexual people, and their allies are not only deserving of rights, but are also deserving of acceptance and God's love.

"We've won rights, and we're not going back," gay-friendly United Church pastor Cheri DiNovo said. "We're people of faith, and the vast majority of faith in this country, be they Christian, Muslim, Jew, Buddhist, Sikh, Hindu, whatever they are, are LGBTQ2S inclusive … That's our Canadian mosaic, and that's our Canadian life and the haters are not part of that and the haters represent a small minority of that faith spectrum."

Still, the community's vulnerability couldn't be ignored.

"It's fragile you know, human rights are fragile," Tory acknowledged. "The kind of respect we've built up here is fragile in a certain way."

The whole affair was as deflating as it was empowering. Fragility. Vulnerability. Division. Anger. Hate. Hadn't the gay community already been through this?

Volatility in the gay community was as alive in 2019 as it was when drag queens were harassed and attacked simply trying to go out to a gay bar in 1969. People are still targeted. People are still vulnerable. There has been one constant. Drag. Queens have been there every step of the way and now instead of being a curious sensation or target of ignorance, they are positive beacons through the dynamic, changing times. Drag is a highlight of the Gay Village and keeps people going to its establishments when it might have been safer to stay home.

"Drag is the fabric that keeps gay bars together," says Sky Gilbert, the co-founder of Buddies in Bad Times Theatre and a drag performer himself. "They are the only reason why some people go to the bars."

Decades after a small handful of performers got their start in places like Oscars and the Global Village, there are almost a countless number of queens. They go by names like Katinka Kature, D'Manda Tension, Juice Boxx, Sofonda Cox, and Baby Bel Bel. Michelle DuBarry and Georgie Girl, performers Craig had known and worked with, still appear. The lights flash for them, the songs play on, and the love and celebration of everything female is shared among them.

Their careers exist largely here in the Village, despite doors opened by performers like Craig who came before them. Outside the bar scene, not many theatres or cabarets have a dedicated space for queens to perform their art. That's surprising. Drag is a popular draw and bars fill up quickly when a queen hits the stage.

"We are the last of the showgirls," says queen Carlotta Carlisle. "You can't go to any nightclub or supper club or restaurant and see a live entertainer. Most people can't afford to go to the theatre anymore. But you can go to a drag bar and, for a five-dollar cover or even for free, see this beautiful creature entertain."

Carlotta, born and raised in Newfoundland, had just moved to Toronto when she found drag. Her act has a heavy emphasis on her transformation from male to female, with elaborate gowns, shoes, wigs, nails, and accessories. She calls herself "a goddess, not a girl … a gorgeous creature who is an over-exaggeration of the feminine ideal."

She's been on the scene for more than a decade.

"Once you hear applause, you can't not hear it again," she says on an afternoon off, out of character and sitting on a patio at a Gay Village café. "Once you know what it is like to have a room full of people adore you and care, that is a validation and that is a rush. It is hard to go without."

When Carlotta is onstage — typically wowing audiences with an anticipated and dramatic entrance, wearing a jaw-dropping gown with a bouffant wig and all the accessories that only the most glamorous woman could have — she launches into song and dance, lip-syncing to singers like Adele, Celine Dion, Gladys Knight, and Alannah Myles. Sometimes she even lip-syncs monologues from fictional female characters she respects, like actress Dixie Carter's character, Julia Sugarbaker, in the TV series *Designing Women*.

Carlotta performs primarily at Woody's, Crews & Tangos, and the nearby Buddies in Bad Times Theatre, from early evening to late at night. The space fills up for her no matter what the time of day. That has been consistent. What hasn't been consistent is the audience before her. It has changed a lot in her time, even more since Craig's days at places like Club Manatee and the August Club.

Belonging is no longer the biggest pull to a drag show in a bar. People once came here because they needed a place of safety and refuge from an unaccepting world. But social progress has opened doors for other places to socialize. The bar scene is inclusive, people can see live entertainers on YouTube or Netflix, gay-friendly bars can be found in other neighbourhoods, and sex is found on dating sites and mobile apps.

Today drag is seen primarily as entertainment and less as a pillar of strength for people in the crowd who feel they can't be themselves. The patrons of formerly gay-only destinations have diversified: some are gay, some are allies, some just want the novelty of a gay bar. Most nights the loudest patrons are straight women, usually in groups, and probably there to celebrate a bachelorette party. Something about that feels cheap.

"Respected? By some," Carlotta muses. "To some we are a novelty. To some we are artists. To others we are people who fight for the cause."

Over time drag has shifted from being a curious and exciting exception to the performing rules, to being mainstream and commonplace. The fun is not limited to after dark. In Toronto drag can be found at family festivals in community parks, at the public library for storytime with children, and at popular restaurants hosting brunch.

Drag has snuck into many films over the years since the groundbreaking *Outrageous!*, when filmmakers Bill Marshall and Henk Van der Kolk were pushing boundaries and taking risks including a queen in the lead role of their movie. There have been small-budget pictures like *Kinky Boots* and *The Adventures of Priscilla, Queen of the Desert*. And there have been more widely distributed films, too, like *To Wong Foo, Thanks for Everything! Julie Newmar*; *The Birdcage*; *Connie and Carla*; and the more recent film *Dumplin'*.

Even in the mid-1990s, films including the fictional Brady family from wholesome 1960s, television, one character (ironically, a guidance counsellor) is played by a drag queen. The actor was RuPaul Charles, an American queen with a career so expansive he is now a household name. In addition to acting in more than twenty films, RuPaul has worked as a recording artist, model, and host of a handful of radio and television programs. He has had his own talk show, makeup, perfume, and podcast, and he is the name behind RuPaul's DragCon, an annual convention for queens.

One of RuPaul's greatest successes is the reality show *RuPaul's Drag Race*, a competitive television series to find "America's next drag superstar." It has aired on multiple networks for more than a decade, launched global drag careers for several queens, and developed a cult following. Some in the gay community claim not to like it; they call RuPaul a sellout or see his persona as a mockery of gender identity. But the rest of his audience doesn't seem to care. The show's celebrity endorsements, spinoff series, suite of awards (from Primetime Emmys to a GLAAD Media Award), and skyrocketing ratings can't be denied.

The Toronto drag community isn't out of touch with RuPaul's reality television world. Queen Brooke Lynn Hytes, an Etobicoke-born performer who once had a regular act on Church Street, competed on the show's eleventh season. Her fellow queens call her "a big fish in a small pond," "a lip-sync assassin," and "a superstar in the making." She has a strong fan base back at home. Several bars, both in the Gay Village and in a west-end neighbourhood affectionately nicknamed "Queerdale," hosted *Drag Race* viewing parties and came out to celebrate when Brooke came in second place, the runner-up to winner Yvie Oddly.

"We feel every ripple and quake that *Drag Race* makes," theatre performer Pearle Harbour told the *Toronto Star*. "The groundswell popularity of the show means there's a bigger and more voracious audience than ever: queers, straight people, tiny tots alike. People are starting to understand that everyone is welcome in drag. Everybody is invited to the party."

Most say they still feel a ceiling in their work and art. No one is buying tickets to see a drag queen headline a show at a venue like the Royal York Hotel or Massey Hall, where Craig got booked. Church Street is drag's only lasting destination, and even there, the pay makes it hard for a queen to sustain that career. Local entertainers make a fraction of what queens in the U.S. market do.

Some are hopeful, some are not. Most find it best to just put everything they have into what makes their act unique and push on to perform wherever they can, no matter what they get paid, who is in the audience, or why they are there. They won't be dissuaded.

"There is a ceiling in Toronto, but I would love to be working to raise that ceiling and moving that top shelf of what we can do," queen Allysin Chaynes told the *Toronto Star*. "When I look at a show like *Drag Race* and I get frustrated that I'm Canadian or hairy or weird, I know that doesn't have to be the end of my journey. Anything's possible in your own scene if you work to make it there."

Allysin is right. Even where the audience is changing and respect is variable, drag has thrived and diversified as an art form. It looks nothing like it did when it first rose in North American gay culture. Today drag comes in numerous styles. If Craig were around today, he would be considered a fish queen because he strived to look authentically female. It takes an even more outrageous, exaggerated female look to be considered club drag; then there is pageant drag, for performers who thrive on competition.

Drag artists today can take part in androgyny (having masculine and feminine characteristics), camp (a clown-like esthetic, with additional emphasis on humour), and activessle (drag with religious imagery, often performing for a charitable or activist function). A newer specialty is faux drag or bioqueen, where the performer is a biological female but performs as a male doing drag as a female.

Few queens sing today, likely because of a lack of suitable available venues. One queen shudders at the idea of singing. She believes audiences would rather see queens looking fabulous and moving to the latest song from Top 40 pop singers like Beyoncé or Ariana Grande. Musicianship as a whole does not seem to be a trendy thing.

There are some exceptions, of course. Entertainer Christopher Peterson spent part of his career in Toronto, and in doing his impressions paired with live singing, Christopher used his talents to open the door to the mainstream, just as Craig did. Christopher has headed many shows; gotten ample television work (he once co-hosted Canadian broadcaster Dini Petty's talk show dressed as Dini Petty); and even performed Craig's part, Robin Turner, when a production of *Outrageous!* was workshopped at a Calgary theatre.

Miss Conception, a queen who built her career in Toronto, also does live singing to recorded tracks or live accompaniment, with costume changes to imitate or parody everyone from Adele, Tina Turner, and Lady Gaga to Disney characters like Mary Poppins and Snow White. Miss Conception's characters aren't all female, either. She does a hilarious take on the character Lumière from *Beauty and the Beast*.

Some queens play instruments rather than sing; Allysin sometimes plays her guitar, banjo, lap steel, and mandolin. She says she's "a mockstar rockstar, but I am incredibly sincere."

Still, musicianship is rare. Drag is ever changing, and some queens see it as part of their work to evolve and push the boundaries. Allysin has been part of a collective group called the House of Filth who try to defy any stereotype or definition of what drag is by incorporating different performers with a variety of styles. They've been called drag terrorists because they are not seen as traditional. They've taken drag and turned it upside down.

Perhaps Carlotta describes the breadth of modern drag artistry best. "Performance-wise, there are as many different kinds of drag as there are artists willing to perform it," she says.

But drag artists do share some things in common: They share a passion for entertaining, music, film, and fashion. All are talented, creative, and driven. And many, like Craig, are in love with the entertainers they emulate.

Gerry Mastrolia is a New York–based entertainer who has dabbled in "the wonderful world of drag" since he was in grade school and sees his impersonations as tributes to the ladies he adores. His impressions include Judy Garland, Liza Minnelli, Joan Crawford, Marilyn Monroe, Mae West, Bette Midler, and Bette Davis — women whom Craig also loved. Through Gerry, these larger-than-life ladies again have a place in an entertainment world oversaturated with divas.

"The power they possessed inspires me in my everyday life and in my drag career," Gerry says. "If I can teach people, or inspire people to keep the memories of these broads alive, I feel like I've done my job. I feel like they are smiling at me from the other side of the rainbow."

Other queens are like Craig in other ways. Some perform to find strength they can't find elsewhere. Drag remains a way to hide from fragile emotions.

"There are people who use drag to get the love and validation they feel they don't get anywhere else," Carlotta says, with a cautionary note. "After you've been denied those things for so long, it does something awful to the human soul."

Carlotta can understand what it must have been like for Craig; how the art form he pursued was both a passion and a cover for pain, his mask for a mental illness he could not define; and how he got lost trying to make the transition from Craig Eadie the sensitive person to Craig Russell the performer.

The separation between the person and performer is hard, even for the most stable.

"Carlotta Carlisle means the world to me; she is a creature of my own creation," Carlotta says. "It's hard to create the separation. People don't know who is behind it all. What happens when they don't know you?"

And what happens when you can't perform your art anymore, the excitement for you dissipates, the theatres close, and the audience changes? Where is the person then?

"Drag is not a lifetime career," Carlotta warns. "What happens when the tides change?"

Craig and Lori have been gone for a long time now.

Some people know them and remember them. Many do not. That's a shame. There's a lot to be celebrated — their accomplishments, their successes, their strengths, and their place and perseverance through gay

Craig and Lori, outrageous star and his No. 1 fan.

liberation and evolving sexual politics in Canada. Above all, they should be celebrated simply for being who they were, no matter what. They were unusual misfits who shunned conformity and strived to be different at a time when people were better off when they blended in.

They also were simply just good people. Lori was loving, genuine, and endlessly generous. Working as a dresser in some of the most elaborate and heralded productions in Canadian theatre history, she worked her fingers to the bone to make others shine in the spotlight. Her work could not have fit her personality better: she was passionate, detail-oriented, and creative — a person of service who gave everything she had to something or someone she admired.

Lori's name echoes in Toronto's theatres to this day. Former colleagues still refer to her and how she did things in her work. They remember her quiet, demure, and eccentric nature; how dedicated she was to both her job and her stars; and her thoughtfulness to those who were kind to her. At the Princess of Wales Theatre, where a locker held her belongings long after she died, a painted mural from a past production above the backstage area has "L. Eadie" written gently in line with other dressers she so respected.

Her contributions to the world around her didn't stop with her theatre work. Lori spent her off hours either working as a caregiver for people with crippling illness or tending bar for patrons in need of a cheerleader and a friend. Anyone else forced to work as hard as she did and juggle the hardships and physical impairments she had would be insufferable, the loudest person in a room. Not Lori. She remained the quiet, diminutive woman who spoke in a whisper and wanted no attention on herself. She was completely selfless.

Lori thought Craig was the one who deserved attention and celebration. That made sense in a way. It was his dream and his purpose to be out on the stages of the world for all to see. He certainly earned his place. He was an impressionist, singer, musician, actor, comedian, host, humorist, and "stark raving genius" who had the ability to dive into the depths of the human psyche, pick out the layers of a person's strengths and vulnerabilities, then emulate them at the drop of a hat. In this he was absolutely unmatched.

"He [was] touched by the gods," friend and former producer Michael Oscars says of him, forty years after their working relationship. "He could think on a dime. He could improvise a line or a moment and he would have you howling with laughter and he could also move you.... He was incandescent. It was wonderful to watch."

Craig was destined to be a star and part of what he called "the star system." He believed we need stars to entertain us, inspire us, and bring us distraction and comfort. He felt that his act made people's dreams come true because he brought beloved stars to life. Craig got accolades, awards, and countless positive reviews for his work, but what mattered most to him was that he reached people who seemed to need him.

Performing as his ladies was Craig's comfort, too. He was deeply sensitive and his emotions were fragile. He openly expressed his sensitivity in his own way fairly often, but few realized just how low his heart could go. He had low self-worth and did not feel loved. That may seem to be an odd assessment for a man who was such a beloved entertainer, but as Craig himself pointed out, he felt his fans loved Craig Russell, not Craig Eadie. The love others had for Craig Eadie could not break through the veil of mental illness they didn't know he had.

Craig was not alone in the way he suffered. Generations of people have suffered from mental illness and were lost to the world by virtue of minimal diagnosis and treatment, but ample stigma and shame. Speaking openly about mental health is a relatively new addition to our daily conversations. The fact that Craig sought help from a doctor and got a diagnosis of manic depression was progressive, but even then it wasn't enough. Not only were the treatment options unsatisfactory, but his illness was also likely more than what his doctor could define at the time. Craig had manic mood swings, unfiltered emotions, and shockingly impulsive behaviour. He responded to many situations in extremes and was often left embarrassed after he acted out in ways he couldn't explain. He felt he could not control himself. That frightened him. Only Lori knew that.

Similarly, few knew he was trying to reshape the very career that had brought him such great success. It is certain Craig is recognized as a female impressionist, a drag queen who made it big. But he wanted to be known for more than that, and he grew ambivalent about his brand. He didn't feel like he fit in to the usually gay-associated world of drag, and he saw impressionism as just one of many talents he had to bring to the table.

Craig wanted to be seen as a respected entertainer, an artist, "a complete original, all things to all people." He had the talent to have that legacy, but he never got to live it. His talents in impressionism were so great, and his antics so outrageous, that it seemed that was the only side of him his audience wanted. He wasn't successful in branching out in his career, and when he tried to make do and find new outrageous antics for his desensitized audience, he offended instead of entertaining.

It all seemed so complicated when, in reality, it was actually quite simple. Craig needed understanding, belonging, and love — qualities that made him just like everyone else.

Lori needed the same things. She was as fragile as Craig. She only really felt she belonged when she was around him. That's what made her so loyal to a man who did not love her the same deep way she loved him. Lori didn't see the difference in Craig's feelings, so it did not dissuade her. She forgot about needing love in return. After all, she'd been trained to feel she was neither wanted nor deserving of love since childhood.

While her husband was able to express his emotions outwardly, Lori couldn't. She kept her emotions in as much as she could. She learned to do what Craig couldn't — compartmentalize — and that allowed her to be more functional and shape the narrative of her life, despite her internal pain. Her life wasn't all sad, though. She was proud of herself for her independence, for marching to a different drum and having "a different way of seeing things," as she wrote in her journal in her last days of life.

This is why, despite their different backgrounds and different personalities, Craig and Lori fit together. Lori's love for Craig gave her belonging, and her loyalty brought Craig understanding. His usual approach to their relationship may have been cold, but it taught Lori strength, and later, when he was a broken spirit and gripped with AIDS, her strength carried him. Decades of their lives, who they were, and what became of them were shaped by that dynamic. They wouldn't have got as far as they did without each other.

What Craig and Lori faced was tragic: parents who rejected them, mental health struggles, sexual assault, alcohol and drug dependency, physical trauma, volatile social and political change in their community, judgment, misperceptions; a lack of understanding about who they were, terminal illnesses, and sometimes just plain bad luck. They didn't deserve any of it.

But here's the thing — if they were here today, Craig and Lori would have few complaints looking back on their lives. They lived on their own terms; thrived in the creative world of the performing arts; reached and touched hordes of people; and achieved their dreams no matter what was expected of them, thrown at them, or understood of them. They revelled in being the outrageous misfits that they were.

If Craig and Lori could sit back and watch everything that happened in their lives play out before them in a theatre, a venue that shaped so much of their existence, they would love every minute. They would toast everything with a cocktail and a nod to Mae and Judy and Bette and Tallulah and all the other entertainers they loved who guided them through their years.

Then they would ask the bartender to pour them another drink. They would share a smile and a laugh, and eagerly anticipate what the next outrageous act would bring.

ACKNOWLEDGMENTS

Thank you to all the amazing people who were willing to be interviewed for this book, to share details wonderful, sad, and outrageous, with a particular thanks to the Hall and Jenkins families, Allison Badger, Dena Jenkins, Shirley Flavell, Phil Buckley, and Tom Veitch. Thank you for allowing me to share Craig and Lori with the world.

Thank you to the team at Dundurn Press for believing in this book. Rachel Spence was a wonderful champion since day one. Scott Fraser, president and publisher, and Kathryn Lane, associate publisher, are absolute gems. Elena Radic has been great to work with through the production cycle, and Heather Wood has been a great support. Copy editor Kate Unrau was fantastic, not to mention likely exhausted after re-entering all of the oxford commas I omitted. Many more on the Dundurn team have contributed to the publishing of this book, including Laura Boyle, Stephanie Ellis, and Ashley Hisson. Thank you.

Thanks to my Toronto Star family, in particular Katie Daubs, Paul Hunter, Deborah Dundas, Peter Howell, Michelle Shephard, Taras Slawnych, Anthony Collins, Josh Rubin, Janet Hurley, Jon Ohayon, Jim Coyle, Scott Colby, Amy Pataki, Kate Robertson, and Jennifer Wells, for their motivating support. Thank you to Sabrina Melchiori and Braydon Holmyard for bringing sunshine to my mornings after late nights with misfits. Thank you to Ed Cassavoy, Mariya Vadera, and Dean Lisk for their assistance, including some of the best visual elements of this book. Immeasurable thanks to Margaret Bream, an incredibly supportive friend, editor, and mentor.

Thank you to the incredible staff at ArQuives (formerly known as the Canadian Lesbian and Gay Archives) and Toronto Reference Library. To anyone reading — support places like these. They hold so many of our stories. And when you are done, support the arts and artists in your community. There are a lot of misfits out there who want to engage, entertain, and inspire you. I met many through writing this book and I will cherish our time always.

Love and thanks to my mom, Cindy Clark, who years ago went to great lengths to find me Roald Dahl and Robert Kimmel Smith books; my dad, Russ Bradley, who is hopeful I'll be as widely read as Allan Fotheringham one day; my distinctive sisters, who are special in their own ways; the Clark, Bradley, Rowcliffe, and Smith families for constant support; Jeff Totman, whose friendship over the last twenty years has never been dull; Tracy Wasylow, for keeping me in line over the years; Miranda McCurlie, for support any time of day and keeping an open door for writing breaks with B.H.; the friends and family members who read different parts and variations of the final product; Ted Mouradian and Megan Mottershead, for introducing me to Toronto's Gay Village, and Michael Hogard and Devon Foster, for reintroducing me to that world after years away.

I would be remiss if I didn't thank my book subjects, Craig Eadie and Lori Russell Eadie. I see you, I understand you, and I celebrate you. I know this is what you wanted.

I'd like to think Craig and Lori were with me as I wrote this book. They weren't alone if they were. Sending love up to Irene and Bill Clark, Chris Clark, Ed Rowcliffe, Pat Openshaw, Mardie Bradley, and Lorraine Chartrand. You were each on my mind at different points along the way. A special call out to Diane (Dinny) Smith for her example to love all no matter what.

And finally, a shout out to the late, great Ian MacDonald for his early enthusiasm and inspiring belief that books, music, and films matter.

BIBLIOGRAPHY

BOOKS

Baker, Roger. *Drag: A History of Female Impersonation in the Performing Arts*. New York: New York University Press, 1994.

Chambers, Stephanie, Jane Farrow, Maureen FitzGerald, Ed Jackson, John Lorinc, Tim McCaskell, Rebecka Sheffield, Tatum Taylor, and Rahim Thawer, eds. *Any Other Way: How Toronto Got Queer*. Toronto: Coach House Books, 2017.

Desjardins, R. Mark. "Saint Mae: Our Lady of Hips & Quips." Unpublished manuscript, 2001.

Dowsett, Gary W. *Practicing Desire: Homosexual Sex in the Era of AIDS*. Stanford: Stanford University Press, 1996.

Duberman, Martin. *Stonewall*. New York: Dutton, 1993.

Ebert, Roger. *Two Weeks in the Midday Sun: A Cannes Notebook*. Kansas City: Andrews McMeel, 1987.

Eells, George, and Stanley Musgrove. *Mae West: A Biography*. New York: William Morrow, 1982.

Empry, Gino. *I Belong to the Stars*. Oakville: Mosaic Press, 2002.

Gibson, Margaret. *Considering Her Condition*. Toronto: Gage Publishing, 1978.

———. *Desert Thirst*. Toronto: Exile Editions, 1997.

————. *Sweet Poison*. Toronto: HarperCollins, 1994.

Gibson Gilboord, Margaret. *The Butterfly Ward*. Ottawa: Oberon Press, 1976.

Hastings, Magnus. *Why Drag?* San Francisco: Chronicle Books, 2016.

Heath, Jeffrey, ed. *Profiles in Canadian Literature*. Toronto: Dundurn Press, 1991.

Marshall, William. *Film Festival Confidential*. Toronto: McArthur, 2005.

McCaskell, Tim. *Queer Progress: From Homophobia to Homonationalism*. Toronto: Between the Lines, 2016.

McLeod, Donald W. *Lesbian and Gay Liberation in Canada: A Selected and Annotated Chronology, 1964–1975*. Toronto: ECW Press, 1996.

————. *Lesbian and Gay Liberation in Canada: A Selected and Annotated Chronology, 1976–1981*. Toronto: Homewood Books, 2017.

Rupp, Leila, and Verta Taylor. *Drag Queens at the 801 Cabaret*. Chicago: University of Chicago Press, 2003.

Russell Eadie, Lori. "What A Drag!" Unpublished manuscript, 2005.

Schmidt-Joos, Siegfried. *Idole*. Germany: Ullstein Taschenbuchvlg, 1985.

Smith, Miriam. *Lesbian and Gay Rights in Canada: Social Movements and Equality Seeking, 1971–1995*. Toronto: University of Toronto Press, 1999.

Street, David, and Craig Russell. *Craig Russell and His Ladies*. Toronto: Gage Publishing, 1979.

Warner, Tom. *Never Going Back: A History of Queer Activism in Canada*. Toronto: University of Toronto Press, 2002.

FILM

Benner, Richard, dir. *Outrageous!* 1977; Toronto, Canada: Video Service Corp. DVD.

Schwartz, Jeffrey, dir. *I Am Divine*. 2013; New Almaden, CA: Wolfe Video. DVD.

NEWSPAPERS

Adilman, Sid. "Craig Russell, author, has new look, too." *Toronto Star*, November 9, 1979.

———. "Craig Russell, phone home." *Toronto Star*, October 22, 1982.

———. "Craig Russell set for European tour." *Toronto Star*, May 8, 1978.

———. "Drag queen gambles on solo turn at Tarragon." *Toronto Star*, June 22, 1996.

———. "Phantom haunts the record books." *Toronto Star*, September 8, 1990.

Allison, Thom. "Outrageousness." *Xtra*, May 10, 2007.

Andrews, Marke. "So-called comedy about AIDS takes bad jokes to the ultimate." *Vancouver Sun*, September 4, 1987.

Anthony, George. "Growing up can be Outrageous too." *Toronto Sun*, August 27, 1987.

———. "Hat trick of showbiz treats." *Toronto Sun*, July 4, 1977.

———. "He's a one-man, dozen-lady show." *Toronto Sun*, n.d.

Arnold, Gary. "Eccentric, Engaging And … 'Outrageous.'" *Washington Post*, August 18, 1977.

Avicolli, Tommi. "When the going gets tough, the tough get Too Outrageous." *Philadelphia Gay News*, November 27–December 3, 1987.

Bailey, Bruce. "Film sequel lacks outrageousness as director misuses Russell talent." *Gazette*, June 3, 1988.

———. "Russell is too outrageous; Straight talk is not part of his/her repertoire." *Gazette*, June 3, 1988.

Balkissoon, Denis, and Tu Thanh Ha. "Death of Alloura Wells tells a story of a vulnerable community." *Globe and Mail*, December 15, 2017. Last updated December 17, 2017. theglobeandmail.com/news/toronto/death-of-alloura-wells-tells-a-story-of-a-vulnerablecommunity/article37356642.

Base, Ron. "Craig Russell sashays down Yellow Brick Road." *Toronto Star*, September 18, 1987.

Battersby, Sarah-Joyce. "Black Lives Matter protest scores victory after putting Pride parade on pause." *Toronto Star*, July 3, 2016. thestar.com/news/gta/2016/07/03/black-lives-matter-protest-scores-victory-after-putting-pride-parade-on-pause.html.

Beebe, Jim. "Curious Alex décor an appropriate Façad set." *Toronto Star*, August 22, 1969.

Bell, Arthur. "Craig Russell: His idol wore a miniskirt." *Village Voice*, August 1977.

Blackadar, Bruce. "Looking back at the kings and queens of an Imperial era." *Toronto Star*, December 3, 1988.

———. "Look Ma! I got married after all." *Toronto Star*, January 12, 1982.

———. "Outrageous Craig, the cowboy and the muu muu." *Toronto Star*, September 13, 1988.

Braithwaite, Dennis. "Craig Russell in fine feather." *Toronto Star*, December 28, 1978.

Brownstein, Bill. "A new 'odd couple' make for a fine film." *Gazette*, October 29, 1977.

Burliuk, Greg. "Toronto Festival of Festivals ten years later, Craig Russell returns to be outrageous again." *Whig-Standard*, September 11, 1987.

Callwood, June. "Talented female impersonators ride high on illusion and fantasy." *Globe and Mail*, March 2, 1988.

Campeau, DuBarry. "An Evening with the 'Ladies' at The Dell." *Toronto Telegram*, August 12, 1969.

Canadian Press. "Crows rally for unity in Toronto as anti-LGBTQ group protests for free speech." *National Post*, September 28, 2019. nationalpost.com/pmn/news-pmn/canada-news-pmn/toronto-mayor-taking-part-in-rally-in-support-of-lgbtq-community.

———. "'Disgusting' West tour by Russell cancelled." *Globe and Mail*, October 30, 1981.

———. "An original, the one and only Craig Russell." *Toronto Star*, September 13, 1988.

———. "Star of Outrageous impersonated actresses." *Globe and Mail*, November 1, 1990.

Champlin, Charles. "A Cannape of Films to Come." *Los Angeles Times*, May 29, 1977.

Clements, Jim. "She's not the real thing but he does come close." *Hamilton Spectator*, May 16, 1972.

Cohen, Nathan. "Monday Miscellany." *Toronto Daily Star*, January 13, 1964.

Colombo, John Robert. "What would your epitaph be?" *Toronto Star*, October 31, 1982.

Conlogue, Ray. "G&S spells success for Brian Macdonald." *Globe and Mail*, June 28, 1983.

———. "Monster bash readies for takeoff." *Globe and Mail*, May 9, 1981.

Corbeil, Carole. "Russell animates sleepy Hogtown." *Globe and Mail*, May 28, 1981.

Crook, Farrell. "The Bath House Saga Drags on 13 ½ Months after Police Raids." *Toronto Star*, March 22, 1982.

Dafoe, Chris. "'I want to get my peer group into the theatre.'" *Globe and Mail*, February 8, 1992.

Dalhousie Gazette. "Crackdown on Gays Violates Human Rights." February 12, 1981.

Doherty, Brennan, and Alina Bykova. "Toronto police to review handling of missing persons cases." *Toronto Star*, December 8, 2017. thestar.com/news/crime/2017/12/08/toronto-police-to-update-public-on-downtown-deaths-disappearances.html.

Downing, John. "Cops, Gays Both Wrong." *Toronto Sun*, February 10, 1981.

Downton, Cheryl. "Craig." *Dalhousie Gazette*, March 22, 1979.

Drain, Millie. "Craig Russell funny man funny lady funny person." *Entertainment News*, March 9, 1978.

Dunford, Gary. "Comin' home to the Imperial Room." *Toronto Sun*, February 24, 1978.

———. "A fine romance?" *Toronto Sun*, November 1, 1981.

Dunning, Jennifer. "Mad for the Movies." *New York Times*, August 12, 1977.

Dunphy, Catherine. "Demons drove gifted writer's career." *Toronto Star*, April 10, 2006.

Durrani, Temur. "Pastor charged with causing a disturbance in Toronto's Gay Village." *Toronto Star*, June 5, 2019. thestar.com/news/gta/2019/06/05/pastor-charged-with-causing-a-disturbance-in-torontos-gay-village.html.

Dykk, Lloyd. "That's Craig Russell on the right. Mae West is below." *Vancouver Sun*, October 10, 1980.

Eder, Richard. "Stage: Craig Russell Rolls His Eyes." *New York Times*, November 3, 1977.

Edmonton Journal. "Barry Westgate at the movies." October 22, 1977.

Egan, James. Public, letter to the editor. *Toronto Daily Star*, January 21, 1964.

Floyd, Meg. "Jazzing up the Genies." *Globe and Mail*, March 15, 1980.

Fraser, Graham. "Female Impersonators Go Public: Out of the Shadows." *Toronto Daily Star*, July 25, 1969.

Fraser, Mary Botsford. "Short forays into a nasty, brutish world." *Globe and Mail*, November 13, 1993.

Fulford, Robert. "The 3 a.m. Craig Russell — again." *Globe and Mail*, March 16, 1994.

Gibson, Victoria, and Jenna Moon. "Toronto police chief dispels rumours of serial killer in Church and Wellesley neighbourhood." *Toronto Star*, December 8, 2017. thestar.com/news/gta/2017/12/08/toronto-police-to-review-handling-of-missing-persons-cases.html.

Globe and Mail. "AIDS robbing arts world of talent and morale." January 20, 1993.

———. "Craig Russell wins best actor award in Berlin." March 7, 1978.

———. "Fanning the flames." January 12, 1982.

———. "Hogtown closing after 2 ½ weeks." June 12, 1981.

———. "Russell plans album of Toronto show." February 16, 1979.

———. "Russell to be host of TV show." December 14, 1978.

———. "Still no pact as Hogtown about to open." May 27, 1981.

———. "Wouldn't that just pop your garters?" September 12, 1987.

Glusovich, Kerry. "Craig Russell in Local Club Bow." *Hollywood Reporter*, December 12, 1972.

Goddard, Peter. "Craig Russell hogs Hogtown." *Toronto Star*, May 28, 1981.

———. "Impressionist Craig Russell works feathers off his boa." *Toronto Star*, February 28, 1978.

Godfrey, Stephen. "An ingenue who wants a touch of evil." *Globe and Mail*, August 15, 1977.

———. "Living off the ladies." *Globe and Mail*, February 25, 1978.

———. "A plushy triumph for Russell." *Globe and Mail*, February 28, 1978.

Goffin, Peter. "TIFF co-founder Bill Marshall, 77, remembered as a pioneer of Canadian film." *Toronto Star*, January 1, 2017. thestar.com/entertainment/2017/01/01/tiff-co-founder-bill-marshall-77-remembered-as-pioneer-of-canadian-film.html.

Green, Robin. "Russell's back, get your spirits up." *Globe and Mail*, September 29, 1978.

Hampson, Sarah. "Let's talk about sex." *Globe and Mail*, September 28, 2000.

Hanlon, Michael. "Homosexual Clubs Worry Metro Police." *Globe and Mail*, August 5, 1964.

Harris, Radie. "Broadway Ballyhoo." *Hollywood Reporter*, July 8, 1974.

Haslett Cuff, John. "Craig Russell's painful Life & Times." *Globe and Mail*, October 25, 1996.

Hertz, Barry. "TIFF co-founder Bill Marshall forever altered Toronto's cultural scene." *Globe and Mail*, January 3, 2017. Last updated March 21, 2018. theglobeandmail.com/arts/film/tiff-co-founder-william-marshall-forever-altered-torontos-cultural-scene/article33480626.

Hill, Charles C. Public, letter to the editor. *Toronto Star*, November 13, 1970.

Horsford, Patricia. "Battle Cry Sounded by Hislop at Rally." *Globe and Mail*, March 7, 1981.

Hoy, Claire. "Homosexuals Recruiting." *Toronto Sun*, January 6, 1978.

———. "Our Taxes Help Homosexuals Promote Abuse of Children." *Toronto Sun*, December 22, 1977.

———. "Radical homosexuals laying siege to society." *Toronto Sun*, January 9, 1980.

Ibbotson, Doug. "Toronto's Craig Russell is an amazing woman." *Topic*, April 22, 1980.

James, Cathie. "Docudrama to explore the life of Craig Russell." *Toronto Star*, July 17, 1990.

Judge, Diane. "Glittering Gold & More Yellow Bricks." *Daily News*, August 9, 1977.

Katz, Sidney. "What Should I Do?: Does Discussing Homosexuality Encourage It?" *Toronto Daily Star*, September 15, 1966.

———. "What Should I Do?: How Can I Tell If My Son, 12, Is Homosexual?" *Toronto Daily Star*, September 17, 1966.

Kelly, Deirdre. "Film-goers' parties bring out the strangest mix." *Globe and Mail*, September 14, 1987.

———. "Russell's hair-razing evening." *Globe and Mail*, March 26, 1988.

———. "'Toronto has really changed.'" *Globe and Mail*, January 23, 1988.

Kirby, Blaik. "Russell: high notes, low humor." *Globe and Mail*, March 30, 1977.

Kirchhoff, H.J. "Schmoozers, producers, and business." *Globe and Mail*, March 7, 1994.

———. "Super vamp." *Globe and Mail*, February 3, 1995.

Kirkland, Bruce. "Cheap, flawed, gimmicky movie is human triumph." *Toronto Star*, September 14, 1977.

———. "Craig Russell: The lady takes a bow." *Toronto Star*, February 26, 1978.

———. "He portrays the women he adores." *Toronto Star*, February 12, 1977.

———. "Hometown boy knows he's made good when the gawkers on the main drag have their eye out for an autograph." *Toronto Star*, February 26, 1978.

———. "Outrageous fortune." *Toronto Sun*, September 12, 1987.

———. "Pressures of stardom K.O. Craig Russell." *Toronto Star*, March 29, 1978.

———. "Provocative impersonator is spicy and entertaining." *Toronto Star*, March 31, 1977.

Kirsch, Jen. "Drag brunch is fun for the whole family." *Toronto Star*, October 11, 2019. thestar.com/life/2019/10/11/drag-brunch-is-fun-for-the-whole-family.html.

Knelman, Martin. "Craig the Outrageous! Audiences never knew when Craig Russell was going to cross the line." *Toronto Star*, September 24, 2000.

———. "Dusty Cohl, 78: Toronto film festival co-founder." *Toronto Star*, January 12, 2008. thestar.com/news/obituaries/2008/01/12/dusty_cohl_78_toronto_film_festival_cofounder.html.

Lacey, Laim. "The latest trend is a real drag." *Globe and Mail*, March 5, 1983.

Lewis, Jim. "Mae West remembers her fans." *Toronto Star*, January 19, 1981.

MacLean, David. "Oops, Reality!" *New York Native*, November 16, 1987.

Maga, Carly. "Brooke Lynn Hytes becoming the first Canadian on RuPaul's Drag Race is no surprise to her fellow Toronto queens." *Toronto Star*, February 27, 2017. thestar.com/entertainment/television/2019/02/27/brook-lynn-hytes-becoming-the-first-canadian-on-rupauls-drag-race-is-no-surprise-to-her-fellow-toronto-queens.html.

Malina, Martin. "Canada made plenty of waves at Cannes Film Festival." *Montreal Star*, May 31, 1977.

Maloney, Mark. "Toronto's mayors: Scoundrels, rogues and socialists." *Toronto Star*, January 3, 2010. thestar.com/news/city_hall/2010/01/03/torontos_mayors_scoundrels_rogues_and_socialists.html.

Martin, Robert. "Canada's profile larger at Cannes." *Globe and Mail*, May 7, 1977.

———. "Outrageous is, under close scrutiny." *Globe and Mail*, September 15, 1977.

Martin, Sandra. "Margaret Gibson, Writer 1948-2006." *Globe and Mail*, March 15, 2006.

Maslin, Janet. "Film: 'Too Outrageous,' a Sequel." *New York Times*, October 16, 1987. nytimes.com/1987/10/16/movies/film-too-outrageous-a-sequel.html.

McCabe, Bruce. "'Outrageous' has glitter." *Boston Globe*, August 19, 1977.

McCracken, Melinda. "Boys Bring Les Girls to Life." *Globe and Mail*, July 19, 1969.

McIver, Jack. "Craig Russell is back in town, folks, and he won't ever let you down again." *Toronto Star*, April 20, 1980.

McLaughlin, Gord. "Outrageous-ly funny as a musical: It began as a book, then became a film. Now Brad Fraser's stage adaptation adds lyrics and music." *National Post*, September 16, 2000.

McPhee, Martha. "Censorship Made Me." *New York Times*, July 27, 1997. archive.nytimes.com/www.nytimes.com/books/97/07/27/reviews/970727.27mcpheet.html.

Mitchell, Elizabeth. "Waking up from a nightmare." *Globe and Mail*, July 5, 1997.

Moon, Anne. "The real Dorothy Poste captains a nice cruise." *Toronto Star*, February 23, 1979.

———. "Singer back on land like a fish out of water." *Toronto Star*, April 5, 1979.

Musto, Michael. "Female Trouble." *Village Voice*, October 27, 1987.

New York Times. "4 Policemen Hurt in 'Village' Raid." June 29, 1969.

Niester, Alan. "New material from Russell mostly chiffon." *Globe and Mail*, March 25, 1981.

———. "Russell rings Twilight Zone changes." *Globe and Mail*, April 18, 1980.

O'Toole, Lawrence. "C'mon, now. Is drag a joke?" *Globe and Mail*, October 19, 1977.

———. "Divine: It takes a man to be a seventies woman." *Globe and Mail*, December 19, 1977.

Ouzounian, Richard. "Mad about the boy." *Toronto Star*, September 29, 2000.

Page, Shelley. "Making art from madness: Author Margaret Gibson's real world of the mentally ill." *Vancouver Sun*, March 28, 1998.

Penfield, Wilder III. "Hoffert has at last hit a high note." *Toronto Sun*, November 13, 1977.

Phillips, Brigid. "Dirty Craig cleans up." *Street Talk*, October 11, 1979.

Pomerantz, Bob. "Craig Russell confirms that he'll marry on Monday." *Toronto Star*, December 24, 1981.

Port Perry Star. "200 attend memorial service for Craig Russell." November 6, 1990.

Rankin, Jim. "Christian group's march into gay village leads to showdown with LGBTQ supporters." *Toronto Star*, September 28, 2019. thestar.com/news/gta/2019/09/28/christian-groups-march-into-gay-village-leads-to-showdown-with-lgbtq-supporters.html.

Rebalski, Nick. "Too Outrageous is something of a drag." *Vancouver Sun*, September 25, 1987.

Reed, Linda. "Craig's women win crowd." *Mirror*, March 1, 1978.

Reed, Rex. "They're an odd couple, but not outrageous." *Daily News*, July 29, 1977.

———. "Travestites Drag; 'S*P*Y*S' Bomb Out." *Daily News*, July 5, 1974.

Reguly, Robert. "A long-lived fan club is hard to find." *Toronto Daily Star*, February 29, 1964.

Rich, Frank. "Even Misfits Can Live Happily Ever After." *New York Times*, August 14, 1977.

Rosenbaum, David. "'Outrageous' is outrageously good." *Boston Herald American*, August 19, 1977.

Ross, Val. "Re-examining Margaret Gibson." *Globe and Mail*, December 2, 1993.

Sadleir, Dick. "Craig Russell Wows 'Em At The Cameo Royal Room." *St. Catharines Standard*, June 8, 1972.

Sanders, Donna. "Craig Russell: Outrageous." *Globe and Mail*, February 24, 1979.

Sarris, Andrew. "Consciousness Razing." *Village Voice*, August 15, 1977.

Scott, Jay. "Cassavetes' fairytale a surprise to him, too." *Globe and Mail*, October 7, 1980.

———. "A comic evening to remember." *Globe and Mail*, November 13, 1984.

———. "David Steinberg seeks a new David Steinberg." *Globe and Mail*, August 18, 1979.

———. "No show? For children it's a heartbreaker." *Globe and Mail*, November 25, 1977.

———. "Nothing too outrageous for Craig Russell." *Globe and Mail*, November 13, 1986.

———. "Russell tops in the he-she field." *Globe and Mail*, December 2, 1978.

———. "Still pushing sex, Mae West is no pushover." *Globe and Mail*, January 27, 1979.

Shaw, Stuart. "All about Craig Russell." *Toronto Star*, August 31, 1979.

Sherman, Betsy. "When things become 'Too Outrageous.'" *Boston Globe*, September 18, 1987.

Simms, Robert. "Violent Attack on Toronto Gays: Thousands Demonstrate Opposition." *Socialist Voice*, February 23, 1981.

Slopen, Beverley. "Gibson emerges from the shadows." *Toronto Star*, January 30, 1993.

Stenham, Polly. "Brutal! Vulgar! Dirty! Mae West and the gay comedy that

shocked 1920s America." *Guardian*, July 5, 2017. theguardian.com/
stage/2017/jul/05/polly-stenham-mae-west-gay-pride-the-drag-
national-theatre.

Taylor, Bill. "Sound death knell for the Dell." *Toronto Star*, July 4, 1986.

Taylor, Kate. "Outrageous doesn't sing." *Globe and Mail*, September 30,
2000.

Taylor, Noel. "Craig Russell looking beyond carbon copies of famous
ladies." *Ottawa Citizen*, November 13, 1987.

———. "Impersonator Russell joins Too Outrageous!" *Ottawa Citizen*,
September 16, 1987.

———. "Too Outrageous: more of the same." *Ottawa Citizen*, November
13, 1987.

Thomas, Kevin. "'Outrageous' Sequel Tops Original." *Los Angeles Times*,
October 16, 1987.

Toronto Daily Star. "Façad to Play at Royal Alex." August 1, 1969.

Toronto Star. "Anti-homosexuals Back Police Raids." February 14, 1981.

———. "Craig Russell named best male and female." November 22, 1977.

———. "Craig Russell plays Imperial Room." August 31, 1988.

———. "Daisy sales aid medical research." June 3, 1985.

———. "Drag in hand worth 300 in bush." May 12, 2002.

———. "Impersonator Craig Russell star of movie." January 7, 1977.

———. "The man styles of Craig Russell." December 16, 1979.

———. "M. Rosenfeld fought illness, 'beat odds.'" July 12, 1990.

———. "'Outrageous' Russell returning for sequel." October 6, 1986.

———. "Police Arrest Hundreds in Steambaths." February 6, 1981.

Toronto Sun. "6 Held in Rally Violence: Five Agitators, One Gay." June
22, 1981.

———. "Badges Removed, Gays Say: Probe Will Seek Cops' Names."
February 9, 1981.

———. "Big surprise in Canadian movie." July 31, 1977.

Toronto Telegram. "Global Village Has Spawned Two Revues." August 2,
1969.

Toushek, Gary. "The most original people buck trends to leave their
imprint." *Globe and Mail*, June 25, 1988.

Train, Sylvia. "Confessions of a promosexual." *Toronto Sun*, n.d.

———. "Goodbye Mae Hello Lori … this wedding takes the cake." *Toronto Sun*, January 12, 1982.

———. "He's Outrageous so don't bring the kids." *Toronto Sun*, n.d.

———. "Russell captures each star." *Toronto Sun*, March 31, 1977.

Turna, Kenneth. "Mae West's crazy about Mae West looking 35 at 85." *Toronto Star*, December 5, 1977.

Valpy, Michael. "Outrageous life was fable for the lost and fragile." *Globe and Mail*, November 6, 1990.

Vancouver Sun. "King of the drag queens as outrageous as ever." September 16, 1987.

———. "Raids Have Gays Steaming." February 6, 1981.

Variety. "Unit Review: Manhattan Follies (Persian Room, N.Y.)." July 3, 1974.

Venn, David. "Councillor Kristyn Wong-Tam raises warning ahead of Christian group's march through Gay Village." *Toronto Star*, September 22, 2019. thestar.com/news/gta/2019/09/22/councillor-kristyn-wong-tam-raises-warning-ahead-of-christian-groups-march-through-gay-village.html.

Victoria Times-Colonist. "Craig Russell Show 'Disgusting, Horrifying.'" October 30, 1981.

Wagner, Vit. "Boys will be girls." *Toronto Star*, April 30, 1995.

Walker, Susan. "30 years later, Russell is still Outrageous." *Toronto Star*, January 21, 2008.

Walsh, Michael. "Outrageous sequel a gem." *Province*, September 25, 1987.

Webster, Bill. "What? Carol Channing here?" *London Free Press*, May 31, 1972.

Whittaker, Herbert. "Local star-makers on the rise." *Globe and Mail*, July 29, 1981.

Wilson, Earl. "The Pantyhose Parade …" *New York Post*, July 2, 1974.

Zarzour, Kim. "Amyotrophic lateral sclerosis organization is run by woman battling odds against her." *Toronto Star*, May 31, 1988.

Zekas, Rita. "Craig Russell is too outrageous!" *Toronto Star*, September 12, 1987.

———. "Makeup man does about-face." *Toronto Star*, October 28, 2000.

————. "Outrageous … to the end." *Toronto Star*, November 1, 1990.

————. "Stars dance the night away at sweaty Outrageous bash." *Toronto Star*, September 14, 1987.

————. "Wilde about the boys; a Walkie-talkie." *Toronto Star*, July 2, 1998.

MAGAZINES

Amiel, Barbara. "Vice Still Has Its Legal Price: Homosexuals Are Confusing Law Enforcement and Discrimination." *Maclean's*, March 9, 1981.

Bastien, Mark. "The man who would be queen." *T.O. Magazine*, July/August 1987.

Bellini, Paul. "Great Ladies 101: Plus Plus Plus!" *Fab*, December 28, 2006.

Bloom, Jessica. "Inside Drag Queen Storytime, the Toronto library's fiercest kids' reading series." *Toronto Life*, January 2, 2018. torontolife.com/culture/books/inside-drag-queen-storytime-toronto-librarys-fiercest-kids-reading-series.

Body Politic. "Gay Freedom Rally Wins Support." 1981.

Darrach, Brad. "Death Comes to a Quiet Man Who Made Drag Queen History as Divine." *People*, March 21, 1988. people.com/archive/death-comes-to-a-quiet-man-who-made-drag-queen-history-as-divine-vol-29-no-11.

Delaney, Marshall. "The drag queen and the schizo." *Saturday Night*, October 1977.

Edwards, Natalie. "Craig finds success in a woman's world." *Screen International*, May 22, 1977.

Fulford, Robert. "The Politics of Homophobia." *Saturday Night*, April 1981.

Hale, Barrie. "The Canadian identity finally revealed!" *Toronto Life*, May 1978.

Hofsess, John. "One Flew Over the Butterfly's Nest." *Canadian*, August 13, 1977.

Hollywood Reporter. "Craig Russell to Mime Movie Queens at P.J.'s." December 7, 1972.

———. "Your Friendly Local Critic." August 26, 1977.

James, Noah. "Craig Russell." *Today*, September 27, 1980.

Katz, Sidney. "The Homosexual Next Door: A Sober Appraisal of a New Social Phenomenon." *Maclean's*, February 22, 1964.

King, Bruce. "The Outrageous Craig Russell." *Gay Scene*, November 1987.

Knelman, Martin. "His Majesty the Queens." *Canadian*, October 15, 1977.

———. "Remembering Craig Russell." *Toronto Life*, February 1991.

Kopkind, Andrew. "The King/Queen of Drag." *New Times*, January 9, 1978.

Lynch, Michael. "Shallow Minds and Shallow Throats." *Body Politic*, 1977, 34.

MacLean, David. "Resurrecting Russell." *Episcene*, October 1987.

Maclean's. "All About Craig." April 17, 1978.

Malina, Martin. "A schizophrenic girl teams up with a gay hairdresser … now that's Outrageous." *Marquee*, September/October 1977.

Miller, Robert. "Sweet smell of excess." *Maclean's*, June 27, 1977.

Miss Chatelaine. "Outrageous." Winter 1977.

Nieuwe Revu. "Craig Russell: Een man als supervrouw." January 18, 1980.

O'Neill, Mark. "You've got to have friends." *Advocate*, October 27, 1987.

Pennington, Ron. "Outrageous." *Hollywood Reporter*, August 18, 1977.

Redfern, Jon. "Gay Television Drama: 'Friday Night Adventures.'" *Mandate*, September 1976.

Rhyne, Brice. "Craig Russell: Outrageous is an understatement." *Mandate*, January 1979.

Rich, Frank. "Mae West 'Sex' Capade!" *New York*, March 30, 2012. nymag.com/news/features/scandals/mae-west-2012-4.

Screen International. "Outrageous — even for Cannes." April 16, 1977.

Sheppard, Gene. "Mae West." *Hollywood Studio Magazine*.

Simon, John. "Imperiled Existences." *New York*, August 15, 1977.

MUSICAL RECORDING

Bonnie Meyer, vocalist. "Just Loving You," by Bonnie Meyer, recorded 1986. Unpublished.

Colm Wilkinson, vocalist. "The Music of the Night," by Andrew Lloyd Webber, Charles Hart, and Richard Stilgoe, recorded 1990, track 17 on *Highlights from Andrew Lloyd Webber's The Phantom of the Opera (Original Canadian Cast)*, Polydor.

Craig Russell, vocalist. "Glamour Monster," by Robert Armes, Tim Tickner, Craig Russell, Syd Kessler, and Marc Giacomelli, recorded 1987, track A1 on *Glamour Monster*, Change Records International.

TELEVISION

Murphy, Dennis, dir. *Life & Times*. "Russell Craig Edie: The King of Queens." Aired October 25, 1996, on CBC. DVD.

Russell, Craig. Interview by Bob McLean. *Bob McLean Show*, CBC, March 1, 1978, MPG video.

———. Interview by Harris Sullivan. *Newshour*, CBC, November 29, 1978, MPG video.

———. *Newshour*, CBC, October 31, 1990, MPG video.

Russell, Craig, and Lori Jenkins. Interview by Bob McLean. *McLean at Large*, CBA, January 27, 1982, MPG video.

———. *National*, CBC, January 11, 1982, MPG video.

VIDEO (INTERNET)

Baxter, Billy. "Who is Billy 'Silver Dollar' Baxter?" October 5, 2011. Video, 7:58. youtube.com/watch?v=EvtFuqTShTw.

"christsforgiveness." "The REAL reason why David Lynn was arrested." June 5, 2019. Video, 6:51. youtube.com/watch?v=QvOjPLhElnU.

"Emerald City TV 1977#40 Roslyn Kind Craig Russell." Interview by

Arthur Bell. 1977. Video, 27:20. youtube.com/watch?v=
D4htHECBHW4.

Feldman, Gene, dir. *Mae West … And the Men Who Knew Her.* Los
Angeles: Wombat Productions, 1993. Video, 57:11. youtube.com/
watch?v=JpcEEyXo7QQ.

Front Page Challenge. Featuring Barbara Hamilton, Betty Kennedy,
Craig Russell, Fred Davis, Gordon Sinclair, and Pierre Berton. CBC,
September 26, 1977, Video, 9:43. cbc.ca/archives/entry/craig-russell-
on-front-page-challenge.

Russell, Craig. *Canada After Dark.* Hosted by Paul
Soles. CBC, 1978. Video, 0:59. cbc.ca/news/canada/
craig-russell-performs-as-peggy-lee-on-cbc-in-1978-1.4905656.

———. *Craig Russell in Concert.* Musical accompaniment by Paul
Hoffert. Recorded in 1979. Hamburg. Video, 48:23. youtube.com/
watch?v=cmjtGlawTZA.

———. *Een avondment Craig Russell.* Musical accompaniment by Paul
Hoffert. Recorded in 1980. Theater Carré, Amsterdam. Video, 48:25.
youtube.com/watch?v=v96Z0U3Tgh8.

———. Interview by Hana Gartner. CBC, 1978. Video, 2:59. youtube.com/
watch?v=KWV9bMndut4.

———. Interview by Robin Young. *Evening Magazine.* WBZ-TV, 1977.
youtube.com/watch?v=IwXgco2okzA.

Smith, Colin, dir. *Behind the Mask.* CBC, c. 1989. Video, 47:33.
youtube.com/watch?v=v2m6Ut2dWsk.

West, Mae. Interview by Dick Cavett. CBS, April 5, 1976. Video, 10:02.
youtube.com/watch?v=WsL7AHCM7PU.

WEBSITES

"A history of HIV/AIDS." *CATIE.* Accessed July 6, 2019. catie.ca/en/
world-aids-day/history.

Benson, Denise. "Then & Now: Club David's." *Then & Now Toronto
Nightlife History,* November 24, 2014. First published *The Grid,* March
26, 2013. thenandnowtoronto.com/2014/11/then-now-club-davids.

———. "Then & Now: Komrads." *Then & Now Toronto Nightlife History*, September 25, 2014. First published *The Grid*, June 21, 2012. thenandnowtoronto.com/2014/09/then-now-komrads.

———. "Then & Now: Stages." *Then & Now Toronto Nightlife History*, October 29, 2014. First published *The Grid*, December 4, 2012. thenandnowtoronto.com/2014/10/then-now-stages.

East, Penny. "Rusty Ryan." *Xtra*, August 20, 2003. dailyxtra.com/rusty-ryan-43407.

"History: Milestones in Telefilm Canada's history." *Telefilm Canada*. Accessed July 6, 2019. telefilm.ca/en/about-telefilm-canada/history.

Knegt, Peter. "Toronto drag queen Allysin Chaynes wants to be your new overlord — and wouldn't that be fabulous?" *CBC Arts*, March 9, 2018. cbc.ca/arts/toronto-drag-queen-allysin-chaynes-wants-to-be-your-new-overlord-and-wouldn-t-that-be-fabulous-1.4568245.

Reiti, John, and Shanifa Nasser. "Pride says it 'never agreed' to exclude police, as Black Lives Matter slams police for 'pink-washing.'" *CBC News*, July 4, 2016. Last updated July 5, 2016. cbc.ca/news/canada/toronto/black-lives-matter-pride-protest-1.3663250.

Roberts, Steven V. "76 – and Still Diamond Lil." *New York Times*, November 2, 1969. Last updated July 27, 1997. archive.nytimes.com/www.nytimes.com/books/97/07/27/reviews/west-magazine.html.

Roche, David. "Craig Russell: 'She Will be missed.'" *Xtra*, September 20, 2000. Last updated October 21, 2017. dailyxtra.com/craig-russell-she-will-be-missed-46785.

"Toronto police Chief Mark Saunders apologizes for 1981 gay bathhouse raids." *CBC News*, June 22, 2016. Last updated June 23, 2016. cbc.ca/news/canada/toronto/police-apology-raids-1.3647668.

IMAGE CREDITS

INDEX